Creativity
And
Common Sense

SUNY Series in Philosophy
Robert C. Neville, Editor

Creativity
And
Common Sense

Essays in Honor of Paul Weiss

edited by:

THOMAS KRETTEK

State University of New York Press

Published by
State University of New York Press, Albany

© *1987   State University of New York*

For information, address State University of New York
Press, State University Plaza, Albany, N.Y., 12246

Library of Congress Cataloging-in-Publication Data

Creativity and common sense.

  (SUNY series in philosophy)
  Bibliography: p.
  Includes index.
  1. Weiss, Paul, 1901–   . 2. Philosophy.
I. Weiss, Paul, 1901–   . II. Krettek, Thomas,
1950–   . III. Series.
B945.W397C74   1987   191   86–19165
ISBN 0–88706–446–9
ISBN 0–88706–447–7 (pbk.)

10 9 8 7 6 5 4 3 2 1

In the arid desert of academic philosophy
in the twentieth century, there is one lovely
flower and one sparkling oasis.
The beauty of Paul's mind is that flower.
That oasis is in Paul's books. Wisdom
can be found there for those who thirst after it.

—— *Mortimer J. Adler*

Contents

List of Abbreviations

The following abbreviations are used for writings of Paul Weiss cited in the text, all published by Southern Illinois University Press, Carbondale.

Beyond All Appearances (1974)	*BAA*
Cinematics (1975)	*C*
First Considerations (1977)	*FC*
The God We Seek (1964)	*GWS*
History: Written and Lived (1962)	*HWL*
The Making of Men (1967)	*MM*
Man's Freedom (1950)	*MF*
Modes of Being (1958)	*MOB*
Nature and Man (1947)	*NM*
Nine Basic Arts (1961)	*NBA*
Our Public Life (1959)	*OPL*
Philosophy in Process	*PP*
Privacy (1983)	*P*
Reality (1938)	*R*
Religion and Art (1963)	*RA*

Right and Wrong: A Philosophical Dialogue between Father and Son, with Jonathan Weiss (1967)   RW

Sport: A Philosophic Inquiry (1969)   S

The World of Art (1961)   WA

You, I, and the Others (1980)   YIO

Introduction

Husserl's effort to stay the rout of ontology with his call to rally to the "things themselves" and to take one's stand with the phenomena was, nonetheless, a retreat from the Kantian divisions, especially that between phenomena and things-in-themselves, and an abdication of the claim to an intelligible depth for realities and an access to that depth. Paul Weiss, however, armed with his own creative understanding and deployment of Hegelian insights, rallies those who would uphold ontology's claim to an intelligible depth for realities and an access to it with the cry, "To the things in themselves!" For him there is to be no rout or even retreat but a counteroffensive grounded in the evidence of common sense. As a result, Paul Weiss is the exception that proves the rule, the rule being the statement by Iris Murdoch that "Modern philosophy is profoundly anti-metaphysical in spirit. Its anti-metaphysical character may be summed up in the *caveat*: There may be no deep structure."[1] Professor Weiss has spent his philosophical life countering reductionistic claims by "evidencing," "adumbrating," and articulating the depth sources underlying the commonsense world. This collection of essays studying the Philosophy of Paul Weiss is intended to make that endeavor more clearly evident.

Weiss only characterizes himself in his claim that the philosopher is one who, concerned with "providing a systematic account of the entire universe," attempts to discover what is irreducibly real and "to grasp those truths that only a divine mind could fully know." His ongoing quest to answer the ultimate question about the nature of the whole of reality is clearly apparent from his first full-length systematic work in philosophy, tellingly entitled *Reality* (1938), to his most recently published "Things in Themselves" (1985). His claim in "Things in Themselves" — that three different things exist in themselves, *i.e.*, realities existing apart from all qualification by anything else, namely, actualities, final conditions, and *dunamis* — is based on almost a half century of reflection on the nature of reality.

Reality is his programmatic work in which are proleptically present

1

many of the notions that are clarified, refined or modified, and articulated in later works, but *Modes of Being*, twenty years later in 1958, provides the metaphysical foundation for the entire Weissian corpus. It proposes to outline a "new viable systematic philosophy which is alert to the basic questions raised by the various sciences, by metaphysics and theology, by history and the arts" that is required "if we are to remain intellectually abreast of the world in which we live" (*MOB*, p. 8).

As a result of reflections and writings following *Reality*, Weiss found himself confronted with the paradox that, although its task is to bring the Good to its complete realization, the human actuality is guilty since it must inevitably fail to realize that good due to its finitude, feebleness, and ignorance. This paradox remains unless four distinct realities — Actuality, Ideality, Existence, and God — are distinguished and their perspectives assumed in turn. Each has to be affirmed as a final, irreducible mode of being possessing its own integrity and career. "The universe they together exhaust requires for its understanding a system in which each is recognized to be as basic, as explanatory, and as incomplete as the others" (*MOB*, pp. 13–14). *Modes of Being* is the systematic and exhaustive distinguishing and clarification of the particular nature of each of these four ultimates and their interrelationships.

Actualities are finite beings in space and time that strive to complete themselves through realizing essential objectives that they variously specify out of a single common future Good (*MOB*, p. 14). Ideality or Possibility is that generic meaning expressing prospects that "the different realities seek to realize for their own benefit and the benefit of those possibilities" (*MOB*, 2.05, p. 109). Existence is a sheer vitality that is simultaneously ingredient in, yet overflowing the bounds of Actualities, "connecting each with every other and coming to focus in the Ideal" (*MOB*, p. 16). Viewed from the standpoint of other beings, Existence is a field that is dynamic and a domain of comparative relations that allows Actualities to be contemporaries and co-present (*MOB*, 1.22, p. 33). By incorporating Existence, an entity is enabled to stand away from, yet remain related to, others. "God is that being who . . . makes a unity of what otherwise would be a detached set of occurrences. He sees to it that the Ideal is realized, and that Actualities are perfected" (*MOB*, p. 15). God, as eternity, is "the locus of the evaluation of whatever there be, no matter what the date" (*MOB*, 1.23, p. 34).

These four modes are dynamically related to one another and are together as intermixed. Each exists in the others as subject to the conditions that they impose, but such subjection does not alter the nature of the subjected mode. Each mode needs, seeks to adjust itself to, partly satisfies, imposes a burden on, and provides testimony to the reality of the others (*MOB*, 4.01–4.10, pp. 277–84). The togetherness of the four modes is simply them as together and not a new, distinct entity. This fourfold division of being, in which each stands over against the others, means that the totality of being is not contained in any one mode. "Only together do they constitute a whole reality" (*MOB*, 1.15, p. 29).

Reality primarily focuses on the mode of being, Actuality. Expositionally exemplifying his affirmation of the circularity of epistemology and ontology, Professor Weiss, beginning with evidence for the reality of the perceived afforded by common sense, moves beyond it to reveal the continuation of Actualities into an indispensable, real, but unknown, depth that can be arrived at through adumbration. This depth factor grounds epistemological and ontological inquiry. In *Reality*, the ultimate answer to the question about the nature of the real is the law of contradiction, which is the category that provides "a universal and inescapable conceptualization of every possible object of knowledge" and that is "capable of being exemplified in both the necessary and the contingent" (*R*, p. 144). Those exemplifications are examined in his ontological considerations of the second part of the work.

The modes of being prominent in the concerns of the two works immediately following *Reality*, i.e., *Nature and Man* (1947) and *Man's Freedom* (1950), are Actuality and Ideality. These two volumes are meant to constitute a single work. *Nature and Man*, reflecting on both Actuality and Ideality, corrects the insular character of Actualities implied in *Reality* by showing them to be occupied with a common future objective (*MOB*, pp. 8–13). It considers "fundamental features of nature, including those of ethics" and is guided by the idea that the essence and vitality of natural beings is grounded in freedom (*NM*, p. v). The freedom that is found in nature is the reason that all things come to be. Human freedom is but one exemplification of that freedom. As a result, human beings are at once both natural and responsible. The human actuality, as a free being in nature, has a unique, irreducible value and a fixed core directed toward a universal good that grounds a responsibility for the Good and the right to be good. *Man's Freedom*, focusing on Ideality, is the companion volume that seeks "to make evident how man through a series of free efforts can become more complete and thereby more human" (*MF*, p. v). It highlights the fact that the human actuality pursues the Good with its own particular freedom — a freedom that is exhibited as preference, choice, and will as the agencies by which it seeks to realize fully the all-inclusive Good — and considers specific issues in ethics as grounded in and supplementing the deliberations of *Nature and Man*.

Our Public Life (1959), appearing the year after *Modes of Being* and benefiting from the insights therein articulated, is the work on politics that was to accompany *Nature and Man* and *Man's Freedom*. Concerning itself primarily with the mode of Ideality, it examines society, state, culture, and civilization as groups to which the public human actuality belongs. It presents the theory of native rights as rooted in the factive existence of the human actuality. Weiss hopes that by clarifying and resolving some enduring issues, some of the ways in which "men might ideally get together and progressively fulfill themselves" might become apparent (*OPL*, p. 18).

Existence is the mode of being that plays a prominent role in Weiss's next four books: *The World of Art* (1961), *Nine Basic Arts* (1961), *History: Written and Lived* (1962), and *Religion and Art* (1963). The first two were originally one volume in which the schema of *Modes of Being* serves to clarify and expound the world and works of art. *The World of Art* "makes evident how existence, speculatively dealt with in *Modes of Being*, acquires concreteness and human pertinence when portrayed and mediated by art" (*WA*, p. x). It considers the similarities and differences between natural objects and works of art, the relation of art to ethics, politics, religion, philosophy, and science, the role of emotions, and the nature of artistic creation. *Nine Basic Arts* distinguishes and examines particular arts on the basis of the nature of their primary interest in one or other of the essential dimensions of Existence, *i.e.*, space, time, or becoming (*NBA*, p. 9). *History: Written and Lived* investigates the public use of Existence by the human actuality. Taking "history seriously, as a domain with a distinctive being and rationale," Professor Weiss examines the motivation, methods, questions, problems, and value of the work peculiar to the historian (*HWL*, p. 4). This is followed by an account of the historic world, which is "one product resulting from an interrelating of the basic realities which make up the universe," as that about which the historian discourses (*HWL*, pp. 118–19). *Religion and Art* is the Aquinas Lecture delivered at Marquette University in 1963 and in it Weiss identifies and examines seven basic relations between religion and art. Focusing primarily on art as religiously qualified, he articulates how it, by making art subject to religious conditions, relates the human actuality to God. He also returns to and develops themes regarding the embodiment of art in space, time, and becoming.

The God We Seek (1964) concerns itself with the mode of being, God. Its focus is "the experience of and concern with God in privacy and in a community" (*GWS*, p. 8). Professor Weiss offers an account of the nuclear, normative dimensions of private and public religious life in an effort to grasp the nature of religion. He also endeavors to isolate the pure, undistorted relation of the human actuality to God prior to its diverse ritualization and specialization in the various religions. Fifteen avenues of access to God outside of any special revelation are considered as enabling one to become acquainted with God, even though they do not provide a rationally sustained knowledge. It supplements the systematic and dialectical speculations about God articulated in *Modes of Being* by disclosing means of access and enjoyment that match those of *Modes of Being* and thereby makes possible a proper grasp that God is, what God is, and how God is involved with other realities. This volume culminates almost twenty-five years of reflection on the question of the nature of reality and completes what amounts to a nine-volume work investigating in depth the issues that *Modes of Being* was written to address.

Before further developing lines of thought already also present in *Modes of Being*, Professor Weiss published three more works that were not specifically a part of the clarification of the exemplifications of the four ultimates. *Right and Wrong: A Philosophical Dialogue between Father and Son* (1967) is just that. With his son Jonathan as coauthor and interlocutor, he develops the interrelationships between human action and ethics as their discussion progressively expands from individual, to familial, to social, to political, to human obligations, concluding finally with a consideration of the universe and law as categories underlying the whole. In *The Making of Men* (1967), Weiss brings to bear on the process of education his reflections on the nature of reality and the basic concepts governing knowledge and actions. The entire life of the individual is taken as an educative process, and he considers the aspects of that process in light of the broader perspective of the life that the individual does and ought to lead. *Sport: A Philosophic Inquiry* (1969) is one of his "best sellers." It considers, within the context of his reflections on the nature of the human actuality, the aims of education, and activities related to sport such as art, the multiple factors — values, goals, requirements, demands, challenges, benefits, and motivations — that are involved with the sphere of sport, as well as the ways in which sport reveals the ultimate depths that are at the source of human life.

Beyond All Appearances (1974) is self-admittedly something of a new beginning for Weiss and is the programmatic work for *Cinematics* (1975), *First Considerations* (1977), *You, I, and the Others* (1980), *Privacy* (1983), and *Toward a Perfected State* (1986). In it Professor Weiss picks up again and develops the epistemological themes that he initially presented in *Reality* and that were implicitly operative in subsequent works. He presents it as "the first part of a two volume study, of which *Modes of Being* is the second — provided that *Modes of Being* be corrected in accord with suggestions and criticisms made in *Philosophy in Process*" (*BAA*, p. xi). The book itself is an effort to show the way in which one can move to the ultimate realities from the "appearances" that are confronted in the everyday commonsense world.

Beyond All Appearances is divided into three parts, the second two of which introduce themes that will be examined in individual works that follow. The first examines and clarifies the nature of appearances and their other attenuated forms as grounded in more basic realities, especially actualities, and shows how appearances function as symbols leading one by adumbration or lucidation into their sources (*BAA*, pp. 96–98). The second part focuses on the second of what Weiss identifies as the three ultimate dimensions of reality, *i.e.*, final conditions (here referred to as finalities), to show how one moves to them by tracing the contexts that connect and govern actualities and appearances back to their sources (*BAA*, p. xiii). This enables him to clarify the nature of "the cosmos" as a law-abiding interplay of actualities and finalities. Prior to this work, the finalities were taken as modes of being correlate with actualities and were examined on the basis of their exemplification in actualities. The present inquiry focuses on finalities as they are apart from actualities. Weiss identifies five common constraints that evidence five finalities. These common constraints make possible a lucidative move to the five, not three as in *Modes of Being*, finalities of Substance, Being, Possibility, Existence, and Unity at their source.

First Considerations continues and refines the epistemological themes of the second section of *Beyond All Appearances*, stressing "the transition from appearances and actualities to ultimate, persistent, conditioning realities — finalities" (*FC*, p. xi). Weiss also sees it as providing a criterion for determining what is worth preserving in his other works. Its conclusions can be supplemented by those in *Modes of Being*, when the latter are suitably modified to bring them into line with later reflections. He offers a systematic and comprehensive account of (1) the evidences of finalities, (2) the process of evidencing that takes one to finalities, (3) the particular character of each of the finalities, (4) the way they affect the individual actualities, and (5) their interplay with actualities to constitute the cosmos.

The third part of *Beyond All Appearances* addresses the nature of the human actuality and its involvement with finalities. Human actualities interplay with, internalize, and instantiate all of the finalities, while also maintaining themselves in opposition to them. Because of this interplay the human actuality "is a substance enriched with a being, nature, existence, and unity" and "is an individual with rights, a trued self, an identity, and an immortality, each of which reflects the result of his involvement with a distinct finality" (*BAA*, p. 309). This leads into a consideration of the nature of the Ideal and the task of its realization. *You, I, and the Others* (1980) continues this theme as it systematically studies the fundamental dimensions and roles of the individual human actuality. By attending to what is commonly accepted about the human actuality, Professor Weiss discovers in the human actuality

a complex private life, continuing into, supporting, and supplementing a public one. Each expresses himself from a private depth, making himself present in a world with other men and other actualities. Each has a self epitomized in an I; each is a person with a limit at a me; each is faced as a you, is one among others, and is encompassed by a common we (*YIO*, pp. xi–xii).

The work itself divides into (1) an examination of the public character of the you as the means of another's access to what one is in depth, (2) the character of the me as that which is attended to by oneself as the means of access to one's own depth, (3) the character of the self as the source of privately initiated acts, (4) the character of the we as offering a number of ways for individuals to be together, and (5) the relationship between the they and the others that presuppose it.

Privacy is the sequel to *You, I, and the Others*. The third of the three ultimate dimensions of reality, *i.e.,* the *dunamis,* first appears in this work as part of the account of the origin of an individual. *Privacy* continues Weiss's effort "to provide a . . . precise and systematic treatment of man, as able to be apart from and to oppose and interplay with final realities" (*P*, p. xi). To understand the human actuality, reference must be made to what is irreducible and unduplicable. This requires an intensive, convergent move to the private origins of the publicly manifested. The book undertakes to identify "evidences of human privacy in the body and the world, to understand what then becomes knowable, and to explore the results" (*P*, p. xi). Privacy is the originative source of human activity and evidence for it is present if there is ever more to an activity than what is bodily contributed. Beginning with publicly available evidences, Weiss uncovers powers existing in the human actuality that are varied epitomizations of a unitary privacy. The first part of the volume examines the person and the self. The former is the locus of the bodily manifested epitomizations of privacy and the latter is the locus of the nonbodily manifested epitomizations of privacy. The insights achieved in this part are employed in the second part to establish the basis for and the character and achievement of human excellence. They also serve to ground a doctrine of native rights rooted in the factively existent human actuality. Weiss's more recent book, *Toward a Perfected State,* works out the various ways that human actualities are publicly together associatively and collaboratively, which togetherness is basic to more complex social and political forms, and is based in part on the insights into accountability and responsibility achieved in *Privacy.*

Cinematics returns to an analysis of the world of art that Weiss had begun in *The World of Art* and *Nine Basic Arts.* In this work he focuses on film as a form of art. He examines the nature of film, the various elements involved in the creation of a film, and the varieties and purposes of film. The two strategic themes of emotions as revelatory of depth sources and the disclosive character of appearances are developed in his philosophical interlude.

Philosophy in Process is the title under which Professor Weiss's philosophical/autobiographical journals are published. These volumes are the ongoing record of the philosophical and personal ruminations that accompany and lead to the formulations of his various systematic works. In them are found the reflective roadways, including dead ends, that lead one through the individual works and the entire corpus. The nine volumes currently published begin in 1955 and are indispensable for an understanding of the continuities and discontinuities, the advances and retreats, what stays the same and what changes, what is and what is not meant in Weiss's thought.

Professor Weiss philosophizes because he is not content with the authority or adequacy of tradition, common sense, science, other philosophers, or even his own philosophy. He is always stretching the limits of received philosophy and attempting to break new philosophical ground. His effort to address the ultimate question regarding the nature of reality, to clarify crucial issues, and to approach definitive answers is, however, neither a solitary undertaking nor one that is ever finally achieved. For him, true philosophic dialogue requires sympathetic attention and critical examination, for only through these is a better understanding of what is and what is known possible.

The essays in this study engage in that sympathetic but critical dialogue with Professor Weiss. Their authors focus on issues that are strategic to the investigations undertaken in and suggested by Weiss's works. They not only raise questions regarding those issues, but also sharpen their features and broaden their application to show how Professor Weiss's insights can serve to resolve problem areas of philosophy.

The dialogue bounded by this study is ordered roughly around the two foci of *Modes of Being* and *Beyond All Appearances* and according to subject matter.

The first three essays are basically concerned with Professor Weiss's philosophical method. The initial essay by George Kimball Plochmann, "Methods and Modes: Aspects of Weissian Metaphysics," offers an analysis of Weiss's philosophic method as it is employed in discovering, clarifying, and articulating his insights and the metaphysics that supports them. Following some opening remarks on the nature and five main elements of philosophic method, Professor Plochmann identifies two stages in Weiss's method and notes that Weiss conceives of it as a complete discipline that begins with what is clearest and then moves to clarify more obscure elements. This is followed by an in-depth and very helpful presentation of the way this method is employed in the presentation and progressive clarification of the four modes in *Modes of Being* and the way it is employed in *The God We Seek* to add content to the more abstract presentation of God in *Modes of Being*. His essay then turns to a consideration of the ways in which *Beyond All Appearances* further develops and refines other elements of Weiss's methodology, particularly, the concepts of appearances and creativity. He examines the methodological employment and import of these concepts as they appear in both *Modes of Being* and *Beyond All Appearances* and as they influence the insights and works that are related to each, especially the works on art.

Robert E. Wood's essay examines and clarifies a strategic but somewhat neglected methodological insight of Professor Weiss, namely, the notion of adumbration. Drawing upon many of Weiss's writings, he shows that the notion of adumbration refers to "a prearticulate level of experience which carries our being beyond itself" and gives access to the "in-itself-ness" of the encountered. This notion is disclosed by art and underlies speculative thought. Through it are revealed both the substantial wholeness of actualities and the totality of all actualities as interinvolved with Existence, Ideality, and God. Wood also distinguishes adumbration from lucidation, the latter being appropriate to reaching finalities rather than actualities.

"The Appearance of Finalities" by Daniel O. Dahlstrom examines Professor Weiss's claim that certain appearances evidence finalities. His examination involves (1) a clarification of finalities through comparing and contrasting them with the Scholastic transcendentals (real but formal attributes of being that are distinguishable but not separable from it), (2) a presentation of Weiss's theory of appearances, as the joint outcome of actualities and finalities, and "evidencing," as affording access to the actualities and finalities at the source of the evidence and evidenced, (3) the problematic nature of attitudes and contexts as evidence of finalities, (4) the fact that emotions, coupled with attitudes and contexts, may ultimately validate Weiss's claims about finalities, and (5) the possible significance of emotions for metaphysics.

The next two articles examine the relation between Professor Weiss's insights and science, the first on the basis of *Reality* and the second on the basis of *Modes of Being* and *First Considerations*.

In "Substantival Process Philosophy: Speculative Common Sense," Peter Miller affirms with Professor Weiss the necessity of a philosophy of common sense, where common sense is conceived of "in the quasi-Aristotelian sense of an operative synthetic awareness of and practical orientation towards the world and oneself." He then asks whether or not such a substantial view should continue as a fundamental element in philosophical wisdom. After evaluating traditional and common objections to a substantial view, as well as the Whiteheadian alternative of an event ontology, he suggests that a new beginning be made on the basis of "a substantival process philosophy that develops the implications of pluralism" and whose starting point is the ontological necessity "that the individuals composing the totality of reality form a multiplicity together." This insight he derives from Book II of *Reality*. This starting point allows Professor Miller to provide an account of field effects, of identity over time, of the freedom and openness of the individual to new possibilities, and to introduce conceptions of value into cosmology.

David Weissman's study, "First Considerations," addresses three issues emerging from his reflection on *Modes of Being* and *First Considerations*. The first is the schema appropriate to a categorial system. The second is the need for a list of categories, with a consideration of the two offered by Professor Weiss, one in *Modes of Being*, the other in *First Considerations*, and their common anomaly. In connection with this issue he offers a possible compromise alternative formulated in terms of (1) "Elements" and "Powers" that give rise to "stabilities," (2) possibility as the categorial complement of actuality, and (3) both as the counterpart modes of existence. The third issue is a discussion of his differences with Weiss regarding the Actuality/Existence relation and Weiss's notions of Substance, Possibility, and Being. These differences are due to their differing estimations of the nature of philosophy, the foundational role of nature, and the place of science.

The next two authors focus on the contribution that Professor Weiss's metaphysical thought makes to ethics. First, Andrew J. Reck, considering the relationship between metaphysics and ethics in his presentation, "Paul Weiss's Metaphysics of Ethics," identifies four waves of modernity — egoism/materialism, the absence of freedom in nature/determinism, the doctrine of total flux, and enduring ontological guilt — that threaten to engulf the ethical. Based on his consideration of the circular relation between metaphysics and ethics formulated in Weiss's *Reality, Nature and Man, Man's Freedom*, and *Modes of Being*, he argues that the insights therein achieved can provide the basis for an adequate response to these threats. He identifies the insights as (1) the concern for a common future, (2) the locating of human freedom in nature, (3) the self as emerging in response to ethical demands, and (4) the mutual completion of the work of each mode by the others.

"Achievement, Value, and Structure" by Robert C. Neville examines Professor Weiss's affirmation of an internal relation between possibilities and values, which affirmation is made along both Platonic and Aristotelian lines and based on a pluralistic solution to the problem of the one and the many. He highlights the presence of this relation in Weiss's thought beginning with *Modes of Being* and continuing through later works. Professor Neville then suggests, on the basis of his theory of value as a harmony of simplicity and complexity, a modification of Weiss's consideration of value that sustains the insights achieved in these works. He concludes, on the basis of the theory of value as articulated by Weiss in *Privacy* and supplemented by his own theory of value as harmony, with the claim that the achievement of structure is value.

Karsten Harries in "Architecture and Ontology" identifies factors contributing to the present confused state of architecture and argues that, if philosophy is to contribute to the discussion about the tasks of building, it must break with traditional aesthetics and the ontology that it presupposes. Challenging the ontological presuppositions of current aesthetics on the basis of Professor Weiss's determination of four modes of being, Professor Harries turns to the insights of *Nine Basic Arts* — that art is not only beautiful but also revelatory of reality and thereby serves truth — as offering the basis for a more adequate philosophy of architecture. The ontological conception of art that is necessary to do justice to the essence of architecture requires Weiss's richer notion of being and kinds of access to beings. Architecture is therein revealed to be the activity of wresting place from space, by bounding and mastering it, and thereby answering the human need for place.

Paul Grimley Kuntz's essay, "Paul Weiss: What is a Philosophy of Sport?" examines another neglected aspect of Professor Weiss's thought, but one of which Weiss is justifiably proud because he subjects to philosophical scrutiny and clarification an unthematized but very influential dimension of human life. Professor Kuntz looks at Weiss's attempt to provide a true and adequate philosophic account of sport grounded in the philosophy of the human person and as revelatory of ultimate realities through its encounter with the four modes, especially Existence and Ideality. He presents Professor Weiss's dialectical consideration of four theories of sport, namely, as play, as discipline, as therapy, and as agon, and concludes that all four are necessary to provide a true and adequate account of sport.

"The Metaphysics of Name and Address: Weiss's Answer to Kant and Frege" by Robert Castiglione argues that Professor Weiss's theory of naming offers an answer to Kant's subsumption of singular judgments under the rule for general judgments and the problems regarding the logical status of such singular judgments to which that subsumption has given rise in light of Frege's concern with the assurance of a *nominatum*. Professor Castiglione claims that Weiss's distinction between expressions that function as signs and those that function as symbols serves to overcome the problems that arise from Frege's analysis in that this distinction grounds a valid intensional logic for evidencing unitary entities. He further claims that Weiss's conception of names as penetrating a depth overcomes the problems arising from Kant's analysis. Weiss's concept of "evidencing" and finalities is the advance that grounds the resolution of these issues.

In "Human Beings: Plurality and Togetherness," after noting the constancy of the theme of the one and the many in both the history of philosophy and Professor Weiss's thought, Richard J. Bernstein examines that theme as it manifests itself in Weiss's consideration of human actualities in *You, I, and the Others*. He offers a systematic exposition of Professor Weiss's account of the unity and diversity of I, you, and me in terms of the public and private. The consequences of this account for the issues of human intelligibility, individuality, identity, uniqueness, spatiality, temporality, embodiment, sociality, politics, and ethics are considered. He follows this with critical comments regarding a lack of clarity regarding the way Weiss's physicalistic language is to be taken and Weiss's slighting of the essential historicity of I, you, me, and we.

Professor Cua's "Queries and Replies" represents the correspondence between himself and Professor Weiss regarding *First Considerations, You, I, and the Others*, and *Privacy*. These exchanges offer important corrections and clarifications of the contents of these works. They also show Weiss as involved in an ongoing dialogue not only with his colleagues but also about other traditions of thought, as well as the need to consult Weiss's nonsystematic and unpublished writings to appreciate fully the content of his works. Their correspondence with respect to *First Considerations* covers (1) the relation of Weiss's Actuality/Finality schema to neo-Confucian concepts, (2) questions about an underlying model of and assumption about agency, (3) whether a vicious circularity occurs in the move from evidence to evidenced, (4) Weiss's account of names, and (5) the character of Unity as a Finality. With regard to *You, I, and the Others*, they touch on the importance of its insights for ethical considerations such as the nature of access to others, the value of others, knowledge of others, and accountability and responsibility. The issues are discussed in light of

Weiss's apparent assumption of a normative model grounded in an ontology of privacy and an objective hierarchy of values, and the impact of these assumptions on the problem of the relation between ethics and metaphysics. Their exchange about *Privacy* is primarily in terms of clarifications for such notions as person and its epitomizations, self and its epitomizations, the idios, and native rights.

Irwin Lieb's essay, "Being and Becoming," briefly reviews the ever-renewed argument over the priority of being or becoming and suggests that, if differently but apppropriately construed, they can both be seen as equiprimordial. He finds this insight in Professor Weiss as well as shows that Weiss's modes doctrine requires it.

Charles Hartshorne in his essay, "Weiss after Sixty Years," reflects on his friendship with Professor Weiss that began with their collaboration on the editing of Peirce's writings and takes up the similarities and differences between his own, Whitehead's, and Weiss's philosophies. His considerations range over their respective approaches to philosophy, the place of human and ethical values, and their ideas of God, freedom, relations, finalities, and individual identity. This essay is of great significance because it offers the mature judgment on Weiss's thought from the "loyal opposition" by its most prominent and respected living representative.

Professor Weiss relishes such dialogue and criticism because his writings are as much a beginning as an end. Through such dialogue he is able to engage in the creative activity that is philosophy. These essays offer evidence that some philosophers do heed his call to preserve ontology's claim to a deep structure for reality and testify to the fact that his philosophy will die neither from sharp criticism nor from neglect (FC, p. 24).

I would like to thank Paul Kuntz of Emory University, Francis Gignac of The Catholic University of America, and especially Jude Dougherty of The Catholic University of America for their invaluable assistance in the collecting and editing of this volume.

Thomas Krettek

One

George Kimball Plochmann

Methods and Modes:
Aspects of Weissian Metaphysics*

I

Paul Weiss looks at the world with deliberate candor. He also brings
to his vision of that world a formal array of concepts. Throughout his
long and distinguished career he has found that the act of philosophizing can end in satisfaction only after the employment of the
perceptual and the intellectual has been balanced. The respect for
orderly procedure must be weighed against the claims of a universe
that, like it or not, is as we find it.

Even if a philosopher decides to arrange and rearrange an array of
abstractions, making it his primary or sole method, it is still evident
that his early stages of development involve a provisional method
that may be no more than an ordinary period of growth. The ultimate
method (which may, if the philosopher progresses further, become
the penultimate method) is willy-nilly predicated partly upon the
provisional, for experience, raw and unlettered, must antedate the
powers of abstract thought in the biological development of each
human being. If a philosopher decides to move on to abstractions
only, the best he can do is to blot out what his natural growth has
given him, and seek for the unbroken calm of a dialectic of concepts
elsewhere. In the writings of Paul Weiss, I find many indications of
this effort, but supplemented, as time went on, by his willingness to
settle the many strident claims of experience.

In order to focus on the main features of a philosophic method as

* I wish to thank the staff of the Southern Illinois University Press for help
in assembling materials for this expository essay, including the loan of copies
of virtually all the reviews that appeared at the time of publication of the
books.

15

pursued by some one thinker, it should be remembered first that a philosophic system must have parts, and that these parts are identifiable as (1) the individual terms or concepts, (2) the propositions in which the terms are joined in specific ways, (3) the arguments that relate propositions and through them the terms, (4) the sciences that combine arguments in patterns intended to insure the highest achievable certainty, and (5) a scope exactly commensurate with the chosen subject matter. Over these structures, with their steeply-ascending levels of complexity, the method must play, conferring an individual character on each of these parts of a system and reflecting the philosopher's choices. Experience can exert its effect at every level.

Philosophers and other writers on philosophy have customarily spoken of method as being unitary, some one kind of procedure set off against the method of science, or the method of history, or even a method in one of the arts. Instead of voicing complaints against these practices here, I prefer the substitution of a recognition that method can first be viewed separately on each of the five levels just now distinguished, and then viewed together. Thus on the level of terms, the methodological concerns all have to do with meanings: whether they are literal or analogical, whether they are fixed or shifting, whether they are conceived as possessing many partially independent meanings or one canopy meaning that, when ultimately arrived at, is found to cover and comprehend all the others. On the level of propositions, the primary methodological distinction is between these considered as affirmative or negative, and in either case whether they are to be taken as true or false and in what degrees. On the third level, that of arguments (accepting this notion in a broad sense as relating ideas), there are a number of technical devices for cogently combining terms so that each one can clarify the position and meaning of the others: hierarchies of various sorts, coordinate categories, types of antithetic pairs and other groupings — these and several other devices loom very large in every philosophical exposition and enjoy a controlling influence in the way philosophy is composed. In science, the main methodological consideration is the order of the topics and therefore the order of the arguments. Lastly, in a system the decision to separate the subordinate sciences or other disciplines, whether temporarily or forever, and the decision to make some one science a starting point for all the others, or to make it the fruition of all the rest — these too are methodological choices, even if their expression takes the form, as indeed it must, of propositions on a much lower level.

Most of the well-accepted logics, especially the symbolic logics of the past century or so, have not much to say regarding method taken in any of these senses. In its most general aspect, and etymologically, method is a way of proceeding. In the working out of a system, it is doubtful whether a philosopher makes a conscious choice of method on each of these five levels separately; and the proper summary of any system usually requires a fusion, as it were, of some of these levels. What is characteristic of an individual philosopher's procedures can be made clear enough by this means.

Paul Weiss, carrying the search for comprehensiveness in philosophy to its final stages, is one of the relatively few thinkers of our century[1] who, skilled in devising and applying refined distinctions between terms, in discriminating degrees of truth and falsity in propositions, and in combining propositions into cogent argumentative structures, has dared as well to fulfill a self-imposed obligation to frame a philosophic system embracing a collection of disciplines that are either sciences or behave as if they were indeed scientific. Not many persons have dealt with such myriad problems and have come so startlingly close to attaining conceptual wholeness. Even so, one of our author's cardinal virtues has lain in his repeatedly working his way beyond the complex solutions to which he himself has already come, now building the newer upon rather than dismissing the older. He has plowed and harrowed his chosen magisterial discipline, metaphysics, many times, thereby enriching its yield as the years have passed. This, I think, is demanded by his method.

In the working out of his open system his very breadth and subtlety makes not well-nigh but totally impossible its characterization with any customary labels — realism, idealism, process philosophy, phenomenology, skepticism, and the rest — that gain currency, lose it for a time, only to reappear with altered meanings and fresh adjectives attached. To pluck a handful of passages from their contexts, which in the case of Paul Weiss turn out to be merged into the whole sequence of his writings rather than his separate essays or even books, would often persuade an inattentive reader that one or other of these labels could be suitably imposed. Another class of shibboleths, those containing the name of some earlier philosopher such as Plato or Aristotle, Thomas or Hume, Hegel or anyone else handy, would fit

Weiss just as poorly. For him, the writing of philosophy does not assume the form of penning isolated hypotheses or queries that, taken singly, resemble traditional pronouncements or hallowed questions; nor does it require that his solutions be cleared first with philologists and historians.

Weiss has been brief with regard to method as a separate topic for discussion; one searches in vain the indexes of most of his books for references to more than a few passing remarks on it,[2] although anyone looking at the texts themselves will find them displaying the results of the closest possible concern for method. This undescribed, implicit, and resolutely pursued method has as its first stage the discovery of the outcome of varied systematic combinations of very general terms. These terms, carefully defined at the outset, acquire richer meanings through those novel combinations, and in this way come to be applied in ever narrower subject matters, which ultimately turn out to be directly experienceable. Through this application, however, the subject matters, themselves isolated at the outset, take on more and more connections with others, so that their new cohesion is at length one reflecting a universal scope, this time more diversified, more articulated, and more concrete than at first seemed likely. A reader may think that this phase of the method is an echo of the Plato of the *Sophist* or *Parmenides* or *Timaeus*, or of John Scotus Eriugena, or Hegel; yet other phases soon enable him to discern the differences, numerous and marked.

The second stage reveals itself especially in the books coming after *Modes of Being*; an extraordinarily vigorous attempt is made to introduce and merge experience into the speculative scheme, the result being that the dialectic of concepts is at first disturbed by the intrusion. The experience begins as a slightly unformed entity that will not go away and that constantly interferes with the formed, the intellectual, the pure. This opposition is largely overcome by the fact that a dialectic of terms, when practiced assiduously enough, becomes part of one's experience, while this very experience, confronted by the play of conceptual reasoning, becomes first a term in the dialectic and then is indissolubly joined to it, eventually permeating it throughout.

As I have said, the system of Weiss is open, for he makes a number of alternative approaches, extensions, and assimilations to the same or overlapping topics and to their interrelations. This gives his chief analogies new force each time, and results in statements that at first blush logic would condemn as inconsistent, though they are not actually so. This openness, or flexibility if you like, or substitutability

of strategies should not be blamed upon caprice; altering the perspective so that the leading terms can be made to give up new secrets
and, concurrently, be tested repeatedly is desirable. No one theory,
no one array of terms, is typical of all of Weiss's metaphysics. To give
a complete account, therefore, one must expound at least a half–dozen
books devoted to that discipline, together with several more that
introduce metaphysical doctrines elucidating other topics such as morality, art, and education. Any exposition focusing on a single work
could render that one faithfully but would, at the same time, falsify
it through failure to consider the entirety of the work and the possibility of contradiction among the many books. Flat contradiction
requires that both sides of an opposition have precisely the same
significant terms if one of the assertions is to be recognizably true
and the other false for that reason alone. The method of absorbing
totalities that Weiss calls for makes it possible to compose equivalent
doctrines whose words may sound the same but whose meanings are
given in diverging contexts, and whose truth or falsity cannot for this
reason be determined by reference to their opposition to supposedly
contradictory doctrines and nothing else.

A method as conceived on the fourth level, that of a complete
discipline, must dispense an order of treatment that begins with what
is clearest and then moves to enlighten the darker patches, or else
begins with what is confused and gradually finds clarification in statement, refutation, and progressive restatements. Weiss commonly follows the first of these orders. In *Modes of Being* he begins with four
modes, the ways or categories in which all things exist, and from
which, in various combinations and modifications, the outlines of
particular existent things, their possibilities and limitations can be
deduced. In *Beyond All Appearances* it is our everyday experience, while
in *First Considerations* there is a further effort to synthesize the approaches of the other two treatises. Among all his books and within
each of them, especially the volumes of *Philosophy in Process*, he offers
a hundred visions and revisions, many of the latter having been
motivated by objections, mild and friendly or harsh as the case might
be, to the body and details of his thinking.[3]

II

Modes of Being (1958) can be called Paul Weiss's watershed book,
dividing two phases of his work, and in it he carries on metaphysical

speculation in the grand style. He begins, as I have already indicated, with the four modes, a list termed neither reducible nor expandable. The first of these modes is Actualities (*MOB*, discussed pp. 21–104), finite beings located in ordinary physical space and time, and thus encountered empirically. Actualities are either active or inactive; that is, either simple causative agents or ineffective aggregates. The former kind interact, or, to use a Weissian phrase, they urge themselves upon one another,[4] but this comes about because the possible holds itself open. Potentiality is real, and a route that an actuality may follow is toward the good, namely a somewhat indeterminate, incomplete condition that must be subdivided into specific goods proper to separate actualities of which man is the eminent prototype.

The second mode is the Ideal, or Ideality (*MOB*, discussed pp. 103–84), which is the Good divorced from any exclusive reference to the particular actualities that seek to realize that good. Whatever is possible cannot be self-contradictory, hence all real possibililties to which actualities can attain must be internally in agreement with themselves. As with Actuality, Ideality manifests itself chiefly in man, and this provides opportunity for an absorbing discussion of law, right, and might, the latter being defined as Existence socialized in an unorganized people habituated to carry on the structure of a whole society.[5] Education as striving for an end enters the account at this point.

The third of the four is Existence (*MOB*, discussed pp. 185–276), or being as it actively divides itself. (No doubt some philosophers would prefer to call this becoming, change, power, or the like, since Weiss thinks of it as a restless force overflowing all the Actualities and connecting each with each.) It is "quite close," says the author, to Plato's receptacle, Aristotle's prime matter, Newton's ether, Schopenhauer's will, Bergson's élan vital, Whitehead's Creativity, and Northrop's Undifferentiated Continuum (*MOB*, p. 185),[6] an indication of the Weissian conviction that a single concept can sustain widely differing and even inharmonious interpretations.

Existence in its subdivisions continually expands, though the expansion is limited by the other three modes. As separated from Actualities it is the spatial field they require in which to exist and interact. As separated from Ideality it is the causal ground for all development. As separated from God it is cosmic vitality. All the other modes fall short of *full* interaction with each other, and this gives point to Existence, which helps to complete the other three and, in turn, is unified by them. We can apprehend Existence, and because this mode is the ground of contemporaneity, we can say that the mode and the knowing of it are brought together at the same time by the very character of the known. In time, Actualities lose their Existence and become facts of which the past is merely a tissue.

The last mode is God (*MOB*, discussed pp. 277–370), who has a reciprocal relation with the others such that they all need God, God needs all of them, and a mutual adjustment is made to the burdens imposed by the others. The reality of God is afforded nine testimonies, three of them basic, the rest subordinate, to the reality of God as unity and ultimate end. Teleology in its substantival, rationalistic, historical, moralistic, directional, providential, architectural, mathematical, and structuralized aspects provides this testimony, although Weiss quickly adds that teleological *proofs* for God's existence are impossible. Again, nine cosmological approaches to God exist (in a quite different list from the teleological), but no uniquely rigorous proofs. To complete the trio of approaches (somewhat reminiscent of Kant's), there can be no specifically ontological proofs either, but some kind of assent to God can nevertheless be given through work (reflecting Existence), faith (reflecting Actuality), and assent following inference (reflecting Possibility and through it Ideality). Further, the three "classical" proofs can be made to operate in tandem, so that a new one can be devised showing that God is also relevant by teleological testimony, and it is possible through a cosmological detachment. This, however, is mere Existence as it operates on the conclusion of a cosmological rule, *i.e.*, what was merely possible is elevated to the rank of something separate and determinate and thus actual. A combination of the modes by an involution and what might be called modes-in-modes yields twenty-seven proofs for the reality of God, nine each for work, faith, and assent following inference (*MOB*, pp. 320–24). And yet all proofs of God beg the question, *must* beg it, for they commence with testimony, but the testimony owes its very presence to God.

The modes all intertwine, cooperate, delimit, supplement, and alter the effects of each other. God as the principle of unity is in a sense unique, binding the others more firmly than if they were capable of existing without him. It is tempting to state, in light of the elaborate correspondences and fixed analogies that Weiss establishes, that all the terms of the metaphysical network at bottom mean the same thing, as appears to be true of the systems of certain other philosophers superficially resembling Weiss — I hazard Eriugena, Berkeley, Bradley, Alexander, and, perhaps, Schelling. In view of Weiss's repeated assertions that the modes are, all of them, irreducible to one another or to anything else, and in view of his careful representations of their uniqueness, however, we must allow them that independence — and allow Paul Weiss the ineradicable complexity that has bade fair to become one of his trademarks.[7]

To introduce the fifth chapter of *Modes of Being*, I will first make some general observations. By most accounts, the book is a dialectical work, but the question of what constitutes dialectic is not easily answered, since both the definitions and the practices of dialectic have varied greatly throughout the centuries. It is safe to say, however, that among its meanings we can have philosophic composition exhibiting all of the following, and these are not impossible to find in selected systems important in past centuries:

1.   terms that alter their meanings;

2.   in altering, they become enriched by the relations established, with meanings left over from earlier phases of the dialectic, much as the present usages will enrich those to come;[8]

3.   the meanings ultimately, or more rarely initially, are the most general ones possible, meanings of the widest comprehension that still convey a distinction from what falls outside the terms. For instance, X does not ordinarily receive a meaning of this distinctive sort, and, hence, is not such a dialectically significant term;

4.   oppositions, chiefly contraries that appear as pairs of terms (if one member of such a pair undergoes a change of meaning, the second will also);

5.   arguments in support of many of the propositions reached, but not of all, for this would result in circularity;

6.   arguments by way of refutation, or attempted refutation, of what is proposed;

7.   hence an emphasis on negation and the *possibilities* that all being can be reduced to nothing, every truth can be shown to be partly false, every good somewhat discredited, every instance of the beautiful revealed at the same time as ugly and disgusting — as a stage, though not the last stage, in a continuing dialectical process; and

8.   since the terms can gain in width, resolution of oppositions

usually arises from generalizations that manage to include both, or all, aspects of a dialectical sequence in which negations have been uncovered.

Given, then, the dialectical character of *Modes of Being*, that a considerable space will be devoted to the negations of all that has been put forward positively is expected. The penultimate set of chapters of the book are given over to these opposites, which Weiss insists are nevertheless parts of the system. They function as negations only when made too specific and treated as independent terms rather than relations. Otherwise, they are absorbed into the system. Verbalized as negations, any rejections of the system begin to appear only when experience is set off against the system, which of itself cannot include experience.

A listing of the full sequence follows, 441 strong, of the affirmative propositions together with the briefest of hints why they should be accepted, the longer proofs having, of course, already been offered with each of the 441 as it first appeared. The negations are now included, but Weiss says in advance that they have force only when stated as if separately, atomically. Otherwise, taken together, they are assimilated into the system.

A philosophy truly adequate must accommodate all other principles as instances of itself, even when those principles are in strict opposition to fundamental theses of the system (*MOB*, pp. 385–86). We may note that in repeating original theses and then offering paragraph-length antitheses, Weiss is limiting the scope of the objections. Thus he cites what might be counterarguments against the individual propositions describing the function of Actuality, both alone and in concert with the others, but finds no need to defend the choice of the number four for his principles (*i.e.*, modes) or the fact that Actuality is one of them, or that the modes combine with changes in their meanings when the combinations are made. Hence some of the fundamental assumptions are left unassailed; but perhaps Weiss would like to call to mind Aristotle's saying that it is the mark of an uncultivated man to demand a proof for everything.[9] On the other hand, the objections Weiss raises to his own views are serious and searching and are made of anything but straw.

One might assume that the next step is to refute each of the objections piecemeal, but Weiss — contrary to the strategy of Descartes, Berkeley, or others who let opponents air their complaints and then set about to trounce them — leaves the objections unanswered. His preference is to discuss, at some length, the character of a philosophic system as a whole, based primarily on the ever-present problem of the one and the many (*MOB*, chs. 10–12). Monism is impossible, and five traditional attempts to establish some dualism or synthesis are all failures, though they furnish some welcome insights.

Because it is independent, each mode has a different kind of relation to the other three and a different kind of multiplicity that it sponsors in things. The question then arises: How is knowledge possible if we speak for a plurality of modes? Perhaps a mode is known only by another instance of itself, otherwise the perspective would be slanted and the knowledge incomplete or misleading. In order to *know*, the I or self must assume four different functions and with them four "positions":

As standing apart, the I is the Actuality of man in his most private recesses; as in contact with the modes it is man in the guise of Existence, as at once one with and over against what is other than himself; as blending with the modes while stressing one of them, it is man in the guise of the Ideal, as taking a position of the possible in terms of which all else is to be understood; and finally, as submerged in the modes, it is man in the guise of an eternal unity in which the knower has lost his individuality and sees only what is to be seen in fact (*MOB*, p. 530).

The end result is that the knower is both a part and not a part of the grand cosmic sweep; he watches the modes in their work and interplay, but then again, he *is* the modes in their isolation and their cooperation, their limitations and powers.

The four modes might (had Weiss preferred to build a system of unyielding rigidity) have indicated fields to be explored separately in subsequent books — as science, ethics, history, and religion, or some such fourfold division, simple and dogmatic. But this seemed unlikely from the fact that the modes interact and cannot profitably be taken one by one. It was made more unlikely still through the fact that the author was a philosopher fully immersed in Existence — in becoming change, development, process. Consequently, though one *could* make something of a case for his having, after *Modes of Being*, composed four kinds of books, this must be modified. Each of the many volumes treats of topics in terms of the interactions of the modes; the later ones also reexamine the status of each mode and often propose different memberships for the list of them and a different status for the modes taken collectively. The three encompassing themes of his metaphysics are diversification, supplementation, and unity, and these cannot be played in ringing tones in an obstinate quartet.

As I remarked earlier, *Modes of Being* was a kind of watershed. Reviewers spoke of it as a masterpiece, and it was likened for its profundity and comprehensiveness — and difficulty — to Whitehead's *Process and Reality*. At that point the similarity virtually ceases, for *Modes* is hardly an essay in process philosophy. At any rate, Weiss called attention to the way his book sums up and transforms his previous *Reality* (1938) and *Nature and Man* (1947).[10]

Philosophy in Process Volume I (1966) puts the four modes through even more paces than does the book devoted specifically to their treatment.[11] They account for four "positions" of categories (p. 6); four roles of self (p. 350); four kinds of knowledge (p. 206); four uses of the modes in drama (p. 209); four remedies for defects (pp. 176–77); four kinds of men (the observer, the rationalist, the adventurer, and the experiencer — pp. 525–26); corresponding to four types of phenomenological object (the perceptual, the formal, the eventful, and the important — p. 546); four strategies (p. 206); and so on.[12] True, however, to the flexibility I mentioned earlier, Weiss eventually relinquishes virtually all of these suggested quartets without repudiating them. Clearly, each of the modes must be examined in several ways, given several meanings. Thus, God could not possibly be the ground for value, for organizing production, for the spectatorial type of interpreter, for the experiencer among kinds of men, for the important phenomenological object, and the like were the word "God" to be held univocal and to designate a being with but one or two demonstrable characteristics. If God is pure being, then the singleness or simplicity necessarily rules; but if God is somehow (and very differently) related to all things, then the unity of God must be maintained and proved despite the evident diversity of his aspects.

III

A fairly common complaint, whose justice Weiss recognized and even anticipated, was that *Modes of Being* remained abstract, recalling to us from time to time Bradley's famous remark in his *Principles of Logic* about Hegel's "ballet dance of bloodless categories." The books on metaphysics, or rather the books whose principal emphasis was on topics traditionally called metaphysical and published after *Modes of Being*, were therefore devoted in part to supplying all that had heretofore been missing: experience, artistic creation, impulse, religious awe, figurative thought and expression, and, of course, the bridges from these to the modes, which themselves underwent numerous changes. How Paul Weiss met this challenge, which is of course not the only one laid down by certain philosophers against certain others, but one made by men and women everywhere against *all* philosophers, will occupy us for a good share of the balance of this essay.

In *Modes of Being*, slightly more than one hundred theses were devoted to God as a mode; of these perhaps fifteen are on religio-ethical matters, in the sense of a search for God and the way to find Him through faith, prayer, humility, and works. A little more than the first half of *The God We Seek* (1964)[13] is occupied with what one might call the interfaces of religion with ethics, politics, and history. The remainder, headed "The Quest," treats of the turn toward God, ordinarily no simple, abrupt, and final tropism but one coming about in stages, with backsliding and retreat; faith, which again is not a once-and-for-all commitment but is tested over and over with doubt and desperation; religious, sacred language, in part impervious to logic and philosophical analysis; and last, the religio-ethical life, in which the first member of this yoked pair establishes desirable goals for the individual, the second demanding obedience. The love that God bears man includes judgment, which may or may not be a conscious, merciful, forgiving judgment in each case: "The religious man in adoration and in devotion presents himself to God for assessment, and deals with what else there is in the light of what he takes God to be, do, and demand" (*GWS*, p. 241).

In *Modes of Being*, experience was, so to speak, an emergent from a dialectical apparatus, while in *The God We Seek*, experience is as fundamental as any dialectic of metaphysical concepts; defining the experience we have of God must be weighed against the more abstract consideration of what God is. Since our knowledge or even faith regarding the nature of God is also buried deep in experience, both the abstract and the personal must be explored together.

Despite the crisp elegance of almost fifty Questions relating directly to God, His essence and Persons, in the *Summa Theologica* of St. Thomas,[14] or the chiselled directness of the first part of Spinoza's

Ethics, writings on God have traditionally been of a somewhat different character from those on most other topics, with the possible exception of love. The infinity of the Being in qualities and in power, the variety of ways that these can become manifested in finite beings, and the ineffability that pervades all these ways and eludes immediate understanding, are reflected in the host of metaphors, the multitude of admittedly second-best strategies, and the expressions of dissatisfaction and failure to discover a unitary method that will properly apprehend the subject and make it intelligible to others.

If God was a mode in the earlier book, then His nature and existence could be treated with equivalent precision in the charting of intertwined concepts as Weiss treated his other three modes. In *The God We Seek* this stringency is somewhat relaxed, as if the author were more ready to recognize that certain subjects cannot be aptly treated by the quasi-calculative method employed earlier. On the other hand, the discussion of God in the later book is by no means a purely subjective one, it is never hortatory, nor does it attempt to borrow the color of historical vignettes regarding worship, mystical experience, conversion, and so forth.

Weiss has two senses in which he speaks of God and is afraid of slipping unconsciously from one to the other: first, the impersonal YHWH, the ultimate Being, God beyond God, the Hidden God; second, the God of Israel and of Wrath, or of Love, and more — *i.e.*, the metaphysical God and the God of ethics and personal, involved religion (*GWS*, p. 11). The purpose of *The God We Seek* is to show those relations that can, and those that cannot, be established between the experiencing but finite man and the God seemingly possessing the two aspects. The volume then becomes a long search for the conditions, character, and effects of the religious encounter, taking God as a Being of both kinds.[15] Experience of this kind is no longer deduced,[16] but becomes the starting point as "the unmediated aspect of whatever is confronted by a conscious being" (*GWS*, p. 20). In *Reality*, published twenty-six years earlier, Weiss said that "the references to God in this work refer not to the object of religious worship, but to a supposed metaphysical being whose nature is described only in the most general speculative terms, where positively describable at all. . . . Philosophical theologies are the last place to look in order to soothe a troubled spirit" (*R*, p. 161, note). In sharp contrast, Weiss now looks upon religion as beginning "with the awareness that there is a distance between man and God that can be bridged by us, or by

God, or by the two of us together" (*GWS*, p. 9). I doubt, however, that this is as much a change of mind about religion as it is a change of plan.

Weiss now introduces what he calls dimensions of experience with the help of pairs of contraries: focal and peripheral, mine and not-mine, private and public, episodic and constant (*GWS*, ch. 2). For our purposes the third pair is the most important, but in all cases it should be remembered that these pairs do not contain barriers that cannot be crossed and interplay exists among the pairs as well.

Private experience becomes a shared experience when viewed as assimilable into a larger public experience. The private is really public experience waiting to be born, and it expands or contracts by turn. A public experience is real and is dominated by rules of language, conventional behavior, etc. A common world arises from the accord of many private beings, but a public world stands over against actions and beings, and it is conceived in order to explain the way private beings interact, while the common world merely summarizes con-current activities. People participate in public experiences as things to which they are subject.

The types of experience are aesthetic, secular, ethical, and religious; this last can be either private or public and, in either case, "brings us into relation with a felt power that assesses what we are and have attained" (*GWS*, p. 52). Here again there is an interlocking of kinds.

Religious men interplaying with one another and with a higher reality produce a public religious experience, but if the awareness of that reality is lacking, the religiosity of the experience fades into something else. Conversely, God can be treated aesthetically, without religious overtones. In fact, religious experience in the most proper sense can easily be confused with eleven other accompaniments of acts "having something to do with religion" (*GWS*, p. 56). The religious experience, rightly conceived, merges the friendly and the alien, the immediately insistent and the distantly awesome, but the remoteness is more of man's doing than God's. Religious experience relates not to eternity but to everlastingness. We "catch faint glimpses occasionally of ourselves and God as outside an everlasting religious experience episodically shared" (*GWS*, p. 66).

The next major section of *The God We Seek* addresses the Sacred (*GWS*, pp. 67–159). Every object, Weiss says, can be approached as sacred, *i.e.*, as having been qualified by God, but the religious emotions tend to separate some of these objects from the others: a temple or an altar, a consecrated goblet, or objects of this sort. The ultimate religious concept, that of a sacred object, is the basic category as pertinent to things qualified by God. Sacred objects are precious because they offer evidences of God and intimations of His sustaining role, in whom they and others are reproduced. From this standpoint, God is the great conserver, the harmonizer of conflicts.

The idea of God — an impure one, it happens — has both weakened and strengthened human beings to become worse fanatics or greater saints than they could possibly be without it. God is always in us, but we do not always, from birth, have a conscious idea of Him. An idea of God is unique and comes not from distilling ideas of other things, although fear, religious experience, and sacred objects do make us conscious of His presence. In fact, we

obtain the most adequate idea of God as a being concrete, self-identical, omnipotent, and concerned by retreating deep within ourselves in the effort to discover what it is we need, already know, and in some sense already possess. . . . Unlike any other idea, it expresses not only something of God's nature as an object of intellect, but something of His being as the object of need (GWS, p. 93).

Partly because of this need, the religious man feels himself closer to God than to the world, even though Weiss makes clear a gulf between the infinite and the finite:

God does not . . . provide the full answer nor the only answer to the questions which are faced by man. He does not really protect man from death, guilt and futility. At most he [sic: the lower case is a slip, no doubt] replaces the effects of these with others, and thereby adds new dimensions to man's being. To reduce the dangers of death, guilt and futility, men must engage in knowledge and action, ethics and politics, art and history (GWS, p. 212).[17]

To safeguard against despair, a man must join what Weiss calls a dedicated community: first, by replacing his secular values with religious ones; second, by living as a "contributive, constitutive member" of such a community (GWS, p. 100). To this group, an individual must have three kinds of relations: effective, acting in ways that the other individuals help to define; affective, uniting with others in more or less intimate ways, thereby acquiring new qualities; and formal, becoming subject to rules over which he lacks full control. God exists both within and outside of dedicated communities, equally though differently. Threefold membership in those communities brings a man closer to God, and with this confers new powers and virtues upon him. The mystic gives himself to the God that is outside the community — a transcendent being. Withdrawal from this community brings reward by adding a good, or forgiveness, by subtracting an evil, or punishment. The dedicated community has relations to the family, school, and state, among other groups. A secular society should promote peace and prosperity, and little conflict with the dedicated communities should occur, although very often conflicts abound. A church-state is a dedicated community constrained by a political system; a religious state is a political system ennobled by its attention to divinely-determined values.

Christianity, Islam, Judaism, Buddhism, and other religions are, when at their best, dedicated communities, as they should be. But with the insistence on uniqueness and superiority — even when that insistence takes the form of allowing for the saints and beliefs of other religions — each one abdicates its status as true and universal. The competing claims of the great religions are to the credit of none of them (*GWS*, ch. 8).

A full decade after *The God We Seek* — a decade punctuated by the publication of eight books, including five huge volumes of *Philosophy in Process* — Weiss again issued a finished work dealing with problems regularly called metaphysical. If *Modes of Being* was, like Hegel's *The Science of Logic*, a logico-metaphysical treatise with tendrils reaching down to the world in which we live, then *Beyond All Appearances* (1974) corresponds roughly to *The Phenomenology of Spirit* by representing itself as a kind of propaedeutic to *Modes of Being* (*BAA*, Preface).[18] Perhaps because of this intention, two further shifts in methodology are found, corresponding to a greatly increased emphasis upon two concepts, among others, earlier relegated to the background. The first of these, appearance, enjoys a careful treatment in the book whose title reflects this emphasis, while the second, creativity, is prominent in the books on art coming both before and after *Beyond All Appearances*.

In *Modes of Being* "appearance" had almost no status at all, and the very few mentions of it seemed to make it synonymous with outright error. In the new work, however, a change has taken place, and the concept now cuts across the categories, the modes constituting all reality. These categories are in turn realigned so that the basic distinction is no longer a horizontal one between modes enjoying virtually equal rank, but a vertical one in which "actualities"[19] are at the base, and "finalities" becomes a collective expression for several other modes toward which the actualities are tending. Part I of *Beyond All Appearances* moves upward from actualities to the finalities, Part II downward between the same two contraries, and Part III deals at greater length with man, who, as in *Modes of Being*, uniquely embodies all the categories within himself.

It is perhaps fair to say that the basic assertion underlying Weissian metaphysics in all its stages of development is that the real is real objectively, real in itself and not because we as knowers or symbol-makers bring it to life and existence. This contention of his is not simply an epistemological anchorpoint by means of which to take aim at a host of phantasms and fancies, but an assertion that reality is so overpowering that even the most fugitive of chimeras has something inescapably real about it. Weiss admits a great many kinds of beings to his world, the universe is a full one, dense with what many other philosophers have dismissed as nonentities or at best enjoying partial reality. I think that he has been aware that a razor-wielding descendant of old William of Ockham might make some slashes, at first exploratory, later on deletive. Be that as it may, we must be aware that for Weiss appearances are as real as anything else, even if not ultimate simples entering in their own peculiar ways into all things. The preposition "beyond" in the title does not imply that the examination of appearances will dissolve them into illusions and nonsense to be corrected, or else resolve them into higher verities to be established. This is no Bradleyan distinction between appearances that are concepts aimed at explaining parts of the whole and, because broken off from that whole, self-cancelling, and reality, which is the Absolute, a generalized experience that includes all things and persists throughout all time. For Weiss, the appearances are basic and are as they are independently of the way we interpret them. Appearances are products of the conjoining of what he calls "controlled contexts and the exhibitions of actualities" (*BAA*, p. xiv). The appearances exhibit sets of features, and every set points to the fact that a finality has become an ingredient in the appearance. Every appearance — note this democracy — is on the same footing with every other. All appearances are subject to laws and are united in a single totality that comprises the actualities —things in the commonest sense — as they move toward finalities, attaining to them or not as the case might be.

Weiss, inasmuch as he is beginning with daily experience, must either be a phenomenologist here or at least take account of this examination of experience offered by a thinker of such tendencies. Against Hegel he intends to look not only at the great movements of thought but at what happens in daily life; against Husserl he plans to include the practical along with those perceptive, cognitive aspects of human life that Husserl so assiduously scrutinized; against Peirce he will avoid excessive categorizing at the expense of the subtler features of existence as perceived. "The true phenomenologist must let what he confronts advance and recede, fade and pass away without hindrance. Consequently, he can hardly do more than live through what happens . . . " (*BAA*, p. 22).

Appearances, as we have said, are real, but not ultimate realities, for they are "too weak to act, too inert to become, too fragile to be" (*BAA*, p. 64). They arise because actualities exhibit themselves and are opposed to, or at least confronted by, exhibitions of the finalities, which are still unspecified at this stage. To arrive at a finality from an actuality, one must ignore the latter's appearance and instead attend to the finality present in a "subdued" fashion. The usual appearance of water, he says, is "biased" toward water as an actuality and is interlocked with the context furnished by a finality, a context governing the way water is related other appearances (*BAA*, p. 80). The context coming from the finality and that coming from the actuality together make phenomena. In this we see that appearances are not veils between perceiver and reality, hence to know reality is not to know something entirely separate from its appearances, but rather to know the appearances with a knowledge "purged and intensified."

Symbols are appearances merging into adumbrations (leading into actualities) and lucidations (leading into finalities). Without symbols we would perceive appearances but would, like the chained prisoners in the most famous cave in philosophical literature, think them the realities, hence would never know the real. But by closely attending to phenomena and by using symbols we can reach not only the actualities but also the finalities, which Weiss now lists for the first time (*BAA*, p. 95),[20] contrasting the current catalogue with that of his earlier treatise:

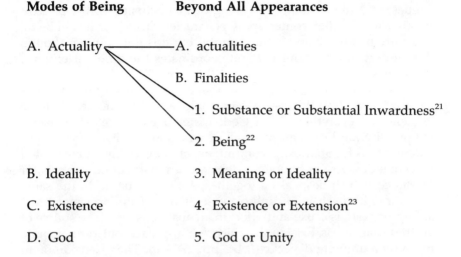

Modes of Being   **Beyond All Appearances**

A. Actuality ————————— A. actualities

                          B. Finalities

                          1. Substance or Substantial Inwardness[21]

                          2. Being[22]

B. Ideality   3. Meaning or Ideality

C. Existence   4. Existence or Extension[23]

D. God   5. God or Unity

Let us, for the sake of clarifying some of the terms connected with creativity, discover what clues are offered in *Beyond All Appearances* to the finalities that loom so large in that theory.

Actualities come to be and pass away, and thus their substantiality is maintained for but a limited time "against the persistent insistence of a constant, final Substance."[24] Each actuality acts to subjectify the affect of the Substance upon that actuality, though the subjectification is incomplete. By internalizing whatever qualifications Substance imposes upon actualities, the actualities make themselves into individuals that oppose and at the same time become instances of that Substance. The best justification for this is that Substance and a universal are in major respects the same.[25] Animality and humanity impose certain characteristics upon Mr. Jones, though they are not Mr. Jones in any exact sense; yet if one removes them, he is removed as well.

Being, elevated in the 1958 book to a status more general than, and possibly superior to, the four modes, is now seemingly accorded a rank coordinate with the other four finalities, though as a matter of fact it was formerly included in the Actualities, not as one of them, but as one of the meanings of the expression. Being is now made ultimate, that which forever is and never will not be. Even if nothing existed, Being would still exist. Every actuality *has* a being. Such an actuality derives limitations from Substance and from the other finalities, and these "taint" the being of that actuality (*BAA*, p. 268). In other words, they confer upon it character, lacking as it is in Being as a pure finality. Being is thus empty, but it is not nothing, though it is unitary and without parts; it coordinates the different entities, regardless of how diverse they are (*BAA*, pp. 276, 297).

Existence of an individual means that its structures control its energies (*BAA*, p. 169). Weiss does not hold with St. Thomas that the existence of everything is in God. Instead, Existence is spatiality, temporality, and dynamism — all of which are divisible into parts. Extension, as for Spinoza, is continuous, but nevertheless demarcated by actualities. As continuous, extensions are parts of or symbols for Existence, which bespeaks a togetherness of the parts. In the same way, time by itself is an unbroken sequence of uniform moments, and dynamism is cause-and-effect in an abstract sense. The source of all these, again, is Existence, which we approach but do not quite reach by a unifying dialectic (*BAA*, pp. 278–80). The extension of an actuality is peculiar to that actuality at that time, though it is also subject to Existence, the abiding continuum.

God as a finality is distinct from God as an object of worship, a personal deity. Weiss makes the interesting observation that the

world in which science is interested is an aspect of the world as it might be seen by God. From this perspective, science can be said to be a part of theology carried on by other means. As such it is to be studied in order to know something of what God has in mind. If we wish to know what exists, we must supplement this knowledge with what is learned in the course of a symbolizing penetration into actuality and other realities (*BAA*, p. 155).

God is infinitely removed from the world, and no finite being can traverse the distance from that world to God, yet God enters into all things, unifying then all, much as in Dante's final, incredible vision. God is one, and one is Unity, both a conclusion and a premise for all thinking.

In his later writings, Weiss maintained that all possibilities become specifications of one particular final Possibility. In *Beyond All Appearances*,[26] Possibility is treated in some respects as a finality itself, although it is not listed with them. Ideality had held a place of honor in *Modes of Being*, as a kind of embracing value or good, but in the work we are now discussing it vanishes from view. It seems wise, therefore, to take up Possibility as *Beyond All Appearances* does, regardless of its status and the capitalization of its name. An actuality has an individual nature, but gains intelligibility the more that this individuality is broken into and merged with other natures. This comes about through Possibility, which, impinging upon the actuality, relates its nature to others, "lifting up the natures" into the realm of necessity. Possibility is specified through the natures, which fill it up and, in this sense, can be understood as an agency in an intelligible cosmos. Thus we see one more instance where Weiss forces his concepts to gain their proper meaning only through interweaving them with others.

IV

If dialectical development and personal biography are two different concerns in philosophic exegesis — as indeed they are in the case of Paul Weiss — then it is permitted to go back in time in order to review another new concept starting to figure prominently in his writings — creativity. *The World of Art* and *Nine Basic Arts*, originally conceived as forming one volume, were published separately in 1961 and were followed by *Cinematics* several years later (1975).[27] The first two books use the fourfold pattern of *Modes of Being*, while the volume on film applies the five-member division of *Beyond All Appearances* and, in harmony with that work, is somewhat more pliant to the demands of ordinary experiences than are its forerunners on art. Even in those books, however, the claims of experience are rarely put aside. As much as any John Dewey, Weiss believes that the theorist on art, his coming to his most abstract and remote formulations, is rooted in experience. Some of this experience is of course common to everyone, but much of it must be extraordinary, being conditioned by the requirements of artistic practice and performance. To write knowledgeably about theatre in *Nine Basic Arts* Weiss authored a play, and discussed theatre from all standpoints with critics, playwrights, directors, and actors; to deal sensibly and sensitively with painting, he studied the tools and media of the art, producing numerous canvases of his own, some of them stark expressionistic representations of Hebraic prophets, with black restless lines and hot colors contrasting; and so on for his involvement with the rest of the nine arts.[28] Before commencing his *Cinematics* he worked at a motion picture studio. In this way, Weiss made as strenuous an effort as any philosopher has ever made to come to grips with the central technical issues of the arts and, at the same time, to see them whole. Yet because of the all-encompassing nature of Weissian metaphysics, it is still something of a truism to say that the other disciplines, numerous and varied, of which he writes, become branches of this metaphysical theory. The intrusion of experience into a system that was originally so luminous is a necessary step, if not one fully foreseen in the early books, through 1958. It means two things: that the explicit metaphysics itself must take an altered shape, and that the other disciplines must bear a relation to that new shape different from what we could expect had none of this alteration occurred. This is a roundabout way of saying that the books on art both are and are not "applications" of the metaphysics of *Modes of Being*.

A principal thesis of *The World of Art* is that an artistic work resembles — but is not really the same as — a natural object, even though both may have aesthetic interest. We can take either kind of object and separate it, physically in some cases, imaginatively in all, and consider its nature in itself, outside of what Weiss calls the web of conventional needs. Art alone, he adds, gives emotions expression and satisfaction, at once restructuring and suffering science, history, and religion, both encouraging and purifying them. Like mere play, art looks to no end beyond itself; but art is a disciplined activity, although unlike established games played by many groups and at many times, it follows no rules (*WA*, pp. 14, 15). Nor is art identical with craftsmanship, which uses skills to produce something merely desired; an art uses *its* skills to bring about what is excellent (*WA*, pp. 16, 17).[29] Employing a technique to produce artistic subtleties in turn alters the very value and role of the technique, and the difference lies in the imaginative character of artistic production, a character that the craftsman as such does not possess. Art, he says,

exhibits something of the spontaneity and self-containedness of play, the law-abidingness of games, the control and purposiveness of work, the value of labor, the arduousness of toil, the weariness of drudgery, the technique of the craftsman, and the excellence characteristic of the liberal arts. But it goes beyond all these. It is a full-fledged creative enterprise making use of material to bring about beauty — excellence given a sensuous body. There is still much more to it than this. A work of art is not only sensuous; it has a rationale; it is not only unified but diversified, many as well as one; there is tension and disequilibrium in it, but also order, proportion and resolution;

it is at once at a distance and immediate, opaque and translucent, novel and traditional (*WA*, p. 18).

Much of the early portion of *The World of Art* is devoted to explicating and detailing this summary. Weiss repudiates one after another the claims of ethics, politics, religion, philosophy, and finally science to rank appreciably higher in the scale of human enterprises. The first four are treated in a group, but the twenty fully-packed pages on science attempt to refute almost every conceivable point urged for the latter's superiority. Weiss concludes:

The most accurate way of relating art and science is to view them as supplements, not as correlatives. Arts conform to the laws science seeks to discover. Science rests on the foundations art discerns. Art is more philosophical than science, science more valuable for practice (*WA*, pp. 59–60).

The two volumes on art were published only three years after *Modes of Being*, so a good deal of the conceptual and methodologic timber was imported from that work. Thus, an object is at once perceptual, corresponding to Actualities among the modes, scientific, corresponding to the (mathematical or nonmathematical) formalities of Ideality, eventful, which stems from the restlessness of Existence, and important, which is a valuation put upon it that rests ultimately with God. The object itself may be a commonsense object, or its interpreted, understood counterpart, or finally a constructed, created substance such as a sculpture, and the four strands, as he calls them, are present in each kind. The importance of a work of art is that it presents objects that are self-sufficient, final, and worthy of man's most passionate devotion (*WA*, pp. 61–79).[30] The first strand under the artist's skilled hand becomes sensuous content, the second becomes rules, the third a dynamic emotional content, and the last transforms importance into overwhelming importance.[31]

The fine chapter on artistic creation is brief and deliberately omits the many recorded episodes of dramatically creative moments and discharges of lightning, so Weiss offers no tales of inspiration's advent while one is mounting the steps of a trolley car or sleeping off laudanum in a remote Lake Country cottage. He speaks only of the general underlying causes of what can then be fixed in a line of poetry, a couple of measures for the violin, or a superlatively drawn eye or hand. What makes artistic creation different from other kinds, and in what way is it the same? This is his question. All art, he insists, possesses an element of creativity, just as all art possesses some organization; these confer unpredictability and predictability, respectively, process and structure (*WA*, pp. 80–82). Artistic creativity is generally the same as other sorts, but has five characteristics making it unique: It is spontaneous, independent of any external cause or rule; it is inventive, using contrivances, chance occurrences, and available materials ingeniously; it is urgent, deeprooted, and overpowering; it is persistent, ceasing only when excellence in a sensuous form is achieved; and it is emotional, from its stimulating inception through to its final satisfaction. These five are insufficient in themselves to produce art of any quality, but they are nevertheless essential (*WA*, pp. 82–83). He continues,

We produce a known substance when, after we purify the abstractions which resulted from (1) a conditioning of common-sense objects by the senses, (2) by scientific attitudes, (3) by an immersion in mere activity, (4) or by an evaluation, we solidify all into a single being (*WA*, p. 84).[32]

The constructed substance, *i.e.*, the art object, shares these traits of perceptibility, intelligibility, dynamism, and value with commonsense objects but surpasses them in being self-sufficient and thus more truly satisfying. If natural objects and art objects have some common origins and traits, they are yet fundamentally different; the latter have both new natures and new careers.

The social root of the artist's activity is his conveyance of part of the meaning of the Good, or Ideality, and this he does through use of a myth. Such a myth is to society as an idea is to an individual, and the artist worthy of the name must use both in a unity. The course of his creativity is guided by this unity, which in every case refers to the beginning of life, or a turning point, or an end. Weiss stresses the fact that for most artists surprises, frustrations, and important changes of plan occur throughout the creation of art — Mozart being an exception he wisely mentions. "Creativity" is thus defined as "an adventure of relating, combining, altering, making, destroying material in an effort to articulate a prospect which is to be made sensuously evident through the emotional use of transformed material" (*WA*, p. 91).

In *Nine Basic Arts*, Weiss restates the essential "dimensions" of the mode Existence as space, time, and becoming or energy, indicating that four ways to approach each of these exist, the four ways being the modes in new guises: through perception, which renders qualities; through science, giving us forms; through action, which is always transitional; and through evaluation. These approaches are suited to nature but not to art, which requires that we take into careful account ideas and creative processes, as well as the art object *per se* (*NBA*, pp. 9, 13–26). Not only are the individual art objects identified in those partly conceptual terms, but the arts themselves under which they fall as individual examples are similarly differentiated. The basic arts are nine, not because they merely loom large in history or are congenial to the author, but rather because each of the three dimensions just now referred to can be assorted in a matrix with three ways of dealing with the materials constituting the subject matters of the arts. These materials can either bound, or occupy, or exhaust a dimension. Hence, when space is bounded we have architecture, when time is bounded we have music writing, which Weiss calls musicry,[33] and when becoming or dynamism is bounded, musical performance. When the material occupies space we have sculpture, when it occupies time there is story, and when it occupies becoming the result is theatre. If, on the other hand, the material is made to exhaust space the outcome is painting, when it exhausts time it is poetry, and when it exhausts becoming the result is dance (*NBA*, p. 34). This very ingenious classification is modified, however, with a series of indications of the way the practice of the arts can and must cross those boundaries, not in reference to a synthesis of two or more arts, as in the German *Lied* or the Italian opera, but simply in the practice of a single art. Thus, the author notes, the spaces exhausted in the paintings of Jackson Pollock and Vincent Van Gogh also contain the traces of energy and its rhythms. But no one art can possibly convey all of the other arts in any immediate sense, let alone convey all of Existence by the means open to them; the materials and the techniques available will not support this strain. Nor can any artist be expected to join all the arts under the heading of one enthralling, comprehensive mastery. Of the hundreds of possible combinations which could be made from the nine arts, no more than a few have been tried. Weiss gives as one example Hans Arp, with his biomorphic shapes of wood raised slightly from a flat background and endowed with lively colors — a combination of bas relief sculpture and painting. Other men and women have joined musicry and story, or music and story. Photography, documentary films, and narrative movies have also achieved combinations. I miss a richer account of opera and music drama (*NBA*, pp. 216–23). On the other hand, Weiss is writing a philosophy of the arts, and little art criticism appears anywhere in the book; his examples are named but rarely described.

In *Cinematics*, the leading principles of *Beyond All Appearances* are still present, but not prominently, the emphasis being on the motion picture with respect to sight and hearing and, above all, making. Throughout, we find a double insistence; first, that film — or at any rate some films — must constitute an art form despite the relatively short history of motion pictures, and second, that film is a unique form, not to be reduced to painting, drama, dance, or still photography. The incidents in a film bear the five kinds of relations (derived from the five realities of post-*Modes of Being* formulations): these are affiliations (through feelings), independence (the integrity of each incident), extensional connections, structures (temporal, spatial, dynamic), and concurrent instantiations (instances of a single unity of the whole film). Such a motion picture as a totality is defined as *"a created (audio) visual ordered whole of recorded incidents*, providing one with a controlled emotional introduction, primarily to Existence, and secondarily to other finalities" (C, p. 22).[34]

V

As I have tried to demonstrate, one should not insist that Paul Weiss has employed a single unitary method throughout his extensive authorship, despite certain pervasive likenesses that show themselves. On each of the five levels earlier distinguished (terms, propositions, arguments, sciences, and system), he has made choices and has varied the selections, not sweepingly but one or two at a time. In *Modes of Being*, the archetypal terms can be fixed by original definition and then altered solely in accordance with a pattern of combination and recombination. The affirmations and negations of the exposition become truer as it progresses, and as they approach closer to concrete reality. The terms in these propositions are initially related as coordinate categories, not hierarchically, and are selected because they are thought collectively to exhaust every universal kind of being. The result is that metaphysics becomes the absolutely primary discipline from which all others derive their meaning and power. As the method carries the discussion through its many phases, the terms take on more and more meanings that are remote from the original ones to which they are related by analogy. This movement progresses further in the books on art. Yet a certain degree of fixity remains, even so: The basic categories remain the same and are recalled in the same relations to one another.

Much of this original methodology remains in the later books such as *Beyond All Appearances*, yet the four primary categories are now superseded by five, some of them the same, some not. The changing from four to five basic concepts has, for purely structural reasons, certain lasting consequences. Four terms can of course be arranged in neatly paired fashion, *a b, a* not-*b*, not-*a b*, not-*a* not-*b*, as contradictories, or, if contraries, hot-dry, cold-dry, hot-wet, cold-wet; or they can be blended through some other device. The fourfold pattern dictates both the pairings and their exhaustiveness. With five, on the other hand, the possibilities of individual pairs are greater and the separation of the entire list into two parts is unwieldy: *abc, de*, or else *ab, cde*. This awkwardness must be overcome by keeping the original terms more nearly literal and fixed in combining them because the pattern is less able to control changes of meaning when the pairings are more nearly random. The analogies can begin to loosen, however, when the terms are applied to other topics such as art, history, and morals or law.

The primary source of truth for the new propositions is not their coherence with others but rather the way in which they reflect both experience and its balancing with the revised conceptual array. These new propositions must also allow for the inevitable concomitant of experience, namely appearance (because we cannot trust all experiences equally), and for creativity together with its prerequisite, possibility. As the discussion becomes less formal and more descriptive, the proofs also become less rigorous in the sense that their grounds are no longer reducible to a small number of primary assumptions but, rather, gather their force from each case specially argued. Metaphysics is still regnant over the other disciplines, but it is more difficult to deduce the starting-points of these disciplines from what has already been laid down as the principles of all things in general. The unity of the system arises not from a formal structure but from a clearly perceived richly textured universe of which the conceptual schematism is now but one aspect.

Perhaps this essay exaggerates the differences between the two phases of Paul Weiss's thinking that I have discriminated, although

I do not believe it does so unfairly. It is necessary, however, to return to a point made very early, that even if a thinker's first works happen to be very abstract, very general, he has still, because he is human, gone through a preparatory period in which experience of a rather elementary and obtrusive kind has dictated most of the content and style of his thinking. Weiss's very general treatment in his first few books was not an escape from this experience, but rather an attempt to reach it and understand it by another route. In the end, then, his philosophic system is oriented toward what is living and what is human. He has tried, with his many gifts, to find balances everywhere, to do justice to each phenomenon and to the principles that themselves are coordinated and balanced in its being and its operations.

Two

Robert E. Wood

Weiss on Adumbration*

Paul Weiss has a special knack for attending to items that other philosophers tend to ignore. Shakespeare's line, "There are more things
in heaven and on earth than are dreamt of in your philosophy,"
though applicable to many thinkers, seems inappropriate when applied to Weiss. In his own way, Weiss is even more ample than the
omnivorous Hegel, who, after all, never elaborated a philosophy of
sport.[1] But then again, many seem inclined to reverse Shakespeare's
line in Weiss's case: "There are more things in Weiss's philosophy
than there are in heaven or on earth."[2]

Where many thinkers — by no means most — are comfortable with
the encountered actualities of Weiss's first book, *Reality*, and many
too are also comfortable with one transcendent addition to such actualities — a God frequently thought of as the highest actuality —
people in general, and the generality of philosophic people as well,
get extremely uncomfortable with four, not to mention five, tran-
scendents or modes of being or finalities, including, and in some
sense coequal with, God.[3]

Now, one of the items ignored by many other philosophers, especially those attracted by logic, is what Weiss calls "adumbration."
It appears in almost all his works, beginning with *Reality*, and continuing to *First Considerations* and *You, I, and the Others*. The exploration of this notion may give us some access to at least one of the
routes that could make Weiss's finalities more palatable to at least
some contemporary thinkers. In the process, it may also reopen access
in a fresh way to the history of speculative thought in the West.

---

*Reprinted with permission from *Philosophy Today*, Winter 1984, Carthegena
Station/Celina, Ohio 45822.

43

I

Adumbration appears initially and centrally in Weiss's first book, and there its use itself adumbrates his later move to transcendent finalities. It appears first in the midst of a discussion of the components of a simple perceptual judgment, such as "This is paper." "This" names what Weiss calls "the indicated," the locatable, the particular, the here-and-now sensorily present, the ostensive object. "Paper" names "the contemplated," the universal meaning, detached from the particular yet oriented toward it as an instance of the contemplated meaning. But the "is" has several functions: first, a synthetic, propositional function joining the indicated and the contemplated; second, a judgmental function referring the propositional synthesis to the encountered object. Weiss detects a third function: adumbration. Adumbration refers to the in-itself-ness of the encountered, standing beyond the reach of the indicated-contemplated surface. Verification that the contemplated fits the indicated is not enough, for we know of the Not and the More than what fits within the clearly articulated elements of the judgment. But knowledge of that More is a kind of nonknowledge, a knowing ignorance (*R*, pp. 32ff., 57, 69; *PP II*, p. 22).

Weiss claims to stand in this matter somewhere between Kant and Hegel. Kant restricts knowledge to a phenomenal circle mirroring the constructive power of the mind, but cut off from the noumenal order of the things-in-themselves. Reference to the object is thus reference to what has been constituted by the mind. But having restricted knowing to the phenomenal order within which alone categories such as existence, causality and substance operate, Kant nonetheless claims to know that the thing-in-itself (1) *exists*, (2) *causes* the sensory material, and (3) *sub-stands* the phenomena that stand "on our side" as verifiable sensory-intelligible content. Kant thus violates his own restrictions. To avoid this violation, Weiss accordingly distinguishes two modes of knowing, one dealing with the verifiable indicated-contemplated surface jutting into our side, another — knowing in a broader sense of the term — knowledge by adumbration (*NM*, p. 50). "We are" he says, "phenomenalists who are aware that there is a truth beyond phenomenalism making it possible" (*R*, p. 142).[4]

Adumbration at this phase of Weiss's thought has two facets: a perceptual facet and a recessive facet. The elliptical presentation of a plate seen from an angle declining from frontality involves a perceptual adumbration of the circularity of the plate (*PP I*, p. 521). Presumably the outer and macro-observation of the body involves perceptual adumbration of the future penetration of physiology, microbiology, and microphysics. The perceptual adumbrative makes possible a move from where we are, within the phenomenal circle of the public commonsense world, to an extended phenomenal circle. But the recessive adumbrative refers to the ultimate private substantiality of the existing thing, beyond even the extended circle (*R*, p. 58).

Contrary to Kant, Hegel claims to "overreach" the phenomena and eventually to stand completely in the place of the *Ding-an-sich*. For Weiss, this errs in the other extreme, although Weiss has great sympathy for Hegel, considering *The Phenomenology of Spirit* to be perhaps the greatest work in the history of thought.[5] However, Hegel's final claim to penetrate fully to the other side through the development of the Absolute System claims too much. Kant, Weiss claims, began in the wrong place, with articulate knowledge, not with that which antedates such knowledge and to which adumbration points. Hegel's *Phenomenology* seems to begin with articulate knowing, but of the most impoverished sort: the here-and-the now sensorily present. But the movement of the dialectic leads to a progressive broadening and enriching of the scope of the investigation to include desire as that upon which the initial knowing rests. So also Weiss. We actually begin with what he calls the *insistence* of our being as desirously moving outside itself to the insistent being of the other.[6] For Weiss, the adumbrated is "correlated . . . with the unexpressed needs constituting our very privacy" (*R*, p. 282), with emotions, with "affective tone," and even, in one way of fullfilment, with mystical experience. All of these expressions refer to a prearticulate level of experience that carries our being beyond itself. Adumbration thus constitutes the acknowledgment of what the irrationalists and the Romanticists have insisted upon and against which the logicians and the rationalists have fought (*R*, p. 31).

But the very obscurity of this move calls for clarification, and is indeed made possible by the prime principle of the clarificatory move: the principle of noncontradiction, which Weiss calls "the category" (*R*, pp. 144ff.). Its evidentiality seems to be immediate and its scope unlimited. When we acknowledge the lowliest, most fleeting aspect of our experience to *be*, *i.e.*, when we not only meet it, but meet it "as being" and judge that it *is*, we recognize immediately that a thing cannot both be and not be at the same time and in the same respect.

And since outside *being* nothing exists at all, "the category" refers us to what exists within and beyond the phenomenal circle: to the whole of what occurs and can occur within that circle, to the whole of what lies beyond it in each thing — ourselves included — and in the absolute totality (*R*, p. 284). But just for the very reason that it includes the totality in its reference, the category is a kind of emptiness that has to be filled in various ways with the encounterable and the inferrable. The law of contradiction, Weiss observes, is "inseparable from a completely universalizable variable 'any adumbrated'" (*R*, p. 147). It involves a kind of Hegelian overreaching of the phenomena that are relative to my perceptual powers, and a standing, though emptily, in the place of the other. Actually moving into the other occurs in artistic penetration, in love, in mystical experience, and in speculative inference (*R*, pp. 99, 261; *PP I*, p. 403).

Art has a special place in this matter for Weiss. "It is the special task of art to express the perceptually adumbrated side of perceptual matters of fact in such a way as to embrace all other adumbrateds" (*R*, p. 99). Art moves into the particular, but in such a way as to open "the whole of reality as substantial and inward" (*R*, p. 116). "Substantial" here means underlying, grounding the phenomena; "inward" expresses a privacy correlated with our own privacy, where the manifestation of the depth of the thing requires and evokes the deeper side of ourselves. Art gives articulation to a special sense of, a "feel" for, the Beyond. But by reason of our structure, if not also the structure of things themselves, disclosure of the inwardness of any thing involves disclosure of the whole of things. Weiss seems quite close to Heidegger's view of the work of art here.[7] Art is more than the production of a pleasing surface, more also than an expression of my subjective reaction to things: art discloses the whole in an inward and substantial way.

To adumbrate then is to foreshadow, to anticipate darkly, but to do so in a mode of feeling rather than in a mode of conceptualization. Speculation follows feeling here as an abstract, and to that extent, inferior mode of expression of the transphenomenal, revealed and concealed in the phenomena. But speculation has its own advantage in that it clarifies feeling to itself by bringing it into systematic relation with all the modes of experience and inference.

What appears within the phenomenal circle has then to be interpreted as showing or hiding what lies beneath. But the underlying has to be repeatedly rescued from the routinized interpretations that settle into a kind of "dashboard" relationship to the underlying.[8] The phenomenal circle becomes a pragmatic circle of knowing how to push, pull, and turn the surface to get the regularized responses required by a culturally mediated need-base (cf. *BAA*, pp. 9–11). This is the surface that I sometimes suspect is what many so-called realist philosophers mean by "reality." Not so Weiss — and rightly not so. Dashboard realism can at best be a starting point. It must be corrected and extended by the deeper realism of love, art, mysticism, and speculation that add the depth dimension to the pragmatic-phenomenal surface.

The rational and the nonrational, the clearly conceived and the lived, the articulated and the nonarticulated are brought together in a dialectical relation where the adumbratively lived, made possible by the clarity of the category, leads on inquiry as the extension of that clarity. Logic, Weiss's own early preoccupation in the time before *Reality* appeared, logic as a discipline of absolutely clear distinctions and relations arises through severing the adumbrative component. When this mentality dominates, everything else tends to be pejoratively relegated to the nonrational realm, locked into the merely subjective. Weiss is more temperate here than Heidegger who refers in this context to the corrosive acid of a merely logical intelligence.[9] Weiss would rather heavily underscore the "merely" and, characteristically, create ample place for logic. But like Heidegger, he would not only refer the logical to the verifiable surface of the indicated and the methodically controlled conceptuality of the contemplated that develops in relation to that surface, but also to the hidden, the underlying, the encompassing mystery of Being that suggests the framework for ontologically construing the indicated and the contemplated.

II

What is adumbrated is not only the substantial wholeness of actualities but also the totality of all actualities. The adumbrated, Weiss repeatedly affirms, is the correlate of the copula "is" in the judgment. But there is also, Weiss claims, a penumbra surrounding the nucleus of each of the elements in knowing — including both the indicated and the contemplated (*R*, pp. 78–79). In *Modes of Being*, Weiss attempts to move speculatively into the penumbra surrounding each of those elements, only to discover a correlate for each that is not another actuality, but rather a realm, self-existent, other than the actualities, in which the actualities participate in various ways.

The adumbrated fringe surrounding a given contemplated universal is a region or mode of being called Ideality or Possibility. The adumbrated fringe surrounding a given indicated is the realm termed — somewhat eccentrically I think — Existence. And presumably the adumbrated that makes possible the unity of Ideality and Existence entering into any given actuality is God as the ground of that unity. Exploration of each of the modes and their interplay with each other and with actualities allows us to clarify the pull which each exerts within the fuller matrix of lived experience.

The Category or the notion of being, articulated for actualities in the principle of contradiction, is not assigned to any mode or treated as a distinct mode in *Modes of Being*. Being is rather the interplay of all the modes, and by reason of possessing, or being possessed by, the Category at the core of our consciousness, we are able to stand in that interplay and grasp it as such (*MOB*, 1.96 and 2.12. cf. *FC*, pp. 157ff.).

In *Reality* adumbration as linked to the Category was filled in concretely by art and abstractly by speculation — although love and mysticism also appear as means to concrete fulfillment. In *Modes of Being*, art is said to move into the realm of Existence, which plays in the inwardness of the artist as feeling and displays itself in various ways. These ways of display are determined by the interplay of Existence with the other modes.

Existence itself is basically an "othering," a dividedness (*MOB*, 3.01).[10] Related to actualities, Existence is expressed as spatiality, the othering of spread-out-ness, the ontological root of varying types of space, from the abstract space of Euclidean geometry, through the tensed but extrinsic space of relativity physics, to the lived spaces of differing organisms and differing consciousness, entering profoundly into human experience in the articulation of the spatial arts of architecture, painting, and sculpture. Related to Ideality, Existence is expressed as temporality generated through reference to the possibilities to be realized in the future, articulated further as chronometric and lived time of various sorts and brought to special articulation in the temporal arts of musical composition, story, and poetry. Related to God as the One, Existence is expressed as dynamism, energy, a restless movement out of what is at any given time and place, seeking in each case and in the universe as a whole a maximal unity and attaining special articulation in the arts of musical performance, drama, and dance. Though itself a tendency to dispersal, Existence is established as a single ground of a single spatial-temporal-dynamic realm by relation to the Divine Unity. The arts thus establish and articulate a concrete feel for peculiar aspects of Existence, but adumbrate as well, in their differing modes, a concrete feel for the underlying encompassing wholeness of Existence.[11] It is a feel directed at the wholeness that lures the theoretical physicist to elaborate a view of the total realm of space-time-energy and clues the cosmologist as to the ultimate mode grounding these pursuits. In Weiss's more recent work, *Beyond All Appearances*, the proper emotional attitude that both opens up and is evoked by the encompassing finality of Existence is awe (cf. *BAA*, p. 17). The dwelt-in adumbrative move past the surface leads on toward speculative comprehension.

Weiss offers several novel approaches to the divine mode. The adumbrative relation to God is lived through in various ways as well as logically clarified. Weiss lays out the geography of nine differing sets of proofs (not nine proofs, but nine *sets* of proofs), only *one* set of which involves traditional logical inferences (*MOB*, 4.14–4.60). There are other and richer vehicles whereby God is "proven" to men long before logical proof was thought of — "proofs" having to do with such things as prayer and work and institutional participation. "Proof" here means something like "the proof of the pudding (which) is in the eating." It is the whole set of relations to God and the multiple ways to God that men live through which Weiss sets out to clarify. Weiss works persistently with the logic of possible relations between finalities in their interplay with actualities. If I understand the general lines of Weiss's analysis of the sets of proof for the existence of God, approximately 729 proofs are possible within the modal philosophy ($9 \times 9 \times 9$: nine teleological beginnings, working through nine cosmological relations, terminating in nine ontological detachments). But again, the adumbratively lived is dialectically related to the logically articulated.

Weiss's later view of five finalities provides seemingly endless logically possible combinations: *e.g.*, in his treatment of the five basic dimensions of the Self, (namely Psyche, Reason, Mind, Sensibility, and Spirit), Weiss sketches out five functions of Mind, subdividing two of these functions into five differing acts, each division corresponding to the five finalities as they ricochet off each other within the interior of each differing type of actuality (*BAA*, pp. 342–48). For our purposes, however, the point is that all this constructive work is not strung over an empty experiential void, but is in constant interplay with an extraordinary alertness to the lived adumbration of each of these areas.

III

After *Modes of Being*, differing facets of adumbration continue to be unfolded, bringing together features to which we have already called attention: intensive adumbration, directed toward actualities; extensive adumbration, directed toward the other modes of being; and cosmic adumbration, directed toward the interplay of both, leading to a sense of the absolute totality.[12] Again, he divides adumbration, from another perspective, into two types: a determinate and an indeterminate type. The determinate involves our lived-through, dwelt-in, concrete rootage. Indeterminate adumbration involves the possibility held open by the presence of "the Category" or the notion of being in us, of leaving our own rootage to enter sympathetically into the life-world of others, though never as richly as in the case of our own (*PP II*, p. 153).

Weiss comes to see the adumbrated as having its own sort of dynamism. The modes of being do not merely stand beyond the circle of our penetration, resisting our complete entry; they also exert a positive pull (*BAA*, p. 97). The more we enter into them, the more they seem to take hold of us. We move from grasping and controlling to being apprehended. In *Beyond All Appearances*, this attracting power is linked up with the power of symbols, distinguished but related to the function of signs. The latter are symbols that have lost their drawing power and are capable of being manipulated by us (*BAA*, pp. 89ff.).

The distinction seems remarkably close to Heidegger's description of the flattening-out process whereby beings lose their Being, *i.e.*, their revealing-concealing power that draws us into intimate presence, and become mere data, equidistant from us and capable of being manipulated.[13]

But in that same work, Weiss distinguishes adumbration from lucidation, the former term now being reserved for our relation to actualities, the latter for our relation to the other modes (*BAA*, p. 89). This shift is actually in keeping with his initial usage in *Reality*. Adumbration there was related to the in-itself-ness of sensorily encounterable entities, of actualities. But actualities exist and enter into the field of our awareness by reason of our mutual participation in the encompassing modes of being. Thus light is thrown upon entities for us in various regions — in science, in philosophy, in art, in politics, in religion, in meditation — through our attending to the interplay between the entity and the region. The entity participates in these regions and thus juts into an illuminated field of awareness. But it also stands irremoveably in itself and thus recedes from that field. We participate in the same regions, but do so in a peculiarly illumined way because we stand in "the Category" — in traditional terms, we are related to being as such. In the premodern tradition, we come to know actualities because of the illuminating activity of the agent intellect, and the groundedness of both things and intellect in the primordial intellect.

Weiss sees that the encompassing regions can come to exert an even stronger emotional pull, in the modalities of awe, wonder, reverence and the sense of mystery, than do the actualities (cf. *PP VI*, pp. 515–19). Hence the total concentrated dedication of the man of religion, the scientist, the artist, the philosopher, etc. But the attitudes mentioned are sustained in a tension between the revealing power of a region and the sense of an even greater concealment in the region itself. The term "lucidation" calls attention to one pole of the relation. But an adumbrative feature to the encompassing regions still exists that is even more pronounced in the emotional stances mentioned than it is in the case of encounter with individuals.

In *Beyond All Appearances* Weiss adds two new modes and renames them all "finalities." Being as the interplay of the modes in *Modes of Being* becomes a distinct finality and is distinguished from a new finality that he calls Substance (*BAA*, pp. 232, 267ff., 272).

Substance, a finality in which all actualities participate as standing in themselves, stands also in itself. It is linked with Weiss's taking seriously the claim of certain mystical types to identity with an impersonal Encompassing reached within the innermost privacy of the self, but linked to all other privacies. This is the kind of mysticism represented by Taoism (cf. *FC*, p. 114, no. 52).

No longer the neutral point of the interplay between the modes, Being too, now takes its place as a distinct finality. But though the finalities are coequal and coeternal for Weiss, Being seems to play a pivotal role (*BAA*, pp. 275–77). For Weiss it is the great equalizer —

a univocal and apparently minimalist notion of being-outside-of-nothing common to absolutely everything. It is Being that man alone of all the actualities internalizes. It affects all his other relations by granting him access to all that is, enabling him to live his life in reference to the Totality, enabling him to be drawn from the surface toward the depth of actualities, and from actualities into the ultimate depth of finalities.

Weiss links mysticism with Being and Substance, as well as with God. His treatment of mysticism thus appears to move like the famous statues of Daedalus, shifting from union with God as a personal Evaluator, to the Taoist impersonal but inward Identity, to a Parmenidean mysticism of the identity of thought and Being. Add to this awe in the face of the overwhelming character of power and spatio-temporal vastness, and we have a list of the essential types of experience that are too often collapsed into relation to a single Encompassing finality, to which many people are perhaps too quick to affix the name "God." Distinguishing different finalities allows us to distinguish different types of experiences that seem to move beyond experience of actualities. Indeed, by reason of their dialectical relation, distinguishing different experiences aids in the clear discrimination of differing finalities.

But even for those for whom the experience of the personal Evaluator is the pivotal experience, by reason of the interplay of the different finalities, one can begin to understand how each distinctive experience becomes for the religious man a symbol of God. Depth experience in each of the finalities can draw us into the others. But once again, just as symbols can flatten out into signs as empty reference when we lose the ability to enter into the drawing power of the symbols (*PP VI*, p. 642), so also real experience of the finalities may be only conventionally referred to the presence of God in relation to Whom we may not be truly dwelling. However, recovering the power of religious symbols would seem to be linked significantly to recovering the adumbrative-lucidative reverberances of finalities — in relations of respect and love directed to other actualities, in the development of artistic sensibility, and in the various forms of mysticism directed to finalities.

IV

Weiss's philosophy is essentially a revised Platonism with the *chorismos* between Being and Becoming and, correspondingly, between soul and body eliminated along somewhat Hegelian lines of mutual inclusion, and with the aristocratic hierarchy of hypostases reestablished in a democratic society joined by the lowly Receptacle as principle of the rabble of plurality. Weiss's democratization of the finalities has the advantage of breaking the grip of privilege accorded the rational realm of Forms in the history of Western philosophy, which provoked periodic outbursts of irrationalist revolution (though Plato's own erotic relationship to the final Good actually anticipates and assimilates the protest). Relation to the World-Soul, recovered by Weiss as the Taoist inwardness of the encompassing Substance, is acknowledged to be as profound and as deserving of attention as the clarity of the Forms. Artistic sensitivity especially has led to a rich articulation of the Receptacle. Art, installing us firmly in this world, nonetheless opens us to a realm of Existence including the transcending actualities, and allowing access to the interplay of the other finalities in it. The lowly Receptacle is elevated by being given its due respect in art and in theoretical physics.

But in Weiss's case, breaking the grip of privilege accorded to the rationalist domain has resulted in a rich development of the rational itself — as if in humbling itself, the rational is all the more exalted. The tandem movement of adumbration and speculation across the finalities has resulted in a dialectical interpenetration of the speculative and the lived. It is this that constitutes the deeper lure of Platonism: its rootage in a more primordial lived relationship to the differing ways in which the phenomenal surface of the everyday world is girt about by encompassing, transcending regions that we cannot exhaust, and whose inexhaustibility is the reason why we can at best achieve *philo-sophia*, a loving pursuit of the final encompassing, why we can never — if we are wise — lay claim to final wisdom. Weiss, like Plato, and in many respects beyond Plato, is keenly aware of the soil in which the tree of metaphysics is planted.[14]

Of course, in relation to Weiss's variation on the themes of Platonism, a metaphysical creationist will have obvious difficulties locating the divine in a democratized pantheon — even as a *primus inter pares*. But viewing God as the creative ground of all the rest — and thus as other than the rest in a radical way — the creationist can still applaud the sensitive way in which Weiss does justice to the other transcending enterprises that have functioned and can still function as routes to God.

In Weiss's thought — and, I think, in fact — we humans can stand open to the presence of finalities as we stand open to the presence of the inwardness of actualities — our own included — by reason of our standing in the region of Being. Expressed in the humblest judgement, the presence of the category of Being in us opens us to the whole of what is, in the differing modes in which things are. But is this Being as empty as Weiss suggests? Is it merely the great equalizer, the lowest common denominator? Does not Being rather include the wholeness of each actuality and finality — partially filled, but emptily for the most part, from the side of our knowing-dwelling? And is it not then hierarchically realizable? Can it not then be realized in a single instance as a Nature, not hemmed in by the various modalities of finitude? Can it not then, like Weiss's Substance, stand over against the beings who, by participating in it, are enabled to stand over against it as well? Might not then all our adumbrations and lucidations finally point to That, not as one among many, but as the ultimate term of our heart's desire? Might It then not be identical with Being Itself, which all others mirror in some way — as awesome Power and Vastness, as eminent Intelligibility and enticing, prescriptive Value, as Inwardness and Encompassment, as Full Actuality, but finally as the Mystery that all of this only adumbrates?

Weissian thought, from a creationist perspective, has the great value of opening us to the experienced symbols that lead us first in a lived, adumbrative way, then by way of speculative comprehension and clarification, into encompassing regions other than God and other than actualities, but pointing to their functioning, in turn, as symbols of God in the interplay of the finalities.

Kierkegaard complained that most philosophers construct magnificent thought-castles, but dwell in miserable shacks nearby. Weiss has surely constructed magnificent thought-castles, but he has been able to do so because he has learned so deeply what it means to dwell in fullest humanness. Adumbration points to that. Weiss holds together the lived and the comprehended in a single system, the lived leading on the comprehension, the comprehension clarifying the lived, and holding open, in a time when so many factors conspire to close it, the space of transcending life.

Three

Daniel O. Dahlstrom

The Appearance of Finalities*

Paul Weiss: a philosopher with sensitivity and a sense of humor,[1] a man of the twentieth century engaged in its desperate project of philosophizing anew yet an anomaly to his age and to the world, an American with a speculative mind[2] who writes successfully for a cultured audience, defying the crippling cliches, cliques, and cults of personality that pass for professionalism and tradition among his cloistered contemporaries, a metaphysician of truly catholic proportions, founding philosophic journals and societies and prodding the philosophic community to turn its attention to the full range of human existence.

If these remarks have too much the sound of a eulogy, let there be no mistake about my intentions. I come not to bury Weiss but to praise him and praise, on the plain of philosophic friendship, is given when the thoughts of another are taken seriously as a possible way to the truth, as a road to be tested, worthy of attention and struggle. Weiss's major insights in his first metaphysical treatise, *Reality* (1938), and twenty years later in his masterpiece, *Modes of Being* (1958), passed through the years of refinement in the journals published as *Philosophy in Process*, and culminated in the mature metaphysical speculations outlined in *Beyond All Appearances* (1974) and *First Considerations* (1976). In this latest stage of Weiss's fifty-year metaphysical odyssey, Weiss recognizes two fundamental sorts of realities, which he calls "actualities" and "finalities." Although they are in themselves opaque, actualities are unique, factual, and expansive units. They become intelligible inasmuch as they are affected by certain conditions. Things, living beings, and humans are able to be distinguished in a hierarchy of actualities according to the degree to which they respectively in-

---

*This paper was delivered at a Symposium on the Philosophy of Paul Weiss at The Catholic University of America, May 18–19, 1981.

55

ternalize those conditions. Weiss does not claim any special intuition for these speculative insights. Rather, they are the result of attending to the appearances of actualities.

Certain conditions of the actualities are permanent and irreducible, transcendent realities, *i.e.*, conditions not traceable simply to the interaction of actualities, including human beings. Making their presence felt universally, these conditions are the finalities, and as with actualities, Weiss claims to know these ultimate conditions through their appearances.

This paper weighs Weiss's claim. I intend to examine and evaluate the evidence that certain appearances are in fact finalities appearing. Since this examination presupposes a clear conception of what a finality is, the opening portions of the essay profile the nature of a finality by comparing it to a celebrated statement by Aquinas on the nature of transcendentals. This is followed by reviews of Weiss's theory of appearances in general and his theory of evidence. Attention then turns to two dominant appearances of finalities, according to Weiss, *viz*, attitudes and contexts, and the leading role assigned to basic emotions in evidencing finalities' appearances. By themselves, Weiss's accounts of attitudes and contexts do not provide, I argue, sufficient evidence of being appearances of finalities. However, the evidence he claims is provided by basic emotions in conjunction with attitudes and contexts is another matter. In this regard, Weiss is staking a bold claim for the role of emotions in speculative metaphysics. The thesis that emotions have metaphysical import is perhaps not satisfactorily established but neither is it easily refuted.

I. Finalities and Transcendentals

Although Plato's blending and division of five major forms in the *Sophist*, Aristotle's remarks on being and unity in Book Gamma of the *Metaphysics*, and even the Cartesian tradition's fascination with attributes and modes all offer interesting parallels to Weiss's finalities, perhaps the most instructive standard of comparison is found in a Scholastic theory of transcendentals. The paths to finalities and to transcendentals alike begin with reflection on and analysis of claims made about the world we immediately confront and experience. In each case, moreover, these ultimate modes of being are closely correlated with first principles of logic and epistemology.[3]

Throughout the centuries, there has been, of course, no monolithic theory for these properties of being, first formally discussed by Philip the Chancellor of the University of Paris around 1225, and apparently labelled "transcendentia" by Suarez.[4] In Suarez's compendious and influential rendition only three transcendentals exist: the one, the true, and the good. Drawing on distinctions in Aristotle's *Metaphysics* and a host of scholastic authors, including Thomas Aquinas, Suarez claims that transcendentals are real properties of being, although they are distinguished by reason alone. That is, the transcendentals are real but formal attributes of being, real features no more separable and no less distinguishable from being than the property of being odd-or-even is from quantity (in a system of natural numbers where zero and infinity are not numbers). While adding nothing that is not already contained in being in fact, the transcendentals explicate its formal or essential meaning via negation or via relation. In terms of negation, each being is one or undivided in itself and distinct from others. In terms of relation, being is true or intelligible in relation to a possible understanding and being is good or suitable in relation to a possible desire.

Yet Suarez recognizes that other nominees for transcendentals are to be found, most notably in texts of Aquinas himself, and he labors to demonstrate that, even for Thomas, only three transcendentals properly exist. An article has appeared in the *Thomist* resurrecting this Suarezian reading (though it is not identified as such).[5]

In the context of the present paper, I certainly intend to leave to scholastic exegetes and philosophers the question of the reducibility of being's proper attributes to the transcendentals of unity, goodness, and truth. However, one text, especially recalcitrant to this project, is relevant to our concerns. In Aquinas's opening article in the first of his "Disputed Questions on Truth," he elaborates five modes of being that bear a marked resemblance to Weiss's finalities.[6]

The purpose of Aquinas's article, it bears noting, is not to establish the transcendentals but rather to distinguish the true from the real. By its very nature, being is not a *genus* to which some extrinsic difference is added. Being is spoken of significantly, then, only inasmuch as concepts or predicates designate some mode of being not expressed by the term "being" itself. The term "being" itself (or *ens*) is the gerund form of the infinitive "to be," expressing the act of being (or *esse*). The modal expression of this being can occur in two ways, depending on whether what is predicated of being is a special mode of being, *e.g.*, substance, quantity, and other categories, or "a mode generally consequent to every being."[7] This latter general mode of being corresponds to what has become known as the transcendentals.

This universal mode of being may refer, in a positive or negative manner, to every being either (1) in itself or (2) in relation (or ordered) to another. (1) Every being is positively identified in itself in terms of a specific quiddity or essence, and, referred to in this way, each being is a "thing" (*res*). Described negatively, every being is undivided in itself or "one" (*unum*). (2) In relation to others, each being is distinct, and this is expressed by saying it is "something" (*aliquid*). Also, in relation to others, each being is suitable, on the one hand, to some purpose or drive, warranting the designation "good" (*bonum*) and, on the other hand to a possible comprehension and hence may be called "intelligible" or "true" (*verum*). Thus, on the strength of this analysis, five transcendentals exist. Each being is a thing, one, something, good, and true. Or, with other words, each being is a kind of thing, integral, unique, purposive, and intelligible.

Are these five universal characters of being, outlined by Thomas Aquinas, isomorphic with Weiss's finalities? The answer is "not exactly." But the differences are as instructive as the similarities and forcefully demonstrate the distinctiveness of Weiss's metaphysics. A review of these samenesses and differences, moreover, will clarify what we must look for when we search for appearances of finalities.

The overlap between some of Weiss's finalities and some of Aquinas's transcendentals—at least in the *de Veritate* passage outlined—is patent. The finality Weiss labels "Possibility" is supposed to provide a universal, compelling condition by virtue of which actualities are intelligible. This finality certainly seems to correspond to the transcendentals Aquinas identified as "the true." Weiss also identifies Unity as a final condition, accounting for all unities, and this finality obviously bears a marked resemblance to the transcendental one in Aquinas's list. A similar correspondence exists between what Weiss calls "Being" and Aquinas calls "something."

According to Weiss's theory, to the extent that an actuality internalizes this finality (being), it has native rights and enjoys the status of a distinct being, on a par with but distinct from all other beings. Weiss's "Being," then, parallels Aquinas's "something," understood as expressing that every being is "something other than something else."

Beyond these parallels the correspondence between Weiss's finalities and Aquinas's transcendentals is less secure. Indeed, even the parallels mentioned are far from exact. Since "thing" for Aquinas designates the quiddity or essence of what exists, some rationale exists for extending Weiss's Possibility to the thinghood, as well as the truth of every being in Aquinas's scheme. On this interpretation Weiss's conception of Possibility would extend over Aquinas's distinction between beings in themselves and in relation to one another. Similarly, what Aquinas means by "something" or "different from another" is captured not only by what Weiss calls "Being," but also by the finality he terms "Substance," the finality by which actualities and appearances supposedly affiliate and *contrast* with one another. Also, what Weiss means by "Unity" is the source, not only of appearances' and actualities' individual integrities, but also of their values, thus overlapping the transcendental goodness of being.

Existence, in Weiss's philosophy, as the finality or universal condition of every actuality's dynamism, resembles the good in Aquinas's list of transcendentals as well. But the morally normative character of the good Weiss locates neither in Existence nor in Unity but in Possibility. Moreover, for Weiss, Existence is a spatially and temporally dynamic condition of each actuality.[8] On this note, the differences between Weiss and Aquinas become especially sharp. In the text from *de Veritate*, the act of existing is not a separate transcendental. Rather, Aquinas distinguishes all the transcendentals from being as its modes. Moreover, Aquinas certainly does not equate existence with spatial and temporal conditions. A superficial similarity is found between the finality Weiss calls "Substance" and the Thomistic *esse*. Substance, for Weiss, is that finality by virtue of which each actuality persists, acts, maintains some control over its parts, and has an irreducible, independent core. While this account of Substance overlaps with the act of existing in Aquinas, Aquinas would not consider being to be really distinct from other transcendental features of being.[9]

This last remark brings us to perhaps the central difference between Aquinas's transcendentals and Weiss's finalities. Whether the fivefold distinction at the outset of *de Veritate* be accepted or reduced to the traditional transcendentals of truth, unity, and goodness, Aquinas considers them only logically distinct from one another and from their foundation in being (*ens*). While interpreting the transcendentals as expressions of, or a power radiating from, a primary act of existing is possible, they do not, as do Weiss's finalities, exercise a control over actualities, independent of the act of existing. Complementing his view of finalities is Weiss's doctrine that actualities in themselves are not substances, beings, or existents, but that actualities are affected by finalities in order, as actualities themselves, to be substances, beings, existents, unities, and intelligible.[10] For a judgment about actualities to be true, according to Weiss, it must acknowledge the intrusion of finalities, as alien conditions, on actualities. For Aquinas, on the other hand, the transcendental features of things are derivative of their being and not really distinct from it. On this point, Suarezian and Thomistic traditions are in agreement and equally inconsistent with Weiss's metaphysical doctrine of actualities and finalities.

In the face of these Scholastic views, the novelty of Weiss's doctrine is readily apparent. Finalities, for Weiss, are universal, compelling conditions of actualities, really distinct from those actualities and from one another. Those finalities are not, like Aquinas's transcendentals, mere modes of being, but rather each is a distinct reality. Is there evidence of such realities in experience? Can their appearances be pointed to? These are questions that must now be answered in order to be able to evaluate Weiss's novel alternative. However, before turning to these questions, it is necessary to determine exactly what Weiss means by 'appearance' and 'evidence.'

II. Appearances and Evidence

Some aspects of experience are so direct and efficacious that attempts to define or explain them in terms of something else are often bound to obscure and confuse. In these instances it is better, as Reid and Hume remarked, to "offer some observations that may lead us to attend to the conception we have of it in our own minds."[11] Weiss, in his account of appearances, wisely adopts this strategy. Appearances are inert and immediate, the inevitable starting point of knowing. Yet, given their inertness, appearances cannot be the only source of knowledge, or else no action and neither the presence nor nature of appearances themselves could be accounted for. Thus, although they have an integrity of their own, appearances are also derivative and biased toward realities that not only produced them but maintain a hold on them. Appearances, in other words, are ways realities present themselves, not to be identified with, but also not independent of, those realities. An appearance is never by itself alone, strictly speaking, but neither is an appearance ever the presence of a single reality alone.

Two kinds of appearances, *viz*, content-biased and context-biased, correspond to the prominence of actualities or finalities as sources of the appearances respectively. For example, a shape is primarily an appearance of an actuality, while a localized extension is primarily a finality's appearance. However, appearances, although so biased and rooted, are always the joint outcome of actualities and finalities, a fact that accounts for their integrity opposite their dominant sources.

Weiss outlines three degrees of ultimacy to appearances: familiar, common, and ontological. The familiar appearances are a daily world overladen by social and individual characteristics. By "common" appearances Weiss has in mind empirically available occupants of a domain such as a particular science, art, religion, and so on. Ontologically, however, appearances are the outcome of actualities and finalities, in a setting in which one of the latter is always dominant. In terms of this composition, we find a "content/context" continuum from a maximum exhibition of an actuality with minimum exhibition of a finality to a maximum exhibition of a finality with minimum exhibition of an actuality.

When we attend to an appearance we impose a boundary between it and what we neglect, whether that boundary duplicates a real distinction or not. In contradistinction to the objective appearance, this bounded appearance is the *confronted* appearance, *i.e.*, the appearance attended to and known. A bounded or confronted appearance is *objectified* inasmuch as it is imagined and construed apart from its boundaries (as objective or confronted). Thus made an object of imagination, an appearance's various facets can be isolated and then re-joined in judgments and claims. "Knowledge is possible," Weiss remarks, "because one has withdrawn not only from a mere interplay with other realities, but also from what is confronted" (*BAA*, p. 85). Thus, in addition to distinguishing appearances in terms of their dominant sources and biases in actualities and finalities, Weiss has a threefold distinction of appearances in terms of their relation to a knower, *viz*, objective, confronted, and objectified appearances.[12]

These distinctions among appearances do not undermine what is perhaps the most important feature of appearances: their symbolic character. Unlike signs, which Weiss considers external to one another and their objects, symbols are continuous with what is symbolized. What mediates an appearance as an actuality's symbol is an adumbrative, while what unveils the symbolic relation between a finality and its appearance is a lucidative.

A crucial difference exists between adumbratives and lucidatives as the experienced mediators of appearances with the actualities and finalities they respectively symbolize. Lucidatives indicate the persistent hold of a finality on appearances by affecting human beings emotionally so that the symbol of the finality is not external to the human being. However, "actualities have no such effect, and men, as a consequence must make use of symbols external to themselves in order to arrive at those actualities" (*BAA*, p. 97). Where for some objectified (*i.e.*, imaginatively isolated, analyzed, and judged) appearance, I make an objective judgment, the truth of that combination of something designated and contemplated is evidenced via an adumbrative. The adumbrative reveals the actual union, in an objective appearance or in actualities, of that combination I remake in a judgment, while also indicating that there is more than this combination.[13] In ordinary discourse the adumbrative is often indicated by a copula, when viewed as more than just a link between terms and meanings. The commonsense claim that there are real states of affairs and real things appearing in ways subject to the things and not just to the perceivers is thus captured by the "adumbrative."

What is important for the purposes of this paper is the difference between the symbolic mediation of actualities and finalities. Lucidatives provoke basic emotions in human beings that cannot be detached from the appearance as a symbol of a finality. Certainly in both forms of symbolization, there must be a withdrawal by the knower into himself or herself and an acknowledgment of the compelling character of the symbolized actuality and finality. In both cases, the knower imposes boundaries on something known that remains continuous with itself apart from those boundaries (*BAA*, p. 143). However, in knowing the appearance of an actuality (*e.g.*, a thing, a living being, or a human being) I immediately symbolize the appearance, recognizing it as evidence of the actuality. In knowing the appearance of a finality, on the other hand, I am myself a symbol and the boundaries I impose in knowing appearances are themselves specifications of some exhibitions of finalities. The knowledge of actualities, then, can be devoid of emotional import whereas basic emotions are part of the very appearance of finalities.[14]

Weiss develops the distinctiveness of finalities' appearances in general and our knowledge of them by introducing a theory of evidencing, which is itself merely a form of symbolizing in reverse.[15] Just as

Weiss tends to use the term "appearance" when he is referring only to appearances of actualities, so he has a tendency to employ the term "evidence," especially in *First Considerations*, to refer principally to finalities. In *Beyond All Appearances*, however, Weiss does speak of evidences of actualities. His definition of evidences as "effects present in something alien and affecting this" (*FC*, p. 62, sec. 1) complements his view that appearances are symbolic since actualities as well as finalities maintain a hold on their appearances. In any event, although the theory of evidencing seems to be but a development of the symbolic character of appearances in general, Weiss's treatment of evidencing centers mainly on the evidence of finalities.[16]

The theory of evidencing is introduced by means of a parallel with knowing. In knowing there is an object both inside boundaries imposed by the knower and yet continuous with itself apart from those boundaries. The object known, then, provides evidence of the object itself. This evidencing, again in tandem with knowing, has two stages: epistemic and ontological, though they are "embraced in a single symbolization" (*BAA*, p. 227). "What is known evidences a known object, and this in turn evidences the object itself" (*BAA*, p. 226). Weiss locates the likeness between knowing and evidencing in the composition of the two processes. Knowing is a selective, boundary-imposing relation to an object existing apart from that relation. Knowing occurs only if a continuity occurs between three factors: what is known, the known object, and the object to be known. Similarly, evidencing is a process involving evidence, evidenced, and the source of both, all in continuity. "The evidence must be related to the evidenced as a known object is to the object to be known" (*BAA*, p. 227).

Further parallels exist between knowing and evidencing whose unpacking lies beyond the scope of this paper. However, a crucial difference must not go unmentioned. "Knowing" is an activity of human beings. "Knowledge is a contingent product; it need not occur and may be blocked by errors" (*FC*, p. 37, sec. 64). There is no knowing without the performer of that activity. Realist that Weiss is, he of course does not consider a human being the sole condition of knowledge. Yet he recognizes the indispensability of the knower in knowing, however much the activity consists in truing conclusions to what lies outside human consciousness.[17] Evidence and evidenced, on the other hand, are related to one another and grounded in a source apart from any knower.[18] In addition, and perhaps more significantly, any use or knowledge is dependent on the evidencing and its source. "No one could return to that source," Weiss affirms, "unless aided by the source itself" (*FC*, p. 67, sec. 35).[19]

Like symbols and what is known, evidence is always carried by something other than its sustaining source.[20] The carriers of evidence are particular actualities or appearances that specify the evidence and which the evidence in turn helps constitute and control (*FC*, p. 64, sec. 16; p. 66, sec. 26; p. 82, sec. 27). While specified by a particular appearance, the evidence itself, once detached from that appearance, is "a limited universal specifying a more comprehensive one, the evidenced" (*FC*, p. 82, sec. 25; p. 65, sec. 24). By neglecting the particular that specifies it and by concentrating on its specification of the evidenced, the user of evidence pairs the evidence and evidenced. This pairing is epistemic and may err, but if correct it accords with an ontologic pairing (*FC*, p. 85, secs. 50–51). In this ontologic pairing evidence and evidenced are objectively relevant to one another, in the sense that each is made for the other. They are thus also correlatives, inseparable from each other (*FC*, pp. 84–85, secs. 46–47). This ontologic pairing, *i.e.*, the mutual relevance and correlatives of evidence and evidenced, is due to a source and that source is a finality.[21]

Weiss identifies five steps involved in making proper use of evidence: (1) the acknowledgment of evidence in appearances, (2) detachment of it from those appearances, (3) correlation of it with the evidenced, (4) consideration of the mutual relevance of evidence and evidenced, and (5) recognition of their submission to a common source. For the user of evidence, in contrast to evidencing, the steps are sequential.[22] With this qualification, however, making proper use of or knowing what is evidenced involves a reproduction of the process by which a source, *i.e.*, a finality, evidences itself.

Of course these steps do not comprise a formal method such that their employment alone ensures knowledge that a finality is evidenced. The user of evidence, Weiss notes, must treat evidence in a manner "consonant" with the way a source subjects its evidence (*FC*, p. 94, sec. 29). The mediation between evidence and evidenced, accomplished by the user of evidence, is a "participation" in them (*FC*, p. 96, sec. 42). These remarks about consonance with and participation in the evidencing process ...e meant to indicate that the knower's reproduction of that evidencing is to be guided by the same source as underlies the evidencing. "A user of evidence . . . could know that the reproduction occurred if he could know that his activity conforms to what in fact operates on both the evidence and evidenced" (*FC*, p. 85, sec. 52).[23]

That the proper use of evidence must be guided by the same power that is the source of the evidence echoes Weiss's claim that the knower's grasp of a finality's appearance must itself symbolize that finality. As he did in his account of the symbolic character of appearances, Weiss stresses the necessity of withdrawing into oneself to make proper use of evidence (*FC*, p. 88, sec. 75; p. 90, secs. 1–2). By freeing itself from empirical involvement, a human being can exercise a speculative mind that is "attuned to the power which ontologically pairs the evidence and evidenced; . . . [and] therefore, necessarily reproduces what had originally occurred" (*FC*, p. 86, secs. 54–57).

None of this, of course, explains how a user of evidence might know that his putative reproduction of evidencing is subject to the very same source of that evidencing. If the user of evidence cannot be certain his use is guided by some finality, he may very well conclude, not that his use is improper, but that the use is accurate and true without need of recourse to a finality. Talk of finalities would then certainly seem to be superfluous and burdensome baggage, casting considerable doubt on claims of their reality. If I can make proper use of evidence, which is to say, I can know appearances, without recourse to a finality as either the source of the evidencing or the guide to its proper use, there is no reason to claim that a specific appearance is the appearance of a finality. How could I justifiably claim to know that there are finalities if I could not demonstrate that and how I know them?

The critical challenge I am raising here is certainly premature. Weiss's theory of evidencing merely provides a framework for demonstrating the appearance of finalities. Finalities are said to be independent and irreducible, necessary and permanent realities, unavoidable conditions always and everywhere present (*FC*, p. 27, sec. 39; p. 171, sec. 64; *BAA*, p. 233). If a finality does appear, its appearance would be evidence of it, correlated with the evidenced finality in a process of evidencing of which the finality is the source. I could make proper use of this evidence only if I could recapitulate it speculatively, or in other words, only if my act of knowing is itself guided by the finality. But to know that an appearance is evidence of a finality, general canons of evidencing are hardly sufficient. To know whether an appearance provides adequate evidence of a finality, turning to the purported appearances themselves and the sort of evidencing Weiss claims they involve is necessary.

III. Attitudes and Contexts

Finalities objectively appear in at least two dominant and related ways: as *attitudes* in human consciousness and as *contexts* governing appearances independently of any conscious mind. Attitudes and contexts are not to be confused with confronted and objective appearances. Both attitudes and contexts are objective appearances of finalities, although the former is located in human consciousness while the latter is not so restricted. Since human beings' expressions of themselves are appearances of actualities, attitudes may be viewed as a special kind of context.[24]

Attitudes

Although we impose boundaries on appearances in knowing them, appearances exist apart from those imposed boundaries. We are generally aware, even if upon occasion somewhat dimly, that attending to certain appearances is always a selective act. This awareness, while confirming the validity of a distinction between confronted and objective appearances, also indicates the existence of an *attitude*. An attitude ignores, without removing, the boundaries imposed by the selective act of focusing on some appearance. More than just an interest underlying those selective acts, attitudes shape the character of a confronted appearance in terms of what is not confronted. Because of such attitudes we are not only able but predisposed in certain ways to deal with appearances, regardless of whether they are confronted.

Attitudes, then, provide a kind of sense of the whole, an intimation that what is being confronted is not all there is, that to every presence there is an absence. Because they reveal objective relations among appearances, *i.e.*, relations that hold for both what is not here and now confronted and what is, the attitudes themselves cannot establish these relations. Rather, these relations guide and prescribe the attitudes. These attitudes, present more or less in every act of attending to appearance, can yield *a priori* knowledge if we examine them. What we know then is something about transcendent conditions of all that appears, confronted or not.

Thus, if fundamental attitudes could be delineated, they would indicate conditions governing appearances objectively beyond the boundaries imposed by the act of knowing something specifically confronted. In this way attitudes represent a speculative turn, within a phenomenology of appearances, towards ultimate governing conditions. Dominated by specific interests, every human being postures itself uniquely in confronting appearances. However, Weiss maintains that at least five basic attitudes can be distinguished within every posture. Not always present together and, like postures, colored by interests, these basic attitudes may together constitute a complex attitude defining a posture.

The first such attitude is a *sympathetic responsiveness* to or *acceptance* of both a confronted appearance and what lies beyond it, *viz*, its source and other appearances. When I am responsive at one moment to what appears, I accept the reality it displays and whatever else might subsequently appear. For example, when I turn my attention to the crashing sound of white water against the rocks in springtime, I accept this as the river's appearance and imagine its likely union with the appearance of the river opening into a deep, still pool downstream.

The previous attitude suggests someone perched on a cliff successively enjoying the appearances of the river in the valley below, but all the while responding sympathetically to those present and absent appearances as a whole. If, on the other hand, you are in a canoe on that white water, a sympathetic response to the dimensions of the river valley as an aesthetic whole is not your primary attitude. The rocks and the white water are together, but they are irreducibly independent and dangerous, and the canoeist dares not treat the appearance of one more lightly than the appearance of the other. The canoeist's awareness in this case corresponds to an attitude of *appreciation*, a sense of an appearance's equal status to our own and other appearances. The whole intimated by this attitude is not so much an aesthetic harmony as a brute aggregate.

Sometimes an *intellectual* attitude can dominate a human posture. Consider once again the individual perched on the cliff, spotting the canoeist, and contemplating the chances of successfully shooting the rapids below. The observer considers what the canoeist has already overcome, its control of the canoe, and the treacherousness of the rocks ahead. Is it reasonable to think that the canoeist can maintain control of the boat in the waters ahead? The observer's attitude thus shapes the appearance confronted at that moment in terms of its coherence with some future appearance, *viz*, the canoeist downstream fighting successfully or unsuccessfully to keep afloat.

Of course, for the canoeist, more than for that observer on the cliff, the intellectual and responsive attitudes are subordinate to a readiness to act. The canoeist confronts white water rapids to the left and low-hanging branches obstructing passage through the calmer waters to the right. Equipped with a readiness to act, the alert canoeist faces this appearance as inseparable from the river's disappearance behind a bend. Such a canoeist's attitude towards the confronted appearance is *pragmatic*, planning for action in a spatial-temporal-causal matrix that continues into appearances not yet confronted.

Why does the canoeist put itself into such potential danger? The observer on the cliff and the canoeist may catch one another's eye, the former admiring or whispering under its breath "What a fool!" while the latter is flattered or embarrassed by the unexpected audience to its craft and daring. Each exhibits an *evaluative* attitude, attentive to what is present and absent in terms of some value. Equipped with an evaluational attitude, the knower approaches a present appearance with a realistic awareness that it may be diminished or increased in subsequent experiences.

In this way Weiss identifies five basic attitudes: responsive, appreciative, intellectual, pragmatic, and evaluational, no one of which is reducible to any other. Although always part of a posture taken towards appearance, and tempered by contingent interests, these attitudes are said to represent objective conditions of a human confrontation of appearances. To put their function in somewhat paradoxical language, they signal the presence of what is absent, together with confronted appearances (*BAA*, pp. 182–89).

Are these attitudes appearances of finalities? Is there evidence that they are? Before turning to these critical questions, let us look at another purported appearance of finalities, *viz*, contexts.

Contexts

Weiss identifies five different sorts of evidence of finalities, but only one of these is an appearance. In the world of appearances, finalities evidence themselves in the form of contexts. "Finalities at their outermost limits" and "dominating, omnipresent powers," contexts connect the appearances of actualities "by affinity, coordination, rationality, extensionality, and by value" (*BAA*, p. 231; *FC*, p. 44, sec. 35). By holding actualities' appearances together apart from human perceivers (and thus from subjective appearances) and apart from actualities (singly or together), contexts render appearances objective.

Pastels go together and their blending can be disturbed or enhanced by dashes of deep red or purple. Certain sounds match up with certain colors. "Classical," "romantic," "baroque," and "impressionist" have a significance for painting and music. Some sounds and colors also have affinities with specific temperatures, odors, and flavors, a fact never doubted by culinary artists and connoisseurs of fine wine.

These affinities and contrasts among appearances can be resisted, modified, and distorted, but their efficacy, Weiss maintains, cannot be denied. However, that compelling character is *not* due to human beings, both because that efficacy is undeniable and because it can be misconstrued. Nor is it due to the actualities that appear, since some incompatible actualities may in fact have quite concordant appearances. Weiss thus concludes that these affinities are the product of a finality's insistence through an *affiliating context* (*FC*, pp. 40–41, sec. 12; p. 113, sec. 41). Although this affiliating context does not exist apart from the particular appearances with which it interplays, it is the most attenuated presence of the finality Weiss calls "Substance"; that source of the insistency, uniqueness, and inwardness of every actuality.

In addition to their contrasts and disposedness towards one another, appearances are *contextually equal*. Voices in the alley, the odor of the fading daisies on the desk, and the cold on my bare feet are all on a par as appearances. None is more or less an appearance than another. The equality of these appearances from one point of view can be the work neither of actualities nor of human beings, all of which may act and have careers quite independently of one another. Hence, Weiss concludes that the context in which all appearances are on a par is an exhibition of "Being"; the finality that applies equally to and thus coordinates every appearance and reality in the cosmos.

From another contextual standpoint, appearances have intelligible relations and structures. "There are laws dictating how one can rationally pass from an actual circle to an ellipse, from one end of the spectrum to another, from *C* to *A* on a violin" (*FC*, p. 41, sec. 18). These laws are based on an *intelligible context* of those appearances.

Far from being invented, this law-abiding or intelligible nature of appearances together is searched out and must be discovered at great effort by human minds. Thus, Weiss reasons that such a context exhibits "Possibility"; the finality that is the source of the meaning and organized nature of all that is.

Appearances, then, are always in contexts that affiliate and coordinate them with one another and provide them with natures and thus real possibilities. In addition to these three final contextual features, appearances are located contemporaries with varying careers. The appearance of the glass outlasts the appearance of the beer, though they are at one point contemporaries and the one is located in the other. These temporal, spatial, and dynamic features of appearances' relations are so many *extensional contexts*. No human mind and no actuality itself can account for these contexts. Thus they are said to evidence the finality of "Existence"; the root of a common space, time, and dynamism.

Lastly, appearances are all relative to some final value. This value, like the contextual extension and intelligibility of appearances, is not traceable to actualities, including human actualities, all of which have distinct and limited careers, spheres of influence, and degrees of integrity. Hence, the *evaluational context* of appearances must, Weiss reasons, be due to some final condition, the finality he labels "Unity."[25]

IV. Evidencing Finalities: the Role of Emotions

I have been reviewing what Weiss considers the appearances of finalities. Attitudes indicate objective conditions of the human experience of appearances, connecting confronted appearances with appearances absent from the confrontation. Contexts illustrate the objective togetherness of appearances, regardless of whether they are confronted. But has Weiss provided a convincing case that attitudes and contexts are appearances of finalities, that they symbolize finalities as their sources?

The answer, it seems to me, is "no," if one relies solely on Weiss's descriptions and analyses of attitudes and contexts. To establish his thesis, Weiss must demonstrate the following three points:

1.   appearances are composed of or include general and objective factors or conditions (*viz*, attitudes and contexts);

2. these objective factors or conditions must be traceable to something other than themselves; and

3. only finalities could account for these objective factors.

Yet, no one point is adequately established.

Weiss makes his strongest case for the first point. Clarifications and refinements can always be made, of course, but we need be neither canoeists nor perched on a cliff to concede that Weiss's theory of attitudes alerts us to a genuine dimension of human consciousness. Some attitudes are certainly as true and informative of and for human experience as are isolated perceptions of colors or of sounds or even of physical objects. Weiss's recount of contexts also has unquestionable merit as a theoretical basis for several endeavors, such as art criticism, structuralism, and psychoanalysis (FC, pp. 115–17).[26]

Yet the virtues of Weiss's account of attitudes and contexts are nonetheless unable to overcome a central obstacle to speculation about their metaphysical dimensions. For convenience's sake, I will label this obstacle the "problem of metaphysical specification." In ordinary life—i.e., not the extraordinary act of thinking and writing metaphysics—we often say we know that something is happening, though we do not know what, how, or why it is happening. Or, perhaps more commonly, we are able to describe what is happening, though we are unable to say how or why it is happening, or how or why we know it is happening. This sort of knowledge by acquaintance is quite acceptable for the often muddled, but practically determined, regions of ordinary experience. However, these sorts of claims are highly suspect when they are metaphysical in character, i.e., when claims about general and objective (or universal and necessary) features of experience are being made. For such metaphysical claims are precisely meant to be explanatory of ordinary experience. If I claim that there is some universal and necessary feature of appearances, I should be able to *specify* what it is and, if not why, at least how it is present.

However, Weiss's claims about the objectivity and universality of attitudes and contexts are based solely on a putative knowledge by acquaintance. He claims, for example, that there is an *affiliating context*, i.e., a way appearances inevitably contrast and complement one another, but he is unable to specify that context in a single instance. It does make a difference to his thesis that in the Orient and in the West different colors signify mourning, that different combinations of appearances are accepted and appreciated by different cultures, and, for some, domains may not be recognized at all. Such indeterminacy and even lack of specification might, of course, signal merely an *ignorance* of the operativeness of the affiliating context. But it might just as well signify the *absence* of an objective and universal mode of the togetherness of appearances. Similar objections might be raised against each attitude and context Weiss identifies.

My criticism does not deny that contexts and attitudes are found in limited domains. But accounts of attitudes and contexts in such domains do not provide evidence that these contexts and attitudes are in fact universal and necessary conditions of appearances. In fairness, I must mention that Weiss has admitted in private conversation that he has not fully elaborated the relation between what he calls the "common" and the "ultimate" degrees of ultimacy in appearance, *i.e.*, the relation between the particular domains of science, art, and the like and the universal claims of his speculative metaphysics. Weiss rightly fancies himself, as he often remarks, as a breaker of new ground. Thus, my criticism is only an indirect challenge to Weiss. Still, ground breaking should only be the result of thorough environmental impact and geological surveys, careful planning by engineers and architects, and a commitment of capital.

However, let us suppose Weiss is able to provide blueprints that specify the attitudes and contexts in various domains. Let us suppose further that there are in fact five distinct attitudes and contexts constituting compelling conditions for appearances in every domain. Is there a compelling reason to trace these objective conditions back to something else, to consider them, in other words, appearances of some further realities? I am referring, of course, to the second point that must be established to substantiate Weiss's claim that attitudes and contexts are appearances of finalities. This second point, along with the third, *viz*, that the realities to which they are traceable are finalities, is not corroborated by mere descriptions of the attitudes and contexts themselves. Is it not conceivable that there simply are some objective and universal factors in the world of appearances and that the articulations of these conditions represent the ends of the analysis of that world? Why must these contexts be viewed, as Weiss puts it, as finalities in their most attenuated state?

There are at least three equally imaginative alternatives to Weiss's appeal to finalities as the sources of attitudes and contexts. The first alternative admits the reality of contexts and attitudes but denies the cogency of tracing them to anything beyond themselves. There simply are objective affiliations in appearances, an art critic might insist, but they are not the products of anything beyond the world of art itself. A second alternative might trace contexts to specific transcendent features, which, to be sure, are in no way the product of individual and contingent actualities, including human beings, but rather are the constant by-product of principles having no status apart from the actualities and appearances they govern. There are objective conditions of appearances, a scientist might maintain, not because there are finalities, but because there are principles having a bearing upon, but no reality apart from, the world of appearances. What distinguishes such scientific principles from finalities is not only their lack of independence from actualities, but also the possibility of their coming to an end or being significantly altered.

A third alternative is presented by Aquinas's theory of transcendentals. Aquinas recognized certain ultimate characterizations, but these were only logically distinct from being. That is, they are real features of being but only distinguishable from being through a mental abstraction. One can imagine Aquinas agreeing with Weiss that contexts or attitudes are not present independently of the appearance of actualities. However, Aquinas would say that a being is one by the fact that it is a being, whereas Weiss attributes an appearance's unity (or that of an actuality) not to the fact that it is but to a reality independent of the appearance's reality or being. Aquinas's alternative, then, I might suggest, would be to trace attitudes and contexts to being and its human articulation. This human articulation corresponds to being's real modes, not to be confused or identified with being itself but, in the sense of contemporary logic, equivalent to it.

Why does Weiss decide against these alternatives? Is there some evidence that demonstrates conclusively any or all of the three points necessary to Weiss's thesis? Has Weiss provided evidence that attitudes and contexts are appearances of finalities? Up to this point, I have urged that Weiss's account of attitudes and contexts does not by itself establish his thesis. However, Weiss claims another sort of evidence for all three points that, if true, vitiates my criticisms and validates Weiss's position. Weiss claims the evidence of basic emotions.

Weiss adds new dimensions to the Aristotelian dictum that philosophy begins in wonder. For Weiss, the role of certain basic emotions as forms of wonder does not end at philosophy's beginning. Appreciation is one form of wonder, the human emotional response to finalities acting on human beings. Concern is a similar form of wonder as an emotional response to actualities. Though there may be a myriad of concerns or emotional responses to actualities, there are five distinctive strands of appreciation, 'emotional vectors,' as Weiss calls them. These basic emotions are not object-less but terminate in a respective finality.

Appreciation terminates in an all-enveloping presence, without evident division or a fixed and clear nature. Openness, humility, interest, awe, and reverence are basic, emotional vectors, specializing the appreciation. Each specification touches and penetrates into a distinctive finality (*BAA*, p. 262).

Weiss's account of these "emotional vectors" is not simply the gilded-edging on his theory. Rather, he ties the very viability of metaphysics to these basic emotions and an adequate reading of them.

Metaphysics would be a kind of fiction or delusion did the basic emotions specifying appreciation have no objects. But they have objects just as surely as sight and anger do. Those objects metaphysics seek to understand in a systematic intelligible account (*BAA*, p. 262).

Completing the circle, the speculative ideas of metaphysics provide such an account, precisely because they are abstract formulations of the objects of these emotional encounters.[27]

Inasmuch as they accompany attitudes and contexts, these basic emotions provide evidence of finalities. Unlike attitudes and contexts, these emotions certainly seem to require the presence of something beyond themselves to which they refer and which draw whatever is emotionally affected towards it. This appeal to the basic emotions explains Weiss's extensive (and often repetitious) account of the theory of evidencing beyond the theories of appearances and symbolization. According to the theory of evidencing, it may be recalled, the user of evidence must himself or herself become a symbol of the evidenced and must replicate sequentially the ontological pairing of evidence and evidenced. Accomplishing this process, however, required the user's submission to the source of that pairing, *viz*, the finality evidencing itself.[28] This submission or appreciation is an emotion that evidences the appearance, in an attitude or context, of a finality.[29]

Time and competence prohibit me from making an adequate examination of this role of basic emotions. In conclusion, it must be mentioned that Weiss is proposing something startling and adventurous, at least for the American philosophical scene. Emotions, he is suggesting, have metaphysical import. They are not to be equated with an itch to be scratched or a blink of the eye, but neither do they belong to a region where philosophers should be silent. Emotions, Weiss is telling us, should be listened to carefully, not only for the sake of self-knowledge, but for the sake of metaphysics.

Four

Peter Miller

Substantival Process Philosophy: Speculative Common Sense

I. Philosophy and Common Sense

Ours is a changing world composed of a plurality of interactive individual entities, themselves changeable and changing, which are related to one another in space through time. The constituent entities of our world are of different sizes, kinds, and behaviors; some of them are themselves microworlds comprised of others; and some, at least, beneficially or adversely affect and are affected by others. The description could continue, but this much is enough to provide some of the main elements of a commonsense categorization of the world in which we live, the world we experience and manipulate, the world of which we ourselves are a part, and, I maintain, the world that we as philosophers should seek to clarify and explain and in which we should ground our own and others' conjectures and theories. In these convictions I follow Paul Weiss, who, in his first book *Reality*, wrote:

Common sense, taken as the common basic faith of mature, active men, is the unyielding confidence that the rejection of such a world, blurred and unarticulated though it be in large part, is monstrous and futile. It is to that world that one must turn to justify, if possible, and clarify, if true, the tacit dogmas of unreflecting men. . . . Should any philosopher substitute for it another, no matter how glorious and noble, he must be deemed a failure.[1]

The wedding of philosophy to common sense in this fashion might seem a recipe for the tedium of restating the familiar and obvious and for a conservative dogmatism that precludes novelty, criticism, flights of imagination, and radical transformations of our understanding. That none of these sorry consequences need follow will be evident to readers of Weiss, but a word of interpretation may help to explain why.

A philosophy of common sense does not consist of a compilation of commonsense utterances or a reiteration of truths of ordinary language, nor does it endorse common opinions or majority viewpoints as necessary truths. These may well be in error. The logic of the position that I am willing to defend conceives of common sense in the quasi-Aristotelian sense of an operative synthetic awareness of and practical orientation towards the world and oneself. It is a modifiable and only partially articulate *a priori* framework of experience, thought, and action. Philosophy needs to appeal to common sense in a twofold way, at the beginning and at the end of enquiry. At the beginning we recognize that philosophy is an attempt to interpret our lives and the world in which we live; that our common sense embodies our current lived philosophy, our categorization of the world; and hence that our current common sense is the starting point for our philosophizing. However, it is not the end, since a part of our common sense is to recognize the potential for ignorance, bias, error, inconsistency, and incompleteness. Driven by doubt, imagination, speculation, rival views, and renewed observation, common sense is subject to extension, refinement, and perhaps radical reformulation by the whole array of human resources and investigations. But, in the end, the outcome sought in this development and revision is an improved common sense still purporting to interpret our lives and the world while better satisfying norms of rigor, coherence, adequacy, and depth.

The centrality of common sense, whether naive or sophisticated, to philosophical pursuits is illustrated by the dialectical maneuver of insisting upon self-referential consistency in philosophical debate. Socrates employed the technique regularly when he drew out the implications of a proposed hypothesis to the point of absurdity, *i.e.*, a conclusion clearly unacceptable to the proponent's common sense. Aristotle defended the law of noncontradiction against potential skeptics in a like manner: they are forced to presuppose it if they wish to advance any definite intelligible thesis whatsoever. And Descartes convinced himself of the certainty of his own existence as the presupposition of his skeptical reflections. Philosophy in this vein, so well-mined and masterfully exploited by Paul Weiss, is a quest for the unyielding presuppositions of experience, thought, life, and action. Whatever else it may become, philosophy must remain a philosophy to live by.

II. Aristotelian Substances

The commonsense world sketched in our opening paragraph was cast primarily in terms of substances. What is a substance? The Aristotelian paradigm of a substance is an individual organism, a man or a horse, for example.[2] These and other kinds of concrete individuals are ontologically fundamental because everything else is an aspect, property, compound, activity, or relation of these.

A substance is not an unintelligible surd or propertyless material substratum underlying the phenomena; rather it is a concrete whole that we can comprehend because we can both confront it in experience and abstract its formal characteristics for contemplation and analysis. Nor is a substance inert; it actively maintains its nature in the face of and imposes itself upon an ambient and often contrary world, and it may develop in accordance with its characteristic potential. Most important for our purposes, a natural substance is essentially temporal because it possesses numerical identity through change, a mutable durability. The abstractable qualities it contains have varying degrees of permanence and temporariness.

In the light of our characterization of common sense as containing the potential for criticism and reformation, we must ask whether a substantival view in the Aristotelian tradition should remain a fundamental and enduring feature of philosophical wisdom or whether it should ultimately be replaced?

III. Problems with Substances

I have claimed that our naive commonsense philosophy of nature is a substantival view in which we take our bearings amongst the reidentifiable and changeable individuals that compose it. Two key features of such individuals are that (1) they have some sort of self-contained, holistic local unity, which enables them to be identified, approached, and distinguished from one another, and (2) they have numerical identity through time and change, which enables us to speak of one and the same entity existing at different times, in different circumstances and with changing characteristics. This account has faced a number of difficulties in its history, including those posed by contemporary physics. The following are a few of these:

1. Eddington's two-tables paradox poses again the perennial issue

of the relations of parts and wholes.[3] Substances come in self-contained and mutually exclusive units. If the solid table of common sense is one of these units, then its component molecules, atoms, and particles must needs be deprived of a sharply individuated, self-determining integrity. If, however, the parts are the ultimate substances, then the table is but an aggregate of these, and the void between them is without an independent integrity of its own.

2. Paradigmatic Aristotelian substances, such as an individual organism, are self-contained within fairly definite and precise self-determined boundaries. But even for common sense operating with unaided perception, most inorganic matter is a "heap," without intrinsically determined shape, and gaseous matter has no determinate boundary or volume apart from what may be externally imposed by containers. In modern quantum physics, the definiteness of location and boundaries for material units vanishes during unmeasured intervals. The model of substances, when thought of as clearly bounded and precisely located wholes, appears to break down at many points in the physical world.

3. Moreover, even when the boundaries of substances are reasonably definite, causal influence between substances whose boundaries are distant seems to be a fact of our world. Although auras, telepathy, and telekinesis are somewhat dubious candidates, gravitational and electromagnetic phenomena are well-established field effects. How shall these be accommodated in a world of individuated, localized substances? One answer, an ancient one, is in terms of the transmission of causal influence, either through chains of intermediate substances or through travelling substances moving from the locus of the cause to that of the effect. However, independent evidence of the existence of such intermediaries does not always exist, and no clear and adequate models of the way they operate exist; therefore, such hypotheses often appear to be *ad hoc*.

4. Empty space poses a problem for substantival metaphysics. Is there such a thing, and if so, what is it? How can the continuous and unitary manifold of space be reconciled with the multiple individuated, localized, and demarcated substances within space? Do these affect one another? Are either substances or space reducible one to the other?

5. Finally, in this brief catalogue, the Humean critique of substantial identity must be mentioned. A substance is supposed to remain one and the same throughout a duration of time. This is its identity.

However, such sameness, and thus identity, is but a fiction, argues Hume, because all substances are subject to change, and if they change they are no longer the same object as before. In our minds we blur small and continuous variations together and think of the object as unchanged when really this is not so.[4]

IV. The Whiteheadian Alternative

Difficulties like the foregoing have led to frequent and sometimes widespread shifts in physical ontologies away from the substantialism of common sense and classical Western metaphysical systems. Ontologies, whether based on immaterial idealism, an absolute spatio-temporal manifold, or a causal network of events, have sought to redescribe the substances of common sense in terms of a system of appearances, intensified portions of a spatiotemporal field, or worm-like sequences and aggregates of events. Insofar as the physical sciences have adopted models that would replace the substantival constructions of common sense with, say, a spatiotemporal manifold or concatenated events, we find ourselves in a cultural circumstance in which common sense, the philosophy we need to live by, and the physical sciences, which we need for our most precise and detailed understanding of physical nature, are profoundly at odds. But this is the sort of challenge that is the lifeblood of philosophy. Under the ideal of intellectual coherence, we must strive to bridge the chasm and overcome the alienation.

This definition of the problem suggests two strategies. One is to enrich the event-based model common in contemporary physics to such an extent that common sense can find within it sufficient material for a philosophy by which to live. The other is to reinterpret the substantival categories in a manner adequate to both critical analysis and scientific extensions. The former strategy is Whitehead's; the latter, that of Paul Weiss. The two strategies may be complementary; alternative descriptions of the world are possible, provided that the scientifically originated account does not contradict conditions essential to common sense. Unfortunately the Whiteheadian account appears to violate some of those conditions.

Although Whitehead formally recognized, through his reformed subjectivist principle, that the experiential base of common sense, naive or refined, must be incorporated into an adequate comprehensive outlook, he also thought he could do this by replacing a substantival ontology with an event ontology.[5] Instead of interpreting the mutable durability of the universe and its parts in terms of the Aristotelian conception of finite, local subject/agents that are self-determining *through* time, he sought to reinterpret the phenomena in terms of actual occasions, which are finite local subjects (but not agents) that are self-determining *at a* time. In other words, in Whitehead's world there is no concrete natural entity that changes; only a succession of novel entities bearing a variety of relations to previous entities.

Space does not permit a full elaboration and critique of the Whiteheadian reinterpretation of nature, but we can note in passing where it apparently fails to do justice to our own experience of perception and action. A proper phenomenology of perception would note that the perception of an object requires a duration of time through which the perception develops and changes. We see an aspect or facet of an object in the moment with expectations as to the way the experience will unfold as we continue to observe and interact with the object. Subsequent experience fulfills and modifies those expectations, while elaborating further expectations for the more remote future. The same "I" who at one moment experiences an object as having a foreshadowed future later finds his prior expectations confirmed and disconfirmed in various ways. I, the experiencer, at least, am a substance, a mutably durable identity through time.

But I am not only an experiencing subject; I am also an agent responsible for my character and deeds. As such, I need time for (1) growth in knowledge of the world's and my potentialities, (2) formation of long-range goals and values, (3) awareness of present circumstances, (4) formation of specific intentions, (5) initiation of actions, (6) feedback on progress, (7) modification of the course of action, (8) evaluation of successes and failures in my attempts, (9) reevaluation and reformation of intentions, and (10) reevaluation and reformation of long-range goals and values, and so on. Thus, the various aspects of my agency, for which I and others hold myself responsible, require that I endure for a considerable stretch of time. No atomic temporal slice of my existence, particularly if it is below the threshold of conscious modification, can be held similarly responsible. If such a slice were self-determining at a time rather than through time, it could be so only in a nonresponsible way. How, then, could a sequence of nonresponsible segments add up to a responsible agent?

V. Weiss's New Beginning

A philosophy to live by must retain its hold on common sense even while transforming it in response to other philosophical norms. In doing so it cannot abandon the experience of an enduring responsible self amidst other enduring and locally changing, individual substances. It is not clear that an event-based cosmology such as Whitehead's, which substitutes a succession of events for changing entities, can meet these demands. In any case, our central aim in the balance of this account will be to explore the alternative strategy of Paul Weiss to reformulate substantialism in a fashion that meets the challenges posed in the preceeding section III. Weiss's initial execution of this project occurred in his 1938 book *Reality*, which provides the main inspiration for my sketch here, although I develop the themes of space and time somewhat differently than he did.[6]

What new beginning can possibly be made on the subject of substance so as to avoid some of the pitfalls exposed above? The key provided by Weiss in Book II of *Reality* is a substantival process philosophy that develops the implications of pluralism. The starting point for this account is that the individuals composing the totality of reality form a multiplicity together. Indeed Weiss seeks to establish that such a multitude is not a contingent truth about the universe but an ontological necessity. Traditionally, a substance has been viewed and described as relatively self-contained, self-sufficient, and complete with its relations to others a contingent or accidental matter. Yet, argues Weiss, to be anything at all is to be determinate, this rather than that, and thus to stand in a relation of contrast to what it is not. This much he reads out of the law of noncontradiction, which every reality that we can meaningfully characterize must illustrate: "*x* is-not non-*x*." Absolute nonbeing and a monistic singular reality by itself fall apart, under his analysis, as self-contradictory concepts incapable of exemplification (*R*, Bk. II, Chapter 1).

What, then, follows? If a plurality of individual entities together is found, they must be both distinct from one another and related. Each individual member of the cosmos, then, must have two aspects: its *privacy*, itself as excluding others, and its *publicity*, itself as linked with others and together with them constituting a shared public existence. Publicity and privacy, it must be emphasized, are dual aspects of one and the same individual. I will designate this union of the public and private aspects of one and the same individual an *intensive unity*, to stand in contrast to the *extensive unity* consisting of the public relations that unite diverse individuals. My claim is that this Weissian model can be elaborated and specified in such a way as to resolve the *aporia* posed in section III and to suggest a framework for interpreting physical theory that is a viable alternative to cosmologies based on events or a singular unified field. Unlike these alternatives, as speculative common sense, it offers a philosophy by which to live.

VI. Plurality and Space

We have distinguished the mutually excluding distinct individual privacies of individuals from their public aspects. The latter together constitute the public relations and public existence between the individuals. I will try to demonstrate that the public existence they share is a dynamic, force-ridden field of interplay that must assume an extensive, space-like form. Public existence itself contains a number of distinguishable characteristics. Any part of the public existence uniting diverse individuals, because jointly constituted by them, can be viewed as:

1.   the intrusion of each in the others;

2.   the adaptation of each to the intrusions of the others;

3.   a mutual accommodation wherein they meet, but which also contains,

4.   a tendency of each to assimilate the others; and

5.   a mutual tendency to resist such assimilations and indeed the intrusions of one another.

For example, the public existence shared by two individuals A and B can be viewed as a public facet of B in which A is a present intruder requiring B's adaptive response and vice versa. The intrusion and adaptation on the part of each toward the other jointly determines the character of their shared public existence. The public existence that A and B share is not simply an indifferent intermediate domain lying between them. It is, after all, an aspect of A, i.e., A's public side, integrated by A into intensive union with A's own privacy. This internal integration of its public and private sides by A at the same time is a tendency on the part of A to assimilate B insofar as B is joined to *A* in their shared public existence. In the meantime, of course, *B* is reciprocally likewise engaged in assimilating *A*. One might think that the end result of such mutually assimilative tendencies would be to collapse the many into one, and so it would be but for a simultaneous contrary tendency of *A* and *B* to resist one another, as they must, if they are to distinguish themselves from one another to constitute a plurality.

Thus the picture that emerges of a plurality of individual substances together includes a domain of public existence crisscrossed with forces of cohesion and resistance between the diverse individuals that are rival owners of the public existence they share. Pressure, repulsion, and fission are phenomena in which mutual resistance predominates. Attraction and fusion display the mutually assimilative tendencies of things. We can attribute relative indifference either to an accommodative balance between the assimilative and resistant tendencies or to a minimal contribution of each to the public existence they share. But presumably some degree each of assimilation, accommodation, and resistance is found as an analytical component of any portion of the public existence that diverse individuals share.

Even at the generic metaphysical level of this analysis there are numerous kinds of relations and interactions that obtain among the individuals constituting a plurality. My focus here, however, is on the spatial features of these relations. The key to understanding space lies in the mutual resistance between diverse individuals, which is the public manifestation of their ultimate distinctness. An individual can allow the intrusions of another to merge with itself only so far as they are stripped of anything alien to its private nature. Otherwise, those intrusions must be resisted. In this manner, individuals each create a *private place* or *absolute location* for themselves, relegating all alien intrusions to the outside. And since this is a reciprocal process, the diverse and mutually resistant individuals of a plurality make a private place for each that is exclusive of and externally related to the others.

Consider further the jointly constituted public existence that lies between the diverse private places of individuals. This shared public existence, and any of its parts, can be thought of as a kind of boundary, a union and a division, between the diverse individuals it relates. Obviously, I am generalizing the concept of a boundary beyond the well-demarcated ones we find it practical to use to reflect the fact that any position in open space, for example, is at least two-sided, dividing nearer from more remote regions. This public division is accomplished, I have argued, by a mutual resistance between distinct entities that keeps each outside the others in its own relatively private place. Yet at the same time, the intrusion of one being in others is not one hundred percent resisted; a degree of accommodation and assimilation also takes place and a partial penetration of the boundary at that point occurs. The penetrated individual, in order to maintain its distinctness from the intruder, must once again further resist the intruder at a more fundamental level. Through the reiteration of partial resistance, partial assimilation/penetration, further resistance, further assimilation/penetration, and so on, a continuum of filter-like boundaries obtains between diverse individuals sharing a common public existence. Each progressively filters the intrusions of the others through the resistance that it mounts as its private core is approached. Thus, it puts its private place at a distance from alien others, a distance consisting of the intervening layers of resistance between them.

My proposal is that public existence, in the form of a continuum of mutual resistance keeping the private places of independent beings at a distance from one another, bears the features that we familiarly attribute to public space. One merit of this approach is that it can give an account of the way space and the substances it contains are related. Public space is an analytic aspect of the coexistence of individuals: their being together so far as they are divided from one another, apart, and unaccommodating. It is a domain of external relations, which is to say that it is a domain of effective resistance keeping beings and parts of beings outside of one another at an extensive distance where the individual natures of each can be preserved distinct. We can be more specific than that, however, by specifying other spatial features in the paragraphs that follow.

VII. Other Spatial Features

Space as a void and a plenum

A classical debate between Aristotle and the atomists concerned whether space was something or nothing. The atomists thought it was nonbeing in contrast to the being of atoms, whereas Aristotle contended that such nonbeing was both unnecessary to explain physical phenomena and nonsensical. I think we can effect a partial reconciliation of their views, however, by noting that "empty" space is at least a partial void from which substantial individuals have largely excluded one another by their mutual resistance. Substances are there only in an attenuated form of public existence. Conversely, they *are there*, effective and minimally interactive. The attenuated being of space falls between the full and the empty of the classical debate.

The two-tables paradox

Which is the really real: the table or the subatomic particles that constitute it? Both, we can say, if we acknowledge degrees of privacy. A macro-object like a table, although composite, is also an individual substance with distinguishable private and public aspects. Together with other macro-objects, like chairs and walls, it structures the space of the room in which it is found, exerts gravitational force, resists penetration by others of the same order of magnitude, and the like. However, as a composite object, its wooden interior, from which other macro-objects are excluded, is only relatively private, *i.e.*, private to a degree, because it is composed of the merged public existence of more ultimate constituents that themselves have more intense privacies. Abstracting from the less intense levels of privacy at which a table has a unitary nature and considering only the more intense levels of privacy achieved by components like electrons, a table is simply a multiplicity of divergent and mutually exclusive individuals that put a lot of space between one another relative to their core size.

Absolute and relative locations

I earlier spoke of the private place that an individual forges for itself in resisting the onslaught of the world as an *absolute location*. I call it such because space is ordered from that point as the *origin* of the individual's uniquely contributed dimension of space and a *limit* to all the others. The more usual observation is that space contains the individual substances found therein, but it is also true that the whole system of individuals contains space. In some sense, every individual exists in its privacy at the edge of space in the unique dimension that it contributes to space. All portions of space, then, are intervals lying between the substances that define the spatial extremes, *i.e.*, they are positioned *relative* to those extremes.

Assimilated space and focal location

To say that individual substances form the limits of space, from and to which all other locations can be referred, is but part of the story of substances and their relations to space. Space lies not only between individuals but also to some extent within them, which in turn endows individual substances with a relative location in the larger matrix. An individual substance must adapt not only to other distinct individuals that intrude upon it but also to the public world, and public space, that they jointly constitute. In part, the alien public world is resisted and held off outside and at a distance. But like other intrusions, it is accommodated and assimilated to a degree as well. Thus a portion of the space obtaining between the other substances of the universe becomes assimilated into the privacy of each individual. Absolutely located within the confines of my body as an origin and limit for the rest of the universe, a "here" from which all else is "there," my interior space is also crisscrossed by lines between other objects about me and lies on actual or potential trajectories for gravitational and electromagnetic forces, radiation, and bullets or spears. We can call this wedding of an individual's proper absolute location with a relatively located region of space a *focal location*.

It is interesting to speculate how, through the same dynamics, the assimilated space internal to an individual can be said to map the external space from which it arose. What sorts of correspondences obtain between the space that is internal to myself and the space of the universe beyond? This is an acute epistemological—as well as metaphysical—issue if we would understand the kind, extent, and accuracy of our perceptual experience's representation of the world.

Boundaries

Finally in this catalogue of spatial features several sorts of boundary must be considered. I previously identified a generic concept of boundary as a unity and a divide that stands between distinct beings or parts of beings. At least five varieties of boundary fit that description. First, a *public face* is the more or less abrupt barrier of concentrated resistance with which an individual surrounds the focal location wherein its privacy is most intense. Second, an *interval* of space both unites and separates the distinct individuals which delimit it. In this sense, the broad expanse of space between, say, the earth and the sun can be thought of as an extremely thick boundary separating them. Third and conversely, when two objects are immediately next to one another and in contact, they form an *interface* of contact. In this circumstance, the interval between them is compacted to the point where it is exhausted by the public faces of the two entities. Even so, we can conceive of different degrees of contact ranging from contiguity to continuity according as the public faces in the interface either form distinct poles or they do not.

The preceding kinds of boundary all exist between either composite or incomposite individuals. The last two exist only for composite individuals. Fourth, an *integument* or *limiting face* is the set of focally located individuals that form the surface of a well-defined material solid. Skin, paint, and the surface molecules of a fluid under surface tension are examples of integuments. Finally, closely resembling an integument is a *divider* or *limiting interval*, which, like an integument, is a set of focally located individuals, but which, unlike it, does not belong primarily to a body on one side of it. Instead, it more neutrally limits and joins the two spatial (or material) regions on either side of it. A container, a fence, the shared membrane between two cells, and glue in a joint are examples of dividers.

One general point to be made about boundaries of all sorts is that they have a certain thickness to them. Only mathematical idealizations have no width. To think of actual boundaries in the real world as instantiating without qualification the breadthless limits of mathematics is to commit *the fallacy of precise location*. Whitehead, in defining and avoiding the fallacy of simple location, nevertheless commits the fallacy of precise location. A theory of spatial extension can never be a purely mathematical theory, I believe, if that means abstracting from the mutual resistance and ecstasis of substances in their public relations.[7]

VIII. Integrity and Temporality

Building on foundations laid by Paul Weiss in *Reality*, I have tried to illustrate the way a substantival process philosophy can meet some of the conundra posed for traditional theories of substance. Because substances are diffusely located in their public existence, although focally located in their privacies, they are capable of field effects, the most obvious of which is the joint constitution of the field of space itself. We have explored various relations between substances and space and noted that the boundaries of substances have varying degrees of thickness and definiteness. Most of the observations we have made apply both to the macro-level of composite substances and the micro-level of subatomic particles. Both are substantially real, I insist, and the apparent difficulties in affirming both together can be resolved by distinguishing degrees of privacy for substances, with the micro-substances having the more intense privacies. There remains to deal with the Humean critique of substantial identity through time and an account of the inner dynamics of mutably durable substances.

Hume's critique of substantial identity rests on the assumption that identity through time requires absence of change: "We have a distinct idea of an object, that remains invariable and uninterrupted thro' a supposed variation of time; and this idea we call that of *identity* or *sameness*."[8] This association of identity with invariance is a common theme, even for those who know better. It is the foundation of the ancient Eleatic school of philosophy and was incorporated into classical atomism, whose ultimate bits of reality were invariant in all properties, save motion and position. Even Aristotle, who offered a better alternative, looked for an invariant substratum or a constant form as the foundation of substantial identity through time. It may be that Whitehead drew the same conclusion as Hume and rather than accept an inert invariance at the heart of concrete reality turned instead to societies and successions of actual occasions.

But the Humean assumption must be challenged. Permanence and persistence are not the opposite of change or exclusive of change. In fact, permanent things *must* change, at least in temporal locus and relations to other changeable things and passing events, and change can only occur to that which endures. Kant and Aristotle were right in noting that these concepts presuppose one another.[9] The contrary of the permanent is not the changing but the changeless, which is confined in nature to a particular condition, time, and circumstance, like Whitehead's actual occasions. What cannot change must perish.

Wherein, then, lies substantial identity if not in the invariance of the whole or of an essential component of the whole? A partial answer might be found in the continuity of change that Hume remarked upon. For example, the ship that is reconstructed a plank at a time is still the same ship even if not a single plank of the original remains. But continuity alone is insufficient, because it is a gestalt quality which can apply to a changing image that is insubstantial in itself, say a character in a film or a reflected image. There must be some sort of internal, self-maintaining integrity to the thing itself, which includes, as we have seen, an active differentiation from other objects. The ship, of course, is a composite, not an ultimate individual substance, but like them it continues to hold itself together and differentiate itself from the pier, the water, and other objects in its universe.

The stage is now set to consider the temporal dynamics of substances. We will discover that the Whiteheadian fear that actualities will turn out vacuous and inert is groundless. The integrity of individual substances is, in part, a given but also, in part, a tendency or "motive" and finally, in part, an achievement. In attributing motives and achievements to individual substances of all kinds, I am not supposing some sort of mentalistic panpsychism but merely a specification of the integrity that makes substances to be distinct, unitary individuals. Individuals exist, and continue to exist, with a distinct identity and self-maintained integrity. Their integrity must continue to be achieved, however, because it is constantly challenged by contrary tendencies towards dissolution, which arise from the individual's participation in a public world co-owned with other individuals that resist one another and diversely attempt to assimilate the public existence they share to their own separate and distinct natures.

The integrative tendencies or motivation of an individual substance can be further analysed into three components or dimensions: the conservative, the responsive, and the innovative. The conservative dimension of integrative motivation manifests itself as resistance to change and an adherence to already existing characteristics and tendencies. Psychological forms of this tendency we might call a sort of self-love and the physical forms inertia. Conservative motives of self-preservation or inertia cannot exhaust the integrative tendencies of an individual, however. Because a substance is enmeshed with others in a public world, its integrity will be expressed in responsive or adaptive motives as well, including the divergent tendencies of resistance and assimilation, which I have already explored in my account of space.

Finally, a principle of unrest and potential for change inherent in integrative motivation should be noted. Because the diverse tendencies within itself and in its public existence are partially divergent and at odds, it is impossible for an individual to be completely identified with all members of the divergent set, which would pull it asunder.

Preserving its integrity requires compromise and an innovative resolution of the divergencies not necessarily like any prior resolution. In this fashion, the integrative motivation of an individual substance contains an element of freedom from its past and its environment that is open to new possibilities. At the same time, however, because the individual is also responsively and conservatively integrative, whatever freedom to innovate there may be is held under constraint, usually in quite stable and predictable ways. Real individuals, then, are complex, dynamic, and multidimensioned substances, even though, for analytical purposes, it is sometimes useful to isolate and idealize one dimension at a time, say, as an atomic inertial mass, a contemporary field of forces, or a spontaneous novelty.

Once the dynamic, motivational side of substances is acknowledged, it is but a short further step to introduce broadbased conceptions of value into cosmology. Teleological theories of value link values to motivational factors, to tendencies and the objects and outcomes of those tendencies. As integratively motivated, substances are (usually unconscious) valuers that value the integrity of their own natures and, in doing so, selectively value what they have already become, features of the public world in which they participate, and possibilities for integration that might be. But value theory should not stop with what is actually valued by individuals if it would recognize comparisons of value and standards of value exceeding not only current realizations of value but current motives as well. For that, the realm of possible values must be explored to learn how individuals singly and together might be enriched.[10] These further explorations of the realm of values exceed the present assignment of sketching the potentialities for a process philosophy built upon the very substantial foundations laid almost fifty years ago by Paul Weiss.

Five

David Weissman

First Considerations

Where most of us would settle for inventing a single metaphysical theory, Paul Weiss has two of them. One theory is proposed in *Modes of Being*; the other one is formulated most completely in *First Considerations*. These two books differ considerably with regard to the categories and their relations. Equally vital, Weiss's notion of a categorial schema has changed.

In *Modes of Being*, Actuality, Ideality, Existence, and God are the complementary modes. Where Being is the totality of things that exist, these are its four reciprocally related and constituent aspects. Rather like the notes of a chord, each one is indispensable to the effect of the whole. But unlike the notes, no single mode is self-sufficient. Each one implies and presupposes the other three. Being is the coordination of these four, categorial natures.

First Considerations is different. There, Weiss distinguishes two kinds of reality. First are the numerous Actualities. Second are the five Finalities. "Finalities" are the categorial dimensions or planes that differentiate an actuality, making it complex. It is the particular that gathers and binds their expressions within itself. With Actuality as the primary category, Weiss lists Substance, Being, Possibility, Existence, and Unity as the finalities. On this schema, actualities are the primary sites of being. Weiss is careful to demonstrate the way each of the finalities is expressed in them, although he says very little about the relations of the finalities to one another. This is a change from *Modes of Being* where the reciprocity of the modes is a principal topic.

The differences between these books is striking; but remarkably, there is nothing in the later book to acknowledge that Weiss has revised the schema on which his categorial system is based. Weiss offers no comparison of the two schemas, no evaluation of their comparative virtues, and no effort is found to show that they are, or are not, compatible.

His silence may be explained in this way. *Modes of Being* affirms, at least once (*MOB*, p. 89) that Being is the "common denominator," with Actuality, Ideality, Existence, and God as its four constituent modes, *i.e.*, its finalities. *Modes of Being* is, therefore, already an expression of the same categorial schema that is applied in *First Considerations*. They differ on matters of content—not form. *Modes of Being* affirms that the concrete totality, *i.e.*, Being, is the elementary fact. *First Considerations* emphasizes the plurality of separate and self-sufficient individuals. The one is Spinozistic; the other is Aristotelian.

I prefer to ignore this possible interpretation. Weiss does say in *Modes of Being* that the primary category " . . . must be one with what is" (*MOB*, p. 87). But he stops short of first saying, and then elaborating on the idea, that Being is the primary category. Indeed, Being almost drops from sight as *Modes of Being* concentrates on the four modes and their reciprocity. Actualities, by contrast, are never less than prominent within *First Considerations*. Every claim about a finality is inevitably referred to them. Accordingly, I ignore the tacit isomorphism of these two books in order to stress their useful differences.

The schema appropriate to a categorial system is one of three issues around which this essay turns. We also need a list of specific categories. Weiss has two lists. I shall suggest an alternative to both of them. Finally, I shall consider one reason for the differences between Weiss's categorial system and my own. He emphasizes the philosopher's autonomy. I suppose that our autonomy is compromised, that our concern for nature obliges us to found our categorial system in the discoveries of science.

My argument is fourfold and develops in the following way: First, I discuss an anomaly common to *Modes of Being* and *First Considerations*. Second, I propose a set of categories that averts this difficulty, joining the two schemas of Weiss's books, proving them compatible. Third, I return to the specific categories of those books. Certain issues are clarified if Weiss's categories are evaluated from the perspective of my list. Fourth, I suggest that Weiss's categories suffer in ways to be described because of the autonomy which he claims for philosophic inquiry. The numbers of the sections which follow introduce these four points.

I

Weiss remarks, on page 223 of *Modes of Being*, that, "Actuality encloses a fragment of existence and structures it in ways other actualities do not." Later on the same page, he writes, "Actualities . . . cannot be separated from their existence without altogether ceasing to be actual." The anomaly is Weiss's supposition that actualities are a mode of being, hence elementary, but that actualities are also derivative because of being the several episodes or substances that are prescinded from Existence.

Which is primary, Actuality or Existence, *i.e.*, particular substances or the dynamic, enmattered space-time where substances are generated and sustained? Within *Modes of Being*, where the categories are complementary and equal in primacy, this question might be ignored. For what looks to be Weiss's indecision may be nothing more than the difficulty of describing categories that imply and presuppose one another.

This explanation does not suffice, however, when the same irresolution appears within *First Considerations*, for there the architecture of Weiss's categorial system is altered: Actuality is the primary reality; Existence is reduced to being one of the five finalities that are categorial modes of Actuality.

The relation of Existence to Actualities is described most powerfully in the last chapter of *First Considerations*, the chapter titled, "The Cosmos":

The cosmos contains complexes, compounds and collections. Actualities there are together subject to common final constraints. These dictate how the actualities are related and how they function with reference to one another. . . . Cosmic units, be they complexes or compounds, have relevance, positive or negative, to one another. What each is and does makes a difference to what others are and do, even though those others are at a great distance and come, go, and act independently of them (*FC*, p. 174).

We need to square these remarks, implying the categorial primacy of a dynamic, enmattered, self-dividing space-time with the insistence that, "Each actuality exists apart from all the others. Each fills out a present of the same kind and duration, but in its own distinctive way, to make this its own present having nothing to do with any other" (*FC*, p. 178).

Weiss's dilemma is the one of assigning priority either to the dynamic processes where particulars are created and sustained or to the particulars that resist intrusion and change. If these dynamic relations and processes are accidental to the identity of individuals, then actualities will be windowless monads. Existence will have withered. There will be no dynamic association of reciprocally related and mutually transforming entities, only the aggregate of relationless particulars. Happily, Weiss has also endorsed the contrary view, *viz*, that particulars are embedded within existence, that each of them is an episode within the dynamic, enmattered, and self-dividing space-time.

It follows from this latter view that nothing is an actuality in Weiss's sense: *viz*, there is no thing that " . . . exists apart from all the others." Every part may have an integrity that exempts it from the intrusions of some other ones, thereby enabling it to develop within itself. But no part will be exempt from those conditioning relations that make its generation and identity dependent on some or all of the other conditions within space-time. This should be, I think, the preferred alternative.

II

I now consider what list of categories might be appropriate for characterizing this state of affairs.

For Weiss's Actualities as described in *Modes of Being* and *First Considerations*, we substitute the dynamic, enmattered, and geometrized space-time. Applying the categorial schema of *First Considerations* as our paradigm, we list as finalities the categorial modes that are constitutive of this primary reality. There are two finalities: Elements and Powers.

There are, tentatively, five Elements: 1. a geometrized space-time; 2. motion; 3. matter; 4. matter's dispositions, as they restrict the changes that interacting matters may produce; and 5. qualitative contingencies, including (a) the distribution of matter, and (b) the constants of nature, *e.g.*, the fact that light has a certain velocity. This list is tentative because matter, as mass, may be identified with certain of the dynamic properties of space-time and because dispositions may be powers for relatedness, which are consequent on the geometrical properties of space-time. There may be three Elements rather than five.

There are four Powers: 1. The complex formed by the Elements is self-perpetuating. 2. This complex is self-differentiating, in three respects: (a) it is self-diversifying, resulting in the generation of myriad properties; (b) it is self-dividing, resulting in a diversity of particulars; and (c) it is self-stratifying, using configuration or aggregation to produce systems which are dominant or subordinate to one another. 3. This complex achieves self-differentiation, *i.e.*, it is self-transforming, because its dynamics are causal. Further properties, particulars, and stratifications are produced by the interaction of differences already current within space-time. This acknowledges that space-time must already be differentiated if it is to be self-transforming. (4) This complex is self-coordinating, implying that each differentiation has value or disvalue for one or more others. The patterns of these values and disvalues are expressed as the harmonies and disharmonies that pervade a region, connected regions, or all of space-time.

The Elements and Powers together have a product. For nature, as the self-differentiating, geometrized, and enmattered space-time is constituted of overlapping and stratified *stabilities*. Each stability is a system of properties having persistent organization and cohesion. It has, as a result, some degree of resistance to external, intrusive forces and a measure of self-regulation, *i.e.*, it has an outside and an inside. Each stability faces outwards with a kind of permeable membrane, extracting energy or information from its environment while sustaining its own organization and processes. This resistent perimeter, with its powers for self-regulation, qualifies the stability for a degree of internality. It can behave as a monad, developing in ways that are determined by its own design. A human being is a stability, but so is a rain storm, a solar system, a government, and a spade. The persistence and organization of stabilities, their exclusion of external influences, and their self-regulation explains their relative autonomy. Every stability may have a developmental history exempt from changes within other, possibly contiguous or overlapping stabilities. Nevertheless, stabilities are coordinated and subordinated to one another, as none is perfectly autonomous because each is generated within, and is nourished by those others which comprise its environment. These dependencies are confirmed whenever radical changes in one stability affect other ones.

The one, fully autonomous and externally unconditioned stability is the whole, although the evidence for a single, all-embracing stability is more speculative than established. It is equally likely that the many separate, overlapping, and stratified stabilities cohere with one another in a way that is imperfectly harmonious, with only space-time and the laws deriving from its geometry to unify the whole.

This categorial system is a somewhat impressionistic description of self-sustaining and self-equilibriating thermodynamical systems. This fact has two implications. First, it suggests that our categorial views about nature should be generalized from the findings of experimental sciences. Second, it suggests that metaphysical theory should be continuous with scientific thinking, so that metaphysical categories may have concrete and specific applications.

I emphasize these two points because our categories apply to nature. We laymen may be adept at describing nature as it appears to us. But we look to science to learn what nature is in itself. The alternative is a set of categories having no basis in scientific discoveries and little application either to scientific theory or to nature.

A system of categories founded in scientific discovery also has this other advantage, *viz*, we are saved from having to express and elaborate our claims in a language that is too often metaphorical. We need not place too heavy a burden on the nuances and evocations of whatever names we give to our categories. We will be able, for example, to supply very precise definitions for what is meant by a "stability."

This first part of my categorial system applies the categorial schema from *First Considerations*. Can we also provide for the schema from *Modes of Being*? That is the system whose categories are complementary, not as in *First Considerations*, a primary category and its constituent categorial modes. What might serve as the complement to a dynamic, self-differentiating, geometrized, and enmattered space-time?

Remember that I have made no provision for the ontological notions of being, existence, and actuality. Weiss writes in *First Considerations* that these are concrete efficacies, each one having a power unique unto itself. I prefer saying that "being" is the generic, determinable synonym for "existence," where everything that is has being, and where the problem is one of specifying the more determinate expressions of being.

Being has two, more specific determinations. One of them is actuality. Space-time and all its differentiations, including all the stabilities are actual. Why? Because the necessary and sufficient condition for actuality is determinacy in respect to quality, quantity, and relation. A property, or complex of properties, having position in space-time is determinate in all three ways; but so is that region of space-time made determinate by being the site for this property's instantiation.

Every particular, including all the stabilities, is constituted exclusively of its properties. Each particular inherits determinacy in quality, quantity, and relation from its properties. It is, however, only in relation to one another and by virtue of having a place in space-time that properties are made determinate in these three ways. Hence, it is the three apples on my window sill, and not the number three or the universal, apple, that are actual.

The complement to the actual, space-time world is near at hand. For properties that are determinate and actual may also be determinable and uninstantiated. *Cousin of* is a determinable property. It is determinable with respect to the terms it may relate and also because its terms may be first, second, or third cousins, one or more times removed. Most uninstantiated properties are determinable in quality, quantity, and relation, but even such a qualitatively determinate property as the uninstantiated middle-C lacks the specificity of number and relation. It becomes this particular and actual note with specificity in all three of the required respects only as it is played.

How can the more determinate expression of being that is common to properties which are uninstantiated, hence determinable, be described? They exist, I suggest, as possibilities. Possibility is also a mode of being, one that differs from actuality as the determinable is different from the determinate. Where actuality is realized in the properties of a self-differentiating space-time, a complementary possibility exists, namely, these same properties existing as uninstantiated determinables. Also counted among the possibles are those many sets of properties that are nowhere instantiated.

Possibility is the categorial complement of actuality. These two are the counterpart modes of being, or existence. Possibility is the notion to add as we supplement the categorial schema deriving from *First Considerations* in order to satisfy the schema from *Modes of Being*.

Weiss has insisted that the complementarity of categories is more than a loose pairing; and that is also true here. For the coordination of actuality with possibility is, more exactly, the prefiguring of the actual world by the possible one. The possible world is a set of definite, if still determinable, differences. These properties are organized. They have a structure that expresses the fact that properties existing as possibles are essentially relational. Structures of possibilities incorporate relations described elsewhere as vertical and lateral. These structures are organized hierarchically, with vertical files and lateral orders. An actual world instantiates both the differences and the structure of a possible world. Therefore, the actual world is more than complementary to the possible one: the identity, hence the intelligibility of the actual world, is founded within the possible world.

To summarize, we have a categorial system that applies the categorial schemas from both *First Considerations* and *Modes of Being*. From *First Considerations* comes the notion of a primary category with its constituent modes. That primary entity is the dynamic and geometrized space-time. The elements and powers are its finalities. Stabilities are their product. To satisfy the schema from *Modes of Being*, we say that actuality and possibility are the counterpart expressions of being, so that the complexes of properties organized as stabilities in space-time exist in the first instance as the structured but determinable properties of a possible world. Weiss's two categorial schemas are compatible.

III

The differences between Weiss's categories and my own help to clarify certain issues. There are four to consider: (1) the relation of Actuality to Existence; in my terms, the relation of stabilities to the dynamic, enmattered, and geometrized space-time; (2) Weiss's notion of Substance; (3) Possibility; and (4) Being.

Actuality and Existence

(1) There is a chicken and egg quality to the question: Which is prior, Actuality or Existence? Weiss considers the tension between these two in a passage from *Beyond All Appearances*: " . . . each [actuality] is a unique individual, maintaining itself against a primal Substance, in the very act of instancing this in the shape of a distinctive substance" (*BAA*, p. xvi). I hold the word "substance" in reserve, using it only when considering the second of these four issues. Weiss's point is clear without it. What he calls Existence is the generative matrix where individuals are created and sustained. Yet, every actuality has an integrity that enables it to resist intrusions while developing in ways appropriate to itself.

The balance between individuals and the self-differentiating whole is well-expressed in *Modes of Being* where the four modes are complementary. The balance is upset, in the wrong direction I believe, when *First Considerations* makes Actuality the primary category, with Existence reduced to one of the finalities.

One reason for exalting individuals is Weiss's conviction that activity and causality are fundamental to nature. Causality, hence activity, presupposes these individuals, for change occurs when individuals are transformed because of their interactions. More emphatically, only individuals act, and only individuals are affected by interaction. The dynamics of our universe compel us to acknowledge individuals as primary.

I agree that the efficacy of particulars is a vital feature of our world; although specifying what will count as efficacious particulars is often difficult, as in the case of moving fluids. It might be better to make Weiss's point by speaking of the localizability of causes. Some causes are discrete and separable while fluids are continuous; but both are localizable. Action and change may devolve upon the dynamic relations of disparate but contiguous or connected locales.

This fails, however, to establish that individuals are the primary category. That is because the very integrity of individuals, as expressed by their cohesiveness, persistence, and resistance is conditional. Every individual has integrity because of being embedded within a field where the current differentiation of stabilities exhibits the balance of forces within the field. Every current stability is conditioned by the environment of overlapping, underlying, and supervening stabilities. Individual stabilities are generated or destroyed as the balance among current stabilities is altered.

Every stability endures for a while because of the least energy principles that make its perpetuation less costly than its dissolution. But eventually, its structure dissolves because of factors within both the environment and itself. Some new stability, incorporating all or parts of the old one, arises in its place. Particular stabilities, from rain drops to galaxies, are ephemeral. Their consolidation and dissolution is the record of self-transformation occurring within the whole.

I do not suggest that the whole is an undifferentiated One. The whole is, instead, the totality of coordinated and subordinated stabilities. There may be no superordinate stability within which the lesser stabilities accommodate to one another. Nor does it follow that every differentiation within space-time is related to every other one in every way. For each stability excludes other ones. The internality of stabilities is, in part, this insistent oblivion to many aspects of the world outside them. Still, there are respects in which every stability does relate to every other one, and these are instances where the very identity of the stability depends on its universal relatedness; gravitation and its consequences being one example. Notice that gravitation is one of the relations that derive from the dynamic, geometrized structure of space-time. This structure might be the all coordinating, highest-order one. But then it might function as only the backdrop, the arena, in which lower-order stabilities separate from others while establishing themselves, all in accord with its constraints. The alternative is that each of the differences in every stability has its necessary and sufficient conditions in this highest-order, all coordinating structure. The identity of every stability will depend, if that is true, on its relatedness to the totality of space-time. But how could that be: How could a single stability relate to all of space-time? Only by relating to all of the other stabilities gathered within it, so that each of the properties in any one stability would be a function of its relations to all the rest of nature. These issues are unresolved.

I conclude that someone who emphasizes causality and the fact that individuals act and interact might insist, in the way prescribed by *Modes of Being*, that space-time and stabilities are complementary, neither one being primary. However, Existence, not Actuality, is the primary category, if we apply the schema from *First Considerations*.

Substance

(2) Weiss often uses the word "substance." He uses it to signify the cosmos, but also to designate individual things. Then too, Substance is one of the finalities in *First Considerations*.

Some nuances of Weiss's vocabulary, and especially those which suggest Aristotle's primary substances, are deplored by Weiss's Whiteheadian critics. He replies that a world without substances, a world of patterned events, would lack power, action, interaction, and efficacy.

Weiss supplies a middle way between the Whiteheadian and Aristotelian claims when he substitutes "substantiality" for "substance" (*FC*, p. 107). Substantiality need imply nothing more than persistence, resistance, and efficacy. Many processes have these attributes, so that we are saved from having to believe that actualities are restricted to the discrete, informed matters which are normally counted as primary substances.

Every stability is substantial if persistence, resistance, and efficacy are all that is required of substantiality. But plainly, substantiality cannot be a finality because it is derivative. Its ingredients are motion, matter, and those equilibriating, causal relations that account for persistence and relative impermeability.

This reinforces Whiteheadian claims about substance, without endorsing either Whitehead's own doctrines or the reformulations of process philosophers. I doubt that process philosophers can provide for the phenomena I am calling "stabilities" because stabilities are founded upon the causal reciprocity of their parts, as a thermostat acts on the furnace while the furnace acts on the thermostat by way of the air it heats. The stability having these parts is not merely a pattern or harmony of constituent events. It is, instead, a system of reciprocally related parts where each part is also a stability.

Process philosophy makes no sense of these self-regulating systems for two reasons. First, process philosophers prescind what they call "events" from the ongoing continuities of motion and change. They do that because Whitehead's "actual occasions" are a generalized version of the discrete moments William James described as the "specious present." When thought has crystallized myriad events from the continuities of motion and change, process philosophers must find ways of relating the newly discrete events to one another. Following Whitehead, they say that every event takes into consideration those others which it prehends. Each successor event shows the efficacy of its antecedents by the ways it provides for their influence within itself. This formulation might clarify several issues, but it ignores the fact of generation. Whiteheadians never explain the way an event is produced by its antecedents. We are asked to believe that every actual occasion emerges from and passes away into nothing.

No stability would ever be established if the relations of its constituents were not more dynamic than this. Whiteheadians, reading "society" where I use "stability," may deny this. But a Whiteheadian society is only that set of individuals where each behaves after considering the interests of the others, as best they are known to it. This society is an aggregate, where each member is a perspective on the others, but a monad in itself. A stability is different. The stability is an effect, *i.e.*, it comes to supervene on its elements because of the generative and reciprocal relatedness of those parts. Whiteheadians ignore the generative side of this causal relationship as they have already erred by reifying events. In both instances, they express Whitehead's too Humean predilection: he declares separate what is only distinguishable.

Process philosophers are right to query Weiss's notion of substance; but their Whiteheadian notions do not provide for persistence, resistance, self-regulation, and efficacy. Weiss, merely by substituting "substantiality" for "substance" does provide for some of these things. But, then, substantiality is derivative. It cannot, therefore, be a finality.

Possibility

(3) In both *Modes of Being* and *First Considerations*, Weiss writes of Possibility. In *Modes of Being*, Possibility as Ideality is one of the four modes. In *First Considerations*, Possibility is a finality. However, Possibility as Weiss understands it is not possibility as I have described it.

To see the difference, we need distinguish material from eternal possibilities. Material possibilities are events that would occur if agents were to interact in specific ways, as summer is possible if the earth goes on spinning about the sun. Notice that entities qualify as causes because of their dispositions. The reality of material possibilities reduces, therefore, to the reality of agents that are qualified for acting in these prospective ways. The reality of eternal possibilities is not reducible in this or any other way. These possibles are properties uninstantiated. Their existence is independent of, and prior to, the material circumstances occurrent within every actual world. This conclusion follows from these assumptions: Whatever is not a contradiction is a possibility; hence, either a contradiction or a possibility. Complexes of properties that embody no contradiction exist necessarily and eternally as possibilities.

The only possibilities Weiss acknowledges are material ones. He correctly identifies eternal possibility with logical possibility, but says, " . . . it has no being except so far as one thinks of it. . . . Apart from our determination of it the logically possible has no reality" (*MOB*, p. 107). This is, I believe, an error. Eternal possibilities are independent of thought and language for their existence and character, as "chiliagon" designates a specific complex of properties whether an actual chiliagon has ever existed. Everyone denying the reality of eternal possibilities ignores the basis for all that is differentiated and structured within the actual world.

Being

(4) The notion of Being is fundamental both to *Modes of Being* and to *First Considerations*. In the earlier book, Being is near to being the primary category. In the later book, Being is a finality.

Common to these books is the idea that, " . . . that which is without specificity must be Nothing, Non-being . . . " (*FC*, p. 123). This is, I think, an important remark. It implies that everything that is determinate in any respect has being. Yet, it is not being that makes things specific. Where every thing is comprised only of its properties, it is these properties that make it determinate. They give it identity, and distinguish it from every other thing. Being, therefore, has very little work to do. Vitally, it is the common denominator of everything that is determinate in any way, but this is close to being trivial when the absence of determinacy entails nonbeing.

Two notions of being are relevant here. The first is being as existence, where the necessary and sufficient condition for being is the fact of being a property or complex of properties which is specific in any way. Where possibility and actuality are the more determinate expressions of existence, we say that everything specific has being in one or the other of these two ways. Second, there is Being, meaning the totality of all the properties that exist either as possibles or actuals. On the first sense of the word, being is the primary and pervasive fact. On the second, only the totality is Being.

It is odd, therefore, when *First Considerations* reduces Being to the status of a finality for actualities. Consider: Does Weiss suppose that Actuality is the only thing to have being, *i.e.*, the only thing to exist? Does he believe that actualities are the only differentiations within the totality of Being? This would entail that motion, space, and time do not exist, and that they are not aspects within the totality of things. What is the status of the other finalities? Does Weiss suggest that Substance, Possibility, Existence, and Unity do not exist, or that they too are not factors within the whole? These are the odd consequences when the role of being is turned on its head, with being reduced to a finality for actualities.

Weiss intends that finalities should be categorial powers, each one contributing some vital aspect to the actualities they inform. Being is included among the finalities because it is a power. Yet the power of being is just the specificity of properties: properties exist because of being determinate. Being, as existence, is the common denominator of everything specific; or it is, as Being, the totality of things which are because of being determinate. All the finalities have being because they are determinate, as Weiss's finalities differ among themselves. Being, however is not a finality. Being, as determination or specificity, is still more fundamental than any of them.

Modes of Being is more sensitive than *First Considerations* to the nuances of being. It allows being to be construed in either of the ways just proposed: as existence or as the totality of things that exist. The four modes can be regarded either as ways of existing, *i.e.*, as primitive or most general kinds of determination; or as the four determinations in whose reciprocity the whole is formed.

All four of the issues to be discussed in this section have been considered. How can they be resolved? Some differences between Weiss's views and my views would be settled in the dialectical give and take where theories converge if irreconcilable differences are not exposed. Our disagreement concerning being would likely be resolved in this way. There might be no agreement between us about eternal possibility. These two issues are decisive for a correct understanding of reality; yet their resolution is likely to depend upon conceptual matters only. My disagreements with Weiss concerning the primary category and substance result from differing views about contingent matters of fact, *e.g.*, that nature is comprised of stabilities rather than substances. How shall we formulate and test those empirical claims which are decisive for metaphysical theory as it speaks to these issues? This is the topic of my last section.

IV

Weiss supposes that metaphysics should be autonomous. As the Lindbergh or Magellan of our time, he will circumnavigate all of Being, alone. Someone must do it, he thinks. Where others lose their nerve, he will do it. Weiss accepts responsibility for the network of theory with which metaphysics discovers and represents all that is intelligible within the world.

Every other endeavor provides islands of content and clarity, but none of them is able to integrate and map the whole. There is only the philosopher, meaning one individual and fallible mind, to do that. Weiss knows the risks, but he continues. His metaphysical system, or systems, are the reflections of a traveler who touches ground everywhere, for he must test his hypothesis that a certain, short list of categories is exhibited within every subject matter, in every practice, science, and art. The scope of Weiss's writing is testimony to his resolve. His every book and essay is a query: will this subject exhibit the interpenetrating categorial notions to which metaphysics aspires?

No one else living today has philosophical courage of this standard. No one else dares to make himself responsible for doing as philosopher what Hegel's Absolute accomplishes as Creator. This is my dissent. It is not Weiss's ambition that I reject. No one should fault him for that. I object, instead, to the idea that the philosopher is autonomous.

Autonomy is essential to us because we must have the right and power to evaluate and criticize. But autonomy of the kind Weiss prizes is, more expansively, the capacity for seeing and representing the universe as it is. Autonomy of this sort is a consequence of the power which Plato claimed for *nous*. For as Plato supposed, a single mind of bold and gorgeous intellect might know the design that is exhibited throughout Being.

I distrust this power. Its application presupposes that all of Being is set before the mind, where it is inspected and reported. But nature is not like that. Appearance is very often different from its causes. Critical reflection upon the appearances frequently suggests hypotheses that specify their causes, but many different hypotheses are appropriate to the many different aspects of the world. Rather than Plato's unitary vision, we have the patchwork quilt of physics, biology, psychology, the other sciences, and metaphysics. We are soon lost in the trees, hardly seeing the forest.

Weiss acknowledges that the world shows itself in disparate ways. These appearances, he supposes, are the evidence of its deeper form. He would have us construe the appearances as signs and effects of their categorial sources. In the beginning, individual evidences are traced to their origins. Later, all the categories are seen as they are integrated within diverse appearances. In the end, our apprehension of the world's categorial form is to be regulative: thought is to anticipate and confirm the immanence of categorial form within successive appearances.

Every other discipline interprets the evidence for a specialized interest. Philosophers alone are responsive to the balance of generality and particularity, contingency, and necessity throughout the knowable world. Certainly, no one of us has this synoptic view as inquiry begins; but we philosophers can rise to it. What is more, we do it on our own. We can, and some of us do, see the world in its categorial simplicity. This is, I suggest, Weiss's belief.

I agree that theory provides depth and range; but what are the bases for true theory? The philosopher, as Weiss describes him, is Everyman turned contemplative. I doubt that the evidence available to us as ordinary citizens is sufficient, by itself, to disclose the world's categorial form. The evidence, uninterpreted, is mute. Although the appearances are evidence *of* their causes, they are not yet evidence *for* any claim of ours. Appearances are significant for thought only as they become evidence for some hypothesis. But there are several or many hypotheses for construing every appearance. This diversity among proposed, or possible, interpretations confounds the hope that appearances must lead us to the one correct and unitary vision of what the world is.

If Weiss believes otherwise, he must be thinking that mind can disregard some of the alternative hypotheses, because the clarity and distinctness of one hypothesis guarantees its truth. This would imply that mind has an *a priori* power for intuiting truths about the world. But there seems to be no faculty for rational intuition; and therefore, no privileged philosophic access to categorial truths. There is no alternative to sorting through the various hypotheses as each addresses one sector or aspect of the world.

Where does one start? Which appearances and which hypotheses seem most appropriate for discovering the world's form? Surely one alternative is conspicuously better than the others. The categorial system should be based in the distinctions discovered and presupposed by the experimental sciences.

I do not say this because of believing that science is the only source of our knowledge about the world. Nor do I believe that philosophy should be handmaiden, underlaborer, or bookkeeper to the sciences. Thinking of Aristotle, and also of Duhem, we can imagine philosophy as their queen. Yet as queen, philosophy needs a consort. We are not, and cannot, be autonomous, because we metaphysicians seek fundamental truths about that nature in which we live as parts. Self-knowledge and experience of other things are a useful beginning for understanding nature. But we should not forget the difference between that which is prior in knowledge and that which is prior in being. Every man can describe something of the world as it appears to him. Science reaches beyond experience to describe the world as it is in itself. Scientific theories are more than descriptions: scientists explain. They identify those variables and relations among variables that have generated the phenomena which laymen describe. It is these explanations which sometimes enable the scientist to reformulate our naive descriptions, enhancing their cogency and accuracy.

Nature, including all the artifacts produced by man, exhausts actuality. Metaphysics cannot ignore science without courting ignorance of nature. The contrary is also true: our metaphysics will be applicable and adequate to nature only if our categorial system is founded upon distinctions science proposes and then confirms.

There are of course many sciences, each one only partially integrated with the others. We shall need to pick and choose, relying upon our critical powers as they are informed by the history of both science and philosophy. The task may be easier when the sciences themselves are better integrated, *i.e.*, when the relation of physics to biology and psychology is plainer than is currently true. It will be difficult, short of that time, to propose a single set of categories that is applicable and adequate both to relativity or particle theory, and to the theory of human action. A metaphysical system having to turn in so many different directions will be imperfectly integrated and provisional. We are encouraged to change it each time that scientific theory is reformed. Yet, we need not bend to every scientific enthusiasm: indeterminism, action at a distance, and quantum jumps being some examples that need review. Still, science does propose, establish, and elaborate on some basic truths about nature. The ones of thermodynamics, as they imply the notion of stable systems, are an example. We philosophers, however scrupulous and critical, can only defer.

Weiss never defers. Of science, he writes,

At its best, the account science provides is partial. It does not explain singular experiences, aberrant judgments, speculations, or the objects of faith. It does not do full justice to the mystical, the formal or to what is practically useful or socially desirable. The scientific approach uses only part of the available evidence, and attends only to a part of reality (*BAA*, p. 55).

I agree that science addresses itself to a part of reality only: it ignores properties existing as possibilities, except for the times when representing them in thought experiments. Science has its domain where properties are instantiated, and here science is a scourge. It does, or can, take responsibility for everything actual. Where nature exhausts actuality, there is nothing falling under the primary category in *First Considerations*, that is exempt from scientific study. Metaphysics, as far as it applies to actuality, could not have a wider base.

Even values will sometimes fall to scientific inquiry, as instrumental values plainly do, *e.g.*, aspirin being shown to be better than alcohol as a cure for headaches. But then some other values do earn the claim that science has nothing to say of them. These are values regarded as ideals, *i.e.*, values existing as eternal possibilities but desired and sometimes chosen for realization. We can represent and reflect upon these values, saying that they ought to be realized without invoking science. Yet some of them may be instantiated, thereby bringing these ideals, as actualities, within the domain of scientific inquiry. Why is the human voice sometimes beautiful to the human ear? This has a nonreductionist, scientific answer, one that acknowledges the aesthetic quality while finding its necessary and sufficient conditions in the timbre of the voice itself and in human learning and physiology.

Weiss sometimes remarks (*BAA*, p. 5) that science cannot be a final authority for philosophy, because scientific knowledge has presuppositions that science, itself, does not consider. This is true to the extent that scientists are not epistemologists. But this is not a decisive issue here, first because scientific knowledge is not peculiar for having presuppositions, philosophy has them too; second, because it is the subject matter of science and not its method which is significant here. Science is the best instrument for learning about nature. Metaphysical categories do presumably have nature as all or part of the domain to which they apply. It is hard to imagine any route to understanding nature that does not pass through science.

We need to write a contemporary metaphysics of nature. It should establish that metaphysical categories are continuous with the ones known to science. It follows that metaphysical claims should be made concrete and specific by way of the sciences they subsume. I anticipate that Weiss, were he to write this essay, would be forced to revise some of his earlier claims. Existence, or being, would supplant Actuality as the primary category, as possibility and actuality would be acknowledged as the counterpart modes of being. Substance, reformulated as stability, would prove derivative. The structures prefigured in one possible world would be discovered as immanent within our world. Scientific hypotheses, experimentally confirmed, would be our most comprehensive specifications of these actual entities. Rather than competing with science for the authority to speak of nature, metaphysics would have accepted science as the basis for its own best evidence regarding nature's categorial form.

Six

Andrew J. Reck

Paul Weiss's Metaphysics of Ethics*

Historically, ethical concepts have been analyzed within metaphysical frameworks of comprehensive, systematic theories of the cosmos and man's place in it. Classical philosophers, like Plato and Aristotle, propounded doctrines of man and morality that ultimately rest upon metaphysical foundations. Modifying the classical tradition, medieval philosophers translated metaphysical foundations into theological foundations, employing terms they had derived from scriptural revelation as interpreted by their religious communities. Modern philosophers have perpetuated these traditions, but the most influential ones, like Spinoza, have altered the foundations to agree not with religious faith but with the mechanistic model of nature advocated by seventeenth-century science.

Whereas the classical philosophers, without explanation or clarification, had assumed human freedom to be indispensable to ethics, medieval thinkers strove, with varying degrees of success, to reconcile freedom with the omnipotence and omniscience of God. By the seventeenth century, Calvinist theologians and scientific mechanists either discarded freedom or redefined it to fit into their distinctive deterministic world views. Meanwhile, psychological individualism and materialism joined in support of a selfish egoism that threatened morality and the possibility of a social ethics. In the eighteenth century, Kant perceived correctly that the categories appropriate to the understanding of nature as required by scientific mechanism could not be applied to moral experience. He saved the ethical by removing it from nature and by supporting it with a metaphysics based on the three practical postulates of freedom, immortality, and God. Kant's

---

*Presented at the thirty-second annual meeting of the Metaphysical Society of America held at the University of South Carolina; Columbia, South Carolina; March 14, 1981.

salvation of the ethical, however, shattered man, bifurcating him, on the one hand, into an empirical being under the total determination of mechanical natural laws and, on the other, into a noumenal being enjoying absolute freedom.

A glance at these responses to the relationship between metaphysics and ethics discovers how complicated it is. In one respect, ethics is discerned to be part of the universe of being that is the province of metaphysics. Then the principles of fundamental metaphysics, the categories of which apply universally, govern the elements of ethics, theoretical and practical. Ethics is tantamount to applied metaphysics. In another respect, ethics as the field of practical thought and action is without explanation or justification unless metaphysical postulates are introduced, and these postulates are the final answers given to the last questions in long chains of questions triggered by reflection on the ethical. In this guise, metaphysics constitutes the absolute presuppositions of ethics. In either respect, metaphysics is deemed foundational to ethics.

Nevertheless, some philosophers have recently denied that metaphysics and ethics are related at all; they have tended instead to link ethics to the studies of human nature pioneered by the social sciences, or, shying away from all objective reference, to confine ethics to the study of moral discourse. In the twentieth century, this trend has culminated in Anglo-American analytical ethics; it exhibits what Iris Murdoch has called "the elimination of metaphysics from ethics."[1]

According to Murdoch, the elimination of metaphysics from ethics is based on three arguments. The first argument defies reduction to a single piece of logical reasoning with premises supported by evidence, valid rules of inference, and conclusions warranted by the premises and the rules. Nurtured by the critique and the analysis of language and knowledge, it is the pervasive antimetaphysical posture of contemporary thought. Another argument, which Murdoch calls "the antinaturalistic argument," stems from recognition of "the naturalistic fallacy" that G. E. Moore invented; it denies that the "ought" can be derived from the "is," that "good" is a natural property and can be defined, that value is based on fact. Moore's doctrine undercuts any effort to establish an essential connection or internal relation between the Good and Being. Murdoch's third argument for the elimination of metaphysics from ethics is a moral argument. If ethics were grounded on metaphysics, it is charged that the moral individual would be locked within a framework that diminishes him, his capacity to make free choices denigrated and his responsibility undermined. Thus, Murdoch views the endeavor to ground ethics on metaphysics as a species of dogmatism that weakens the entire fabric of human morality. Therefore, the Anglo-American severance of ethics from metaphysics is justified because, first, it is theoretically impossible to base ethics on metaphysics, and, second, if it were theoretically possible, it would be morally wrong to do so.

Epistemological empiricism and moral individualism are the two major tendencies of recent philosophy that shape the background for the elimination of metaphysics from ethics. From this background we are inclined to assume that, as Murdoch says, "Nothing . . . can *contain* the individual, except possibly his habits and his traditions, and these are merely facts like other ones, and capable of being reflectively examined."[2] As she quickly adds, this is "only one way . . . of conceiving morality."[3] The alternative, which she calls "the Natural Law" morality and which she extends to embrace the diverse company of Thomists, Hegelians, and Marxists, regards the individual "as held in a framework which transcends him, where what is important and valuable is the framework, and the individual only has importance or reality, in so far as he belongs to the framework."[4]

Murdoch's discussion typifies an attitude shared by analytic and existential thinkers that systematic, speculative metaphysics is meaningless or inimical to the individual engaged in moral choice and conduct. She neglects to observe that her account of what "contains" the individual — "his habits and his traditions" — intrudes upon, instead of shielding, his freedom and responsibility. Habits and traditions threaten to sap his freedom and erode his responsibility, unless there are dimensions of his being that are not reducible to the facts investigated by empirical psychology and sociology. The discernment and the delineation of these nonempirical, transcendental facets of human nature are tasks for the metaphysician.

Notable marks of the historic greatness of Paul Weiss, as metaphysician *par excellence*, are (1) that he approaches and treats the major philosophical questions with a firm mastery of the techniques of formal logic and with the incomparable expertise of an ontological analyst;[5] (2) that he articulates his philosophy by working his way through the process metaphysics of Whitehead back to a renovated substantialism originating with Aristotle and perpetuated by the medieval scholastics;[6] (3) that his own systematically speculative enterprise is inspired and advanced by a profound ethical concern. Here, it is the third mark that stirs my exploration of Weiss's thought. The exploration centers on the relation in Weiss's philosophy between ethics and metaphysics, a complex relation all the strands of which might never be unravelled. The explorer, sheltered by the defenses of abstract conceptualization, is baffled, startled, and shaken by the fusion of life and thought in the career of Paul Weiss.

For Paul Weiss, philosophy is not an occupational profession separated from the rest of his life; rather, it is for him as it was for the ancients and for a few contemporaries — a way of life, incessant, vibrant, and passionate. Thought and action are interwoven for Weiss, so that it would be misleading to construe his work as abstract metaphysics with a subset of ethical implications and applications. No one can study *Right and Wrong*, the philosophical dialogue Paul Weiss coauthored with his son, Jonathan, without appreciating the interplay of the ethical and the metaphysical in his personal life and thought, and without concurring in the sentiment expressed by the reviewer for *Time*: "Its only precedent may be *De Magistro (On Teaching)*, a dialogue recorded in 389 A.D. between St. Augustine and his brilliant fifteen-year-old illegitimate son, Adeodatus."[7] Weiss's works illustrate that, while metaphysics furnishes the foundations of ethics, the completion of the metaphysics involves consideration of ethics. Often when Weiss proposes and amplifies what may appear to be the most abstruse theoretical thesis, it proves to be a theme redolent with ethical import. So, in a sense, ethics is foundational to metaphysics.

The circularity of ontology and epistemology, which Weiss recognizes and elucidates in his early book, *Reality*, has its counterpart in the circularity of metaphysics and ethics. The former circularity is manifest in the fact that ontology, which inquires into the nature of being, presupposes that there are valid ways of knowing, while epistemology, which investigates the processes, range, and validity of cognition, presupposes that knowing is a real activity occurring in a real world. The latter circularity is demonstrated by the acknowledgments, on the side of metaphysics, that ontology discovers modes of being imbued with moral quality, that epistemology discerns the norms of validity and truth, that cosmology clarifies the network of relations, including moral relations, that hold between kinds and/or modes of being; and, on the side of ethics, that moral agents, rules, values exemplify and implicate modes of being and their togetherness.

Herein, therefore, I propose to examine the relationship of ethics and metaphysics in Weiss's philosophy. Difficult as this task is, I am fortunately not obliged here to pursue and criticize the countless, diverse, and intricate ramifications of Weiss's metaphysics in its pre-modal, modal, and postmodal formulations.[8] Rather my task is the more restricted one of sketching the lineaments of the bearings of metaphysics on ethics, and of ethics on metaphysics in Weiss's philosophy. Now it is in his premodal thought that these reciprocal bearings first surface.

In *Reality*, Weiss proposes the metaphysical formula that *"to be is to be incomplete"* (*R*, p. 209). Detected in the course of his critique of Whitehead's doctrine of the temporal atomicity of actualities, this principle denies that realities (or actualities) are confined within the span of the moment and so perish with the passage of the moment, and it affirms that they persist through change, since, although they are wholly present as actual, they are still future as virtual (or potential). Metaphysically, this principle not only preserves an Aristotelian substantialism by revising the temporalism of process philosophy; it also guarantees radical ontological pluralism. Furthermore, the description of being as fundamentally incomplete discloses that reality has a character subject to ethical interpretation, analysis, and governance. As virtual, each actuality has a side of its being which it strives to realize, and this realization would make it complete. Now in the sort of cosmos portrayed in *Reality*, each actuality seeks completion by acquiring values already possessed by other existing actualities. Hence, each actuality is bent on robbing and devouring others in a world of unmitigable selfishness and unrelieved strife. In this model of the world, the ethical is overwhelmed by what I call the first wave of modernity — selfish individualism, or egoism, and its companion, materialism (or actualism).

At times, Weiss, who recognized that in such a world the individual is doomed to frustration and self-destruction, suggests in *Reality* that knowledge offers man sufficient solace. "Man is capable of a vicarious completion through the medium of knowledge, for to know is to possess in the mind those things which one in fact lacks" (*R*, p. 294). However, he did not succumb to the illusion that man could live by theory alone. Like Peirce and the American pragmatists, he emphasized that, to be integral, knowledge must not be divorced from action. "Until his [man's] knowledge seeps through his being, it is not he, but part of himself that is complete. . . . To be actually, formally and materially, though still vicariously complete, he must, through the agency of virtuous acts, integrate his knowledge with his being" (*R*, p. 294).

When Weiss went on from his early metaphysics to examine the practical dimensions of human reality, he faced the question that has haunted modern thought: "Can an ethics be grounded deep in the bedrock of nature and still do justice to the fact of duty, the nature of the good, the problem of guilt and related topics?" (*NM*, p. v). During the course of responding to this question, it would become clear to him that no affirmative answer was possible as long as egoism and materialism (or actualism) dominate nature. The question, moreover, has a special urgency in the climate of post-Kantian thought and of antimetaphysical analytic philosophy. For Kant, the answer was negative, and by analytic philosophers in mid-twentieth century the question was dismissed as meaningless. But, after all, these thinkers were victims of what I call the second wave of modernity to threaten the ethical — determinism and its undertow that human freedom has no home in nature. In grappling with the question, Weiss authored two books: *Nature and Man* and *Man's Freedom*. Although each is self-contained, they comprise complementary volumes in his endeavor to establish a naturalistic ethics. The endeavor pressed him to abandon the egoism and materialism (or actualism) of his early ontology, and to discover modes of being that transcend nature.

Nature and Man is an essay in philosophical anthropology. Weiss approaches the problems of ethics only after "an antecedent mastery of the principles governing and exhibited in causation, action, being, life, consciousness, mind, will, and self" (*NM*, p. v). For "an ethical being must utilize powers analogous to those exhibited everywhere and by everything, and . . . he ought, therefore, to be dealt with as illustrating nonethical principles of universal application" (*NM*, p. v). Human ontology shares features with general ontology. All beings, including man, have an inside and an outside, a private nature and a public nature, and are free.

Housing freedom in nature, Weiss drew upon the teachings of the process metaphysicians who, nourished by the findings of evolutionary biology and the new physics, envisaged nature in a way that turns back the second wave of modernity against the ethical. In declaring all beings free, Weiss defined a free activity as an "occurrence which, over and above what the past determines, is self-determined. . . . The agent is compelled to act by what has gone before, but the action is his own, then and there made to be what it is" (*NM*, p. 33).

In *Reality*, Weiss observes that a being ceases to be merely private and becomes public when it is "concerned with that which lies beyond it, and thus as continuous with a virtual region, it has a temporal spread as well [as a spatial extent]" (*R*, p. 222). *Concern* is held in *Nature and Man* to be a universal ontological feature of actual beings. "Each being has a *concern*, a way of reaching from the concrete present into the abstract future" (*NM*, p. 53). The concern of the individual being is its power to focus "the future, as common to all beings, . . . in the shape of a limited, pertinent possibility" (*NM*, p. 53). The future common to all beings is, in Weiss's words, "a single harmonious totality of all that can be"; it is identified, moreover, with "the good as possible and all-embracing" (*NM*, p. 53). Weiss's view of the future is not an envisagement of what will happen, nor even of what may happen, but rather of *what the good for all can be*. Concern specifies this general good; it concentrates on "a specific limited good. The specific good with which a being is concerned is a single, cosmic, absolute good, congealed and individualized in one of many possible ways" (*NM*, p. 53). The formula of being presented earlier — "to be is to be incomplete" — is joined, if not replaced, by another formula: "to be is to be concerned with a pertinent good" (*NM*, p. 53).

Weiss's view of the common future anticipates his subsequent apprehension of a principle, a mode of being that can turn back the first wave of modernity to threaten the ethical; it portends his vision of ideality, which would prove to be an impregnable bulwark against egoism and materialism (or actualism). But the perspective of the author of *Nature and Man* is cast in the mold of evolutionary naturalism. Of course, he departs from ordinary naturalism when he explains the emergence of life by reference to ethical categories, such as freedom and concern for the good. A few selected sentences underline the distinctiveness of Weiss's value-suffused evolutionary naturalism. "The living arises from the nonliving when the latter freely alters its concern. . . . A living being is one whose activities are sustained by a concern, not only for its own good but also for the good of other beings" (*NM*, p. 74). "Life is the result of the exercise of freedom" (*NM*, p. 75). "Freedom is the power behind evolution" (*NM*, p. 102).

Weiss's evolutionary naturalism is distinctive not only because of its stress on the primacy of freedom, but also because, unlike those process metaphysicians who gain creative freedom for nature at the cost of the enduring substantial self, he traces the evolutionary origin of man back to the emergence of the self. Man is born in response to the ethical demand. When a being is *concerned* with the good pertinent to others, this being undergoes changes in the structure of its body, consciousness, and mind; it develops a self. Such a being is man! His single, constant essence is the self. Weiss ascribes seven characteristics to the "self of a natural yet ethical man. It is (1) constant, (2) active, (3) concerned, (4) unique, (5) beneficial to the body, (6) responsible, and (7) sensible to values" (*NM*, pp. 252–53). By means of a metaphysical doctrine of the substantial human self Weiss turns back what I call the third wave of modernity to menace the ethical — the preoccupation with flux, becoming, change, process that renders the human person too unstable, too fragile to shoulder responsibility. Unless there is an enduring self capable of standing fast in the pursuit of the good and of remaining essentially the same through the course of its action, there is no subject of moral agency and responsibility, and ethics drowns.

The theme of freedom became central to Weiss's speculations. Whereas in *Nature and Man* he shows that freedom pervades all the different types of things in nature and that man is "a crucial event in the history of evolution and the history of freedom, the apogee of nature, with traits, powers, promises, a career, and opportunities different from those of other beings," in his next work, *Man's Freedom*, he tries "to make evident how man through a series of free efforts can become more complete and thereby more human" (*MF*, p. v).

Weiss conceives freedom to be present in the temporal duration when action occurs. Prior to the completed action the specific character of the act and its outcome are unpredictable, while possible courses of action may be envisaged. Weiss describes freedom as "an intelligible process by which the indeterminate, the possible, the future, the good, is made determinate, actual, present; it is an activity by which the general is specified, specialized, delimited, given one of a number of possible concrete shapes" (*MF*, p. 71). Man's preference of some means over others in the pursuit of his goals, his choice of some goals or ends instead of others, his willing the good — all these actions are expressions of freedom. As a process, freedom requires an agent acting in time plus possibility. It also requires a situation in which to occur, a situation that energizes yet constrains the process.[9]

As free, therefore, men confront possibilities that lure them onwards into the future as goods which they desire. Whereas Weiss's ontology in *Reality* may be construed as an expression of egoism and materialism (or actualism) because the goods actualities seek are particular values possessed at present by other actualities, his later ontology meets and turns back this first wave of modernity against the ethical. While the ethical appears within nature where, indeed, it is rooted, it rises above nature. In its quest for completion, metaphysics does not merely uncover the ontological foundations of ethics; it also discovers the ethical as itself a region of fundamental being. Thus, Weiss's later ontology posits the Good as a nonactual (or possible) ideal mode of being. He describes "the summum bonum, the greatest possible good" as a cosmic would-be.

It would be a totality in which each being was at its best in perfect harmony with all the rest. Such a cosmos does not now exist. It is an ideal, an excellence applicable to all that is or can be, an absolute "ought to be," *the* good, enabling us to judge what is good and bad, right and wrong, virtuous and vicious. Every single "ought to be" specializes and is subordinate to it (*MF*, p. 199).

The obligation man has to the Good surpasses his capacity. The Good is absolute, and its demands are infinitely comprehensive, so that, regardless what a man does, he cannot perform all that is required of him. As Weiss says, "Man is the guilty creature, a being who can never entirely live up to his obligations, and knows it" (*MF*, p. 259). Now the doctrine of man's inherent ontological guilt, a guilt which is inescapable and can never be salved, entails the futility of all moral endeavor since a man remains guilty no matter what he does. It is what I call the fourth wave of modernity to engulf the ethical. Each wave of modernity brings in its wake a discontent of civilization — the first wave of egoism and materialism (actualism), perpetual warfare; the second wave of determinism, alienation; the third wave of unending and total flux, the fragility and instability of the personal self; and the fourth wave of ontological guilt, madness.

Weiss, at first, does not attempt to resolve the problem of a cosmos that dooms man to ineradicable guilt, and, by consequence, destroys the import of the distinctions between good and evil, right and wrong, upon which sanity depends. Rather, he calls upon man to follow the absolute injunction to create. This injunction requires man, on the one hand, "to reduce wrong-doing to an absolute minimum" and, on the other, "to enhance whatever he can, to perfect things by changing them so that they are more receptive to their own objectives as enhanced by the absolute good than they were before" (*MF*, p. 308). Thus, he equivocates on his doctrine of the inescapable, ineradicable ontological guilt of man when he writes: "Unable to realize fully and everywhere the absolute good to which he [man], to be a man, freely obligates himself, he is, in the end, free only to be guilty for the wrongs it was beyond his power to gainsay, for failure to realize goods outside his reach and capacity" (*MF*, p. 308).

Nevertheless, the moral predicament of man located in a cosmos that burdens him with ontological guilt was a major spur to Weiss's reconstruction of his philosophy into the mature system of the modal metaphysics. In the modal metaphysics, the realities of the earlier ontology are analyzed into two distinct, irreducible modes of being: Actuality and Existence; the good is amplified and assimilated to the mode of Ideality, and the mode of God is introduced. Weiss's systematic reconstruction of his metaphysics was, it will become plain, inspired in large measure by ethical considerations, and to this extent it illustrates the circularity of ethics and metaphysics.

In the modal metaphysics, men and women, the moral agents for ethics, are embraced under the modality of actuality; they are actualities. Within this modality what is most crucial for the possibility of ethics is the ontological nature and status of the self. It has already been observed that Weiss turns back the third wave of modernity that threatens to engulf the ethical — and which shipwrecks process philosophy — when he recognizes the substantiality of the self. Unless the person who commits an act remains the same throughout the course of his action and even afterwards when the outcome of his action is assessed by reference to an ideal standard of obligatoriness, he cannot be held responsible; he cannot be praised or blamed, rewarded or punished. Instead of the inconstant, unstable, fragile, and therefore nonresponsible self proposed by process philosophy, Weiss presents a substantial self, a constant individual agency that possesses the body, expresses itself as mind and will, and is concerned with the good of others as well as of itself.

Is this self immortal? The metaphysics of ethics seems to require immortality, otherwise there can be no final estimation of the moral quality of any agent. Yet, if immortality signifies temporally unending existence, there can be no final accounting still, for there would be, in endless time, no terminus to the consequences of any act and no last day of judgment. In *Nature and Man*, Weiss has much to say about death, little about immortality. In *Modes of Being*, however, he opens the door to immortality. "The death of the body does not demand the death of the self. . . . It [the self] has a natural origin, exists in this life in the body, and yet has a capacity to act and eventually to exist apart from that body" (*MOB*, pp. 51–52).

The creativity of actualities, advocated by Weiss as the absolute injunction at the end of *Man's Freedom*, is of course the concrete manifestation of human freedom. In the modal philosophy it evinces the distinct ontological modality of Existence. "An irreducible mode of being, Existence is sheer vitality, forever passing from one position or guise into another. By encapsulating a portion of Existence within the confines of its own nature, each entity is enabled to stand away from all others at the same time that it is caught inside a wider realm of Existence, where it is kept at a distance from others" (*MOB*, p. 185). Thus, Existence functions both as the field embracing all actualities and as the internal vitality of each being. Existence "marks the fact than an entity . . . (1) is present, (2) is in a process of becoming, or (3) has more implications than those that follow from an idea of it" (*MOB*, p. 200).

As has been noted, the conception of the Good presented in *Man's Freedom* is the idea of a nonactual, universal objective and norm for all action, and it repairs the disunity and immorality portrayed and implicated by the metaphysics of *Reality*, when it integrates all actualities within one cosmos by virtue of their common direction toward its realization. The Good is the principle by which the first wave of modernity — the threat of egoism and materialism (actualism) — is broken. In *Modes of Being* Weiss amplifies its ontological basis as possibility, or Ideality. The Good is the first guise of Ideality in the order of discovery. Other guises of Ideality are the Future and the Principle of Perfection.

The fourth mode of being described in the modal metaphysics is God. Whereas the modes of Existence and Ideality were adumbrated in the premodal metaphysics, it becomes apparent that the mode of God responds to the problem that beset the premodal philosophy — the inescapable, ineradicable ontological guilt of man, which I call the fourth wave of modernity to threaten the ethical, and which issues in madness. Weiss turns back this fourth wave when he conjoins the proposition that "ought" does not imply "can" for man, although man is not released from the obligation, with the further proposition that cosmically "ought" must imply "can."

"One can because one ought" is not true; but "This can be because this ought to be" is necessarily true. What ought to be is that which can be, because what ought to be is the Good, and this is possible. Or, to put it another way, the Good is cosmic in import; its "can be" has cosmic range (*MOB*, p. 104).

Thus when man fails, as perforce he must, according to Weiss's mature system, he is ontologically guilty, and although this ontological guilt is inescapable and ineradicable, solace may be found in the consideration that other modes of being will realize the Good that he leaves undone. Otherwise, the normative possibilities made obligatory by the Good for all actualities, once passed over, would cease to be and would no longer operate as standards for assessing the achievements and failures of actualities. Furthermore, the cosmos, having rejected these possibilities in its existential course, would dissipate the Good. To avoid the dissipation or annihilation of the Good, Weiss insists that what actualities and Existence fail to realize of the Good, God realizes.

Tracing the circularity of ethics and metaphysics in Weiss's philosophy culminates in the discovery that ethics is pressed into the arms of theology. But the climactic embrace is neither easy nor without paradox and irony. As Weiss writes:

That God does satisfy the Good not satisfied by Actualities, even when helped out by Existence, we know. But we do not know whether what we, as ethical men, take to be the Good is identical with what he takes to be the Good. We may have misconstrued just what-ought-to-be, or he may satisfy it only within a context, only as supplemented and modified by him in such a way as to make it have quite a different import from what it had before.

In the end men must look to God to complete their work, but this God and his work is not to be defined in ethical terms. There is no need to refer to God in ethics then except at the point where all human and natural powers fail, and then one cannot be sure that what he does will sustain what ethics demands. And in any case what he does on behalf of the Good becomes a man's, only so far as man accepts that work as his own, translates it into ethical terms (*MOB*, p. 364).

At the risk of declining from the high point of thought and expression represented in the preceding quotation from Paul Weiss, let me reiterate that Weiss's philosophy illustrates the circularity of ethics and metaphysics and that it meets what I have called the four waves of modernity. Each of these waves, itself metaphysical, has threatened to engulf the ethical. Against the first wave of selfish individualism and materialism, Weiss introduces the Good or Ideality. Against the second wave of determinism and its undertow that human freedom has no home in nature, Weiss locates and traces freedom in nature. Against the third wave of unending and total flux that dooms the self to instability and irresponsibility, Weiss affirms the substantiality of the self. Against the fourth wave of inescapable human guilt, Weiss offers the prospect of a saving God. However, Weiss's theological inference is to a God who is neutral, indifferent, perhaps hostile to human moral concerns. This conclusion, perplexing as it is, is by no means peculiar to Weiss. It may be the fault of any monotheism that is not mediated by a presumed divine being who assumes human form. Thus I close my exploration of Weiss's metaphysics of ethics in a mood of bafflement and perplexity, and I observe that Weiss, in his penetrating latest work, *You, I, and the Others,* turns his gaze inwards upon the metaphysics of men and women in their public manifestations and private experiences.

Seven

Robert C. Neville

Achievement, Value, and Structure

In *Modes of Being* (1958), Paul Weiss took the prescient and courageous stand of affirming both sides of the ambiguity in his name for
the mode Ideality: that it consists of possibilities, and that it consists
of values. The stand was prescient in anticipating a ground-swell of
philosophic dissatisfaction with the positivist separation of facts (and
possibilities) from values. It was courageous because the detailed
analysis of the internal relation between possibilities and values was,
of course, a promissory note. In the more than twenty-five years since
the publication of *Modes of Being*, Weiss has addressed that note again
and again, each contribution making progress toward satisfying it.
His studies of this topic indicate the extraordinary extent to which he
is the synthesizing heir of the Western philosophic tradition.

In that tradition, two general approaches to the claim that things,
by their very structure or possibility, have value are, respectively, the
Aristotelian and Platonic. (I use these generalizations about Aristo-
telianism and Platonism for heuristic purposes only — they will be
made specific with respect to Weiss's own language.) The Aristotelian
approach has supposed that value is completeness or self-sufficiency.
Remember, for instance, Aristotle's discussion of the perfection of
the divine mind as thought thinking itself with no external potency
and of the imitation of this in the virtue of contemplation; circular
motion is perfect, imitated by rotation of the seasons, by reproduction
of the species in individuals, and so forth. An Aristotelian final cause
is what fulfills or completes a substance.

The Platonic approach, by contrast, construes value by means of
what, in our impoverished language, we call aesthetic considerations.
The Form of the Good is what makes determinate forms normative
for what they form, "normative measures" as the *Statesman* has it, or
the "cause of mixture" according to the *Philebus*. The Platonic ap-

proach tries to explain the way a thing is good simply by virtue of having form or structure; that is, as embodying possibilities. Change, likewise, is always normative, one way or another, because better or worse possibilities are realized. By contrast, the Aristotelian approach tries to explain the way a thing is good by fulfilling some lack in its structure, by attaining completeness according to the needs of the formal cause.

Weiss has been attracted to both approaches. Specifically, he often has employed Aristotelian rhetoric to make points that are more fundamentally Platonic. My purpose here is to persuade him to develop the Platonic side more directly and to use it to encompass the truth in the Aristotelian. The first section below will discuss these points in Weiss's *Modes of Being*, and the second will extend the discussion through later works. The third will present a theory of value as harmony, suggesting that Weiss should adopt it as the underpinning of his remarks about value. The remaining section will develop the theory of value in terms of Weiss's most recent book, *Privacy*, combining the treatment of value with Weiss's theory of epitomizations to sketch a view of the integrity of human individuals through time. The conclusion will be that things, even human beings, have value by virtue of having structure. To wit, value is the achievement of structure.

I

Modes of Being may well be the most powerful book of systematic philosophy in the twentieth century, drawing its power from several sources. The most obvious source is its systematic character expressing Weiss's solution to the problem of the one and the many; his is the most cogent defense of metaphysical pluralism the American community of pluralists has produced. Among the other sources of the book's power are his often brilliant reflections on specific problems. As he later clearly stated, his view of philosophic method is to articulate common sense, and then alter that only when forced to by overriding considerations (FC, pp. 223–37).

Weiss's commonsense consideration of possibilities motivated his first approach to Ideality in Chapter Two of *Modes of Being*. The first section treats Ideality as possibility and in this context argues that only some of the many possibilities are desirable values.

Plato himself thought that what I have been terming "the possible" was essentially a desirable value, and therefore found himself forced to deny that there was a possible mud or a possible dirt. Yet a possible mud or a possible dirt is as clean and good as a possible light or possible life. But also, since the possible lacks the determinateness and career characteristic of the Actual, it is equally correct to say that a possible light or a possible life is as impoverished, is as incomplete, has as little value as a possible mud or a possible dirt (*MOB*, 2.05, p. 108).

Weiss developed his criticism of Platonism, not in the direction of further defending non-normative possibilities in addition to normative ones, but in the direction of the problem of the relevance of the possible to the actual. He argued that the Platonists err by construing possibilities as complete in themselves and independent, irrelevant to actualities except when made relevant by a third agent, *e.g.*, the Demiurgos. It seems clear to common sense that if it is possible to do other than the good, there are other than good possibilities. Weiss said that "The Good is a possibility which ought to be realized" (*MOB*, 2.10, p. 112). *A* possibility.

In the same place just quoted, however, Weiss argued that what ought to be, can be; and therefore if the primary agent to which the obligation belongs fails the obligation, it passes in secondary form as an obligation to other agents. In some form or other, the Good *must* be realized. This suggests that the Good is the general possibility that gets realized one way or another. Common sense might insist that there are good and bad possibilities and that when the bad possibilities are realized an additional burden is to realize the otherwise failed good possibilities in yet a further actualization — if you have to eat your cake today, you'll have to bake another tomorrow. Weiss sometimes spoke as if there is a tremendous build-up of obligations caused by moral failures, and invoked God as the final realizer of missed good possibilities.[1]

But this position has grave difficulties with the timeliness of so many normative possibilities — one cake may be as good as another, but it is hard to compensate for the sacrifice of a child by the begetting of another. Weiss realized this and appealed to the systematic character of Ideality relative to the other modes. Only one vague possibility faces all actualities. Each actuality specifies a portion of that possibility and, by virtue of the dynamic power of Existence, makes that portion more and more particular until it becomes actualized as wholly definite. Better and worse ways of particularizing and finally actualizing one's portion of our common ideality might exist. The question is whether Ideality as a whole is normative, with better and worse, but no non-normative specializations. Or is Ideality as a whole non-normative, with normativeness entering only among certain specific alternatives for realizing the vague possibility? If one gives the latter answer, then value is demoted from the ontological dignity of a mode of being, and to introduce it among certain of the specializations of possibility is rather *ad hoc*. The history of modern thought indicates the difficulty if not impossibility of saying, on the one hand, that possibilities are just noncontradictory forms that might be actualized and, on the other, that maybe some of these are good. The normativeness is nearly always reduced to the emotions or will of observers.[2]

Weiss himself gave the former answer, that Ideality as a whole is normative, with better and worse specifications. In the first place, he argued that "real possibilities must be realized somehow and somewhere" (*MOB*, 2.13, p. 116). His account of how this takes place appeals to a temporally thick notion of possibilities as the future, becoming more specific as their dates approach the present of actualization. On this account only one possibility exists, one future, in the vague sense, and this can be realized only in determinate senses of which many specifications can be found; each specification is just as much a version of the one vague possibility as its alternatives. I am in thorough agreement with the view that the future is temporally thick and is transformed through degrees of specificity (whether the future is vaguely unified for all things is a complicated issue that should be left open at this point).[3] Weiss went on to say that, not only are all real possibilities realized somehow and somewhere, but also

The Good is an all-inclusive possibility, or Ideal, as relevant to Actualities. The ideal or possible is a reality which has the guise of the Good in its relation to Actualities, the status of the Future for Existence, and the role of a Principle of Perfection for God. . . . The Good is always realized, for every determination is a determination of it. It is therefore the most inclusive, the least determinate, a perpetually fulfilled possibility. But it is realized in specific Actualities, which may themselves be internally in conflict and more often than not will be in conflict with one another. The realization of the Good by diverse Actualities allows for the production of multiple evils (*MOB*, 2.15, p. 120).

This quotation affirms something at the heart of the Platonic tradition, that all possibilities are good just in being possibilities and that evil consists somehow in the misplacing of possibilities (which are good in their own way) in the actual world.

A further question must be pressed here. Did Weiss take the normativeness of Ideality to consist in some intrinsic property of Ideality, in some aesthetic-like harmony or primitive quality of possibility as such, after Plato's fashion? Or did he think of it as completeness, as structural wholeness, as perfection after the manner of Aristotle? The answer, I argue, is both.

In the passage last quoted, Weiss said Ideality is the Principle of Perfection as it relates to God, and this expresses the Aristotelian approach. In *Modes of Being*, God is given the job of completing the realization of all the goods that actualities have missed, and the metaphors describing this are all those associated with completion, wholeness, totality. Often in discussing human normative matters, Weiss appealed to fulfillment and realization of potentials that give individuals their identity.

Note, however, that even in the passage quoted, Ideality is not Perfection for actualities but for God. The reason is that actualities are too local and specialized to have much to do with completeness or perfection. Perhaps people jointly can bring something to completion or perfection, but Weiss's poignant point is that usually they do not — hence the need for God to approach Ideality with regard to Perfection. Rather, Ideality, if it is normative at all, is normative because of something intrinsic, essential, and in itself for Weiss. This normativeness expresses itself determinately with regard to other modes of being as the Good, the Principle of Perfection, and the Future. Here Weiss draws upon the genius of his solution to the one and the many. A thing (*e.g.*, a mode of being) has two components — an essential core and a conditional expression relative to other things; it cannot be or have one without the other, and hence it is an intrinsic harmony of these things. We cognitively approach a thing through its connections with other things, and so may assume that the thing is only its conditional relations; but it is able to relate those ways only because those are the ways its essential core can relate to the other things. Hence Ideality relates to the other modes as good possibilities, as the Principle of Perfection, and as Future; but all of these are specifications of some essential normativeness.[4]

Thus, in *Modes of Being*, Weiss held to a Platonic approach to value on the one hand, claiming that all possibilities are good in their way, all expressing normativeness, and that normativeness in some primitive sense is essential to Ideality. But he also gave expression to the Aristotelian approach, claiming that only some possibilities are good, namely those that foster the completion or perfection of something. What has been the fate of these two approaches in his later work?

II

Shortly after writing *Modes of Being* in the mid–1950s Weiss turned to a series of topical studies. *Our Public Life* (1959) focused on the intersection of people as actualities with their common future, and presented a political philosophy centered on a theory of rights. "Man's native rights are the claims inevitably made by him by virtue of what he is. He, and his essential parts and capacities, have a right to be, and to be fulfilled" (*OPL*, p. 65). In analogy with his theory of possibilities, Weiss explained that each person has a general right to be fulfilled as a person, with specific rights deriving from the specifics of fulfillment; in addition, since people change both personally and in their social roles, rights might shift, but they are normative when and where they apply. The rhetoric of this book was Aristotelian, stressing rights as claims deriving from the need to fulfill the nature one has. But why is fulfillment good? Does not the theory immediately fall prey to the naturalistic fallacy? Underlying the argument, though unacknowledged, is the conviction that the fulfilling is normative because of some quality making it normative, not because it is fulfilling. *History: Written and Lived* (1962) stressed the relation of people to the structures of existence. When it spoke of values for individuals (*e.g.*, *HWL*, p. 60), it used the Aristotelian language of completion. But when it spoke of norms for history, the "historical ought-to-be," it was reaching for the bearing of Ideality on history and used the language of pure normativeness. The normativeness was not spelled out on its own, and this perhaps accounts for why the book has been neglected by historians who would like to surmount efforts at value-free historiography; but the normativeness was presupposed.

In *The World of Art* (1961), Weiss took a frankly intrinsic approach to value. Introducing the notion of the good by citing Plato (*WA*, p. 123), he argued that the special norm for art is beauty, the good made relevant to a work of art as art.

Beauty is a special case of the Good. It is that Good when it has been subdivided and then subjected to the limitation that it have a particularized sensuous being. The artist makes the division of the Good permeate, be effective in every part of his work, by working over his material more thoroughly than the ethical man does or needs to. While working he can be said to take a moral holiday in the sense that he does not then concern himself with the fulfillment of the promise of the objects on which he works and does not try to make anything measure up to the external standard of the ethical good (*WA*, p. 125).

Whereas ethical activity is contrasted with artistic by means of the applicability of language of fulfillment, even in ethics the point is to measure up to an "external" standard, not just fulfill an inner lack or incompleteness. What art shows, as Platonists have often said, is that beauty or artistic goodness has its worth in its very being or expression. Weiss brilliantly argued that works of art are for the sake of beauty or the good, whereas ethical activity uses ethical norms for the moral improvement of the world.

The God We Seek (1964) was strangely silent on the question of value. It adroitly distinguished approaching things as sacred from approaching them as aesthetic, anthropomorphic, or valuable (*e.g.*, *GWS*, p. 81). But it gave little hint about the nature of value (except to refer to it because the argument called for analysis of divinity from the standpoint of Ideality). In this regard, we can suppose that Weiss assumed the intrinsic normativeness underlying value-experience, just as he argued for the intrinsic quality of the sacred in the "ultranatural" quality of things. Instead of Ideality being characterized as a Principle of Perfection, it was hardly characterized at all in this book; the language of perfection was used in a systematic context to allude to how each mode of being is imperfect and is perfected by the others.

That point leads to a summary of this period of Weiss's thought as it bears upon the Aristotelian or Platonic approaches to value. The dominating motif in Weiss's thought was his pluralistic solution to the problem of the one and the many. To be a thing is to have a dual nature in relation to other things that also have dual natures. Part of one's nature is an essential core, and the other part is how that core expresses itself toward other things or is conditioned by them. Ideality then, if it is a basic mode of being, has an essential normative core, indeterminate in itself but made determinate with respect to actualities as normative possibilities, made determinate with respect to Existence as a normative structure for the existential field, or Future, and made determinate with respect to God as the Principle of Perfection. This is formally analogous to Plato's point that the Form of the Good is not in itself a determinate object capable of being known determinately, but it is what makes finite things determinately good, provides ideals for them, and makes them articulable objects of attention and knowledge. For both Plato and Weiss, other things are what give determinateness to the Good/Ideal by specifying unitary norms. But determinateness is not contributed solely by the other things. For both Plato and Weiss, the Good/Ideal is the source of structure for the other things. Without the contribution of the Good/Ideal, "other things" would be sheer chaos or otherness, what Plato called "the Indefinite." The phenomena of our world are thus mixtures of the Good/Ideal and the other things. If the core essential characters of the Good/Ideal and the other things were fundamentally unrelated, both would be indeterminate. But then neither would be itself because each side is both its essential character and its conditional connections with its others.

Unlike Plato, Weiss went on to use the language of fulfillment, completion, and perfection to explain the relations between the modes. That is, he said each mode *needs* the others to be itself and is perfected by them. This would be innocent metaphoric biologizing were it not for the ease with which the metaphor extends to the rest of the Aristotelian approach. One could as easily say that each mode or thing is what it is simply by being together with the others, without suggesting that there is some prior potentiality that needs to be fulfilled by the company of the others. On the ontological level such a potentiality surely could not exist since the essential core of a mode of being is impossible without its togetherness with the others, without its various conditional aspects. Each mode is a harmony of its inner essence and its relational conditions, not more truly the inner essence with the conditions added as an afterthought: this is the genius of Weiss's position. The use of completion language at the ontological level, however, led Weiss to suggest that the modes are like biological actualities with potentialities for the future. This then reinforced the rhetoric of completion as an explication of value. And it turns the modal solution to the problem of the one and the many into a merely structural pattern, representable by x's, y's, "." and ","; this sells short the particularity of the modes.

In the 1970s, Weiss took a new approach to fundamental philosophy, in part as a response to criticisms of the modal solution to the problem of the one and the many. At that time, I was one who objected to the ultimacy claimed for the modes, arguing that being itself had not been taken into account.[5] Weiss reoriented his whole approach, however, now asking the way to find the ultimate realities in the obvious mixture of phenomena in which we live.

Beyond All Appearances (1974) was the first major systematic expression of this new approach. Its treatment of Ideality, unfortunately, abandons the laudable ambiguity of *Modes of Being* with respect to joining structure and value. Except for an early reference (*BAA*, p. 95) equating Ideality with meaning, the systematic treatments of the modes, now called finalities, drop the language of ideality in favor of plain Possibility (*e.g.*, Chapters 12 and 13). This terminological shift was carried forward in a companion book, *First Considerations* (1977). Furthermore, Weiss treated value issues almost exclusively in terms of completeness. For instance, human rights were described as specializations of the basic right to be self-complete (*BAA*, Chapter 15). The glory of human beings, Weiss said there, is that through knowledge they can internalize both other actualities and the finalities more nearly completely than other beings can. *First Considerations* contrasted the actual cosmos with an ideal cosmos, but defined the latter as "embracing the possible unrealized ways in which actualities and finalities could have been together" (*FC*, p. 182). Weiss reaffirmed the obligatoriness of such completeness, and the language hints of the earlier points that every possibility contains some good, and that the exclusion of some possibility is the exclusion of some good. There is an obligation to include, somehow and somewhere, all the goods. But there is no hint that the reason completeness is good is because of some essential normativeness in Possibility. Rather, completeness is obligatory because anything less would be incomplete. Perfection, the "final ideal condition," of course has one guise for actualities, another for Substance, another for Being, another for Existence, another for Possibility, and yet another for Unity or God (*BAA*, p. 364).

Perhaps this is an overreaction to the seeming demise of the normative, or rather the reduction of the normative to mere structural completeness, in Weiss's thought of the 1970s. He indeed continued to talk of obligations, of standards, and of perfection. With regard to perfection, he employed the language of harmony. Consider the following "controlling summary" from *Beyond All Appearances*:

The final condition is the minimal possible juncture of actualities and finalities in the role of a demand that it be enriched by the full harmonious presence of the actualities and finalities. The demand is a constant, measuring what is and what is to be done.

Some enterprises, such as religion, make one aware of depths to finalities not previously noted; others, such as biography, make one aware of unnoted depths to actualities; still others, such as celebrations, produce new appearances which open up unsuspected depths in both. The most adequate grasp of the final condition is mediated by these; they make evident the realities that can most completely satisfy the condition's demand. Philosophy encompasses those realities in a systematic conceptual account. It is therefore able to state the nature of the condition that those realities constitute when they are minimally together and which they can satisfy only by being maximally harmonized (*BAA*, p. 365).

It is possible to read this passage in a Leibnizian way, regarding harmony as the most efficient way to have the most being. This would be an aesthetic conception of value of the Platonic type, and it would make it possible to say that Weiss still during this period acknowledged an ontological normativeness not reduced to structural completeness. Now I believe that he should indeed have intended such a reading. But there is too little reinforcement in the rest of the writings of this time to justify that conclusion.

You, I, and the Others (1980) marked a significant departure for Weiss's philosophy. In it he turned from a preoccupation with identifying finalities and their relations with ordinary life to a detailed and thoroughgoing phenomenology.[6] The structure of the finalities lurks in the background, but more as an organizing principle than as a filter for phenomenology. From the wealth of reflection in that book, let me select only the points having to do with the problem about possibilities and value. Weiss returned with full force to the Platonic view that values are intrinsic to structure. "Value," he wrote, "is a constant, expressing the degree an item approximates the state of a final excellence" (*YIO*, p. 83).

A value is the worth of something, marked out by its place in a hierarchy of greater and greater excellencies. The holding all men to be intrinsically equal in value attests to the recognition of them as occupying the same rank within the hierarchy. . . . They, and things as well, have values no matter what our evaluations, or whether we evaluate them at all. Each has a place in a hierarchy determined by the degree to which it conforms to the demands of a final excellence (*YIO*, p. 84).

The book proceeds to explain how participation in the final excellence takes place for human beings through responsibilities, self-identity,

normative behavior, etc. The focus here is not on completion or fulfillment, but on the objective, absolute value of people and things
simply in themselves. It is their being that is valuable. Furthermore,
Weiss wrote,

> Values are unities governing multiplicities. They are both locatable and
> extended in space, since they are where the multiplicities are. In being spa-
> tialized, the values are not altered, but they do acquire new roles. Spatialized,
> they are reordered, without thereby losing their relative positions in a hier-
> archy of excellencies. . . . Whatever value I have is presently possessed. The
> value itself, though it is the value of an I that exists for a while, need not
> have been temporalized. As a mere value, it is related to other values re-
> gardless of any date or duration (*YIO*, pp. 253–54).

The view of value expressed here arises from a close examination of
the surfaces and depths of people in relation to each other and to
themselves. In this context, Weiss returned clearly to what Plato took
to be the fundamental value phenomenon: the worth of each existing
thing resident in its structure that expresses normativeness in some
sense. There was a clear-cut return here to the view in *Modes of Being*
that a thing is valuable because of the ideality in it, pure normativeness
or value "spatialized" by actualities in which it is resident.

III

I urge that Weiss sustain these insights by adopting the following
abstract theory of structured value. The function of this appeal to
theory is to undergird and display the assumptions of the phenomenology of value he achieved in *You, I, and the Others*.[7] The exposition will move through several levels of abstraction.

Let us begin with the Platonic proposition (from the *Philebus*) that
things in the world are mixtures or harmonies of an indefinite multiplicity of contents on the one hand and patterns of order on the
other. Each contained item is itself a harmony of its own contents
and its patterns. Hence, in describing a harmony, one can isolate
many patterns from its constituents, and patterns of patterns which
integrate these, up to the overall pattern. One can also focus on the
multiplicity for each contained pattern and on the multiplicity of the
whole. Whether analysis moves downward, as it were, from pattern
to contents or upward from identified multiplicity to integrating pat-

tern, any identifiable, determinate thing is itself a harmony of pattern and contents. In Weiss's language, this is to say that everything is internally multiple and conditioned by Ideality. The internal multiplicity comes from the fact that each thing is a harmony of its essence and its conditional relations. The Ideal conditioning consists (in part) in the fact that the multiplicity is structured so that it hangs together. Everything in Weiss's world, from evanescent phenomena through actualities to the Finalities themselves, is a structured multiplicity.

What was just said does not strongly distinguish an allegedly Platonic view from that of Aristotle who, after all, said that substances have both form and matter. What Plato added to his ontology of Mixture, Order, and the Indefinite was the "Cause of Mixture," which is the normative element pursued at length in the *Philebus*. The Cause of Mixture was not conceived as an efficient cause. Plato could account for efficient causation as simply a temporally discursive kind of harmony whose earlier and later parts are determinately related. Nor is the Cause of Mixture an Aristotelian final cause fulfilling a substance or bringing it to completion or satisfaction; a final cause is, in a sense, metaphysically subsequent to a substance with combined form and matter whose essential potentialities it is to fulfill. A Platonic Cause of Mixture is itself the crucial metaphysical condition for the mixture. The Cause of Mixture is very close to what Weiss calls the excellence of something, the intrinsic value achieved by harmonizing this multiplicity with this pattern. To put the point most directly, the Cause of Mixture is the achievement of specific value in harmonies. How can we make sense of this point?

Let us examine the notion of harmony in more detail. Because the components of a harmony are themselves harmonies, they have an integrity of their own. Perhaps their integrity is such that they could exist on their own without each other. Or perhaps their integrities severally require each other so that they can exist only in mutual harmony. Perhaps they are partially independent and partially dependent; perhaps dependence is on the other's function, or part of the function; perhaps the dependence is on something, anything, occupying the other's position. Since harmonies can have temporal patterns there may be greater or lesser determinism between earlier and later parts. And since harmonies are harmonies of harmonies, some levels might be tightly harmonized (much interdependence), some loosely harmonized. Harmonies can be tight organic unities or loose configurations of particles in a cloud chamber, necessary trajectories or chance meetings. A given harmony might be a component of several other harmonies only remotely related to one another (perhaps only through the component harmony). Something which is only a component of a larger harmony in one context might become the dominant integrating element of the same set of components in another context.

Some kinds of harmonies are relatively stable and others shift rapidly. The maelstrom of life consists of many shifting harmonies arising when conditions are right to sustain them, giving rise to higher harmonies that contain them, and then disappearing when their own components dissolve or their ordering patterns are no longer possible. The Chinese go so far as to say that the world should be conceived of, not as things in trajectories (an Aristotelian universe modernized by Newton), but as shifting patterns of changes. We need not decide this issue except to call attention to the variation in tightness of harmonies, and the frequently temporal structure of harmony. It may well be that the universe is a very loosely connected bunch of pockets of high-grade order with little of importance to connect them. The point of this quick sketch of the multifariousness of harmony is that a harmony is a togetherness of a multiplicity.

The formula "togetherness of a multiplicity" is meant to signify a rejection of the view that a multiplicity is held together by some determinate transcendent "third thing." If two things need a third to unite them, then each needs yet a fourth and fifth to unite it to the third, etc. Rather, things are together simply because their characters are such as fit together. This is the genius of Weiss's approach to the one and the many. To say that the things just fit together because of their characters, however, is to say they harmonize. What then is harmony?

Let us reconsider Weiss's categories of the essential and nonessential or conditional. The essential features of something are those it has by virtue of which it is self-reflexively itself. But if the thing were only its essential features, it would not be determinate with respect to anything else (and the essential features would not even be determinate with respect to each other if they had no conditional features relative to one another). A thing is also a group of conditional features, those it has by virtue of other things. If a thing were only conditional features, it would in fact reduce to the sum of the other things. A thing must be a harmony of essential and conditional features if it is to have any determinate identity (which is to allow that it might be indeterminate in respect to some things). Each essential feature, and each conditional feature must itself be a harmony of essential and conditional features, and so on.

What, precisely, is an essential feature? It is one that contributes to the way the harmony integrates its conditional features. Whereas conditional features arise from (or are) other things, what is essential or ownmost about a harmony is what it does to integrate them. Essential features are those that (singly or collectively) determine the roles of the conditional features, paring them down, eliminating potential conditions, constraining, and elevating; in general, giving relative importance to the conditional features. Since a harmony is a hierarchy of harmonies of harmonies, each harmony has essential features for its conditional ones. The essential features of the harmony under analysis are those that determine the togetherness of all the component harmonies with their essential and conditional features. This is to say, by virtue of having this set of essential features, harmonized together, all the components are allowed to be together this way. An artist sketches the outline of a person's face, and those chalk lines, filling but a small fraction of the area of the paper, make possible the recognition of the whole. By virtue of a few (essential) words, a theory is conveyed. "Importance" can be defined as what is essential, or the essential functions, for and in a larger harmony.

The set of essential features harmonizes the components by integrating two aspects, complexity and simplicity. Complexity is the variety of different things that can function as components of the harmony. Integration is easy with little diversity; hard with more diversity. Simplicity is the way by which the diverse elements reinforce one another in an ascending hierarchy of levels so that the top level has sharpness of contrast. The top level togetherness can be the unsimple mere conjunction of a complexity — a and b and c and n. Or it can be an intense simple togetherness of x and y sharply distinguished, with the lower levels of harmony arranged in hierarchies to produce and reinforce the x and y. Integration with great simplicity is difficult; with little simplicity easy. Harmony is the integration of complexity and simplicity, achieving a degree of both. Harmonic dissolution has two extremes: Maximum complexity with minimum simplicity is a and b and c, etc.; maximum simplicity with minimum complexity is x and x with only x's homogeneously contained throughout. Harmonies are better or worse to the extent they maximize both complexity and simplicity. Not variety alone nor purity alone but both, integrated so as to achieve sharpness of contrast, intensity of difference at the highest level of harmony. Of course, with two variables, complexity and simplicity, one can emphasize one or the other, and theoretically it would be possible to get a trade-off point where the value is the same with "more" complexity and "less" simplicity and vice versa. The degree of value in a harmony is the degree to which it maximizes complexity and simplicity. This is close to what Weiss meant in *You, I, and the Others* when he wrote that a thing's value consists in the level it occupies in a hierarchy.

The analysis of harmony now has become explicit about value. To be a harmony is to be valuable because the harmony has some degree of complexity and simplicity. A higher degree would make it more valuable, a lesser degree less.

Before continuing, I would like to comment on the kind of claim at stake. This theory of value as harmony is a speculative hypothesis (with a complex history from Plato through Weiss); it should be believed if it can justify itself as coherent, dialectically adroit relative to other theories, applicable to experience and adequate to it — the criteria we employ for any speculative hypothesis. The theory hypothesizes, however, that value is something we simply recognize in harmony, by intuition as it were. If we grasp the components and see how they are together, then *ipso facto* we appreciate the value. A value judgment is always fallible because we might misconstrue the nature of the components or the pattern of harmony, and the number of components is indefinitely large. But the nature of perception and cognition is to grasp things as harmonies (this part of the hypothesis is implied but has not been, and will not be, spelled out here), which is to appreciate them as valuable. Weiss agrees that experience is thus infused with value.

The harmony a thing has in fact is its *de facto* value. But those same components might be harmonized in different ways, producing different values, perhaps better, perhaps worse. In description we note at least four things: what the components are, what the integrating patterns are, what the *de facto* harmony is, and what the alternate harmonies would be. Description is thus always evaluative if taken far enough, and it arises out of an initial experience that includes a valuation. Reflecting on human affairs, we attempt both to assess the value of the actual and to imagine the ideal. An ideal is an imagined pattern that might be mixed with the components at hand to produce a valuable harmony, a more valuable harmony than which cannot be imagined.

We can express within this theory Plato's point that the Form of the Good is what makes other things good, itself being indeterminate, and Weiss's point that Ideality is what makes other things normative, being indeterminately normative in itself. Normativeness (the Good, Ideality) is what makes *de facto* harmonies and their alternatives valuable, each with its own value according to its disposition of complexity and simplicity. Normativeness has no determinate character outside of its expression in patterns harmonized with content. But the patterns cannot be taken to be merely factual, non-normative, without abandoning the value we in fact appreciate in harmonies. When Weiss pointed out that, if some possibilities are good, and we choose the others, there must be non-good possibilities, he correctly saw that some goods are less good than others, and that the normative component of choice is to realize the best good in the circumstances; his argument did not prove that the alternative possibilities to the good are non-normative. To deny that normativeness is ontologically basic requires rejecting the harmonious character of things. It is one thing to reject the theory of value as harmony; it is another, and much more difficult, to reject the valuational character of our experience. The virtue of the theory of value as harmony is that it makes *prima facie* sense of our value experience, and it resonates with the treatment of value and structure in the Platonic tradition from Plato to Weiss.

This section presents a theory of value that Weiss can embrace directly so as to be true to his insight that Ideality is both structural and normative at once without the onesidedness of some of his accounts subsequent to *Modes of Being*. Let me try to make this theory persuasive by developing it in accordance with certain major themes of Weiss's most recent book, *Privacy* (1983).

IV

In *Privacy*, Weiss argues that a person is an enduring actuality with an inner source of action and expression; privacy is this "initial source of a man's activities" (*P*, p. xi). Through growth, maturation, and interaction with the physical and social environment, this privacy becomes epitomized in certain structures Weiss analyzes in detail:

sensitivity, sensibility, need, desire, orientation, sociality, mind, resolution, the person, autonomy, responsibility, the I, the self, and the
idios. Weiss has long argued against the atomism of process philosophy, and in this book shows the fruit of his position, namely, a
thorough account of the cumulative but temporally spread out structures of human life. Process philosophy has had great difficulty giving
importance to the temporal thickness of these growing and dynamic
structures. Weiss's discussion of value in *Privacy* continues the Platonic emphasis on excellence. Indeed he discusses human health and
excellence in terms of harmonizing all the epitomizations, relative to
context. But he does not attempt a theoretical account of value. I
argue that the theory begun in the previous section would serve well.

It is necessary to distinguish among the temporally spread out
harmonies those that have the kind of tight harmony enduring through
an extended stretch of time that we find in human life, and at the
same time, it is necessary to acknowledge the modal differences between past, present, and future that are essential to temporal harmonies. Some temporal harmonies are very loose, such as the
development of an historic event. Others are tighter, such as a rigidly
determined causal sequence. Yet others are even tighter in some aesthetic senses, such as singing a song. A person is a highly integrated
temporal harmony, with the complexity of many kinds of component
temporal harmonies — some deterministic like the heartbeat, others
indeterminate such as chance and free will — and the simplicity of
bringing all these to conscious, responsible focus in specific, historically apt, actions and enjoyments. How is this kind of harmonic
integrity to be characterized?

A person can be called a discursive individual. The discursive element indicates that the person's life is played out through time, always occupied in a present but with a past and (maybe) a future. The
individual element means that it is the same, unitary person from
beginning to end, despite the changes and despite the absence of
past and future from the present.

In an actual present moment conditional features are integrated
with essential features into a definite harmony. The subjective immediacy of the moment consists in the coming to be of the definite
harmony. The conditions may have been actualized before, but their
integration into this moment's harmony is what is taking place in the
subjective immediacy of the moment. If the harmony is not an ex-

tended harmony, but an atomic individual, then its essential features that achieve the integration are spontaneous, emerging with the integration itself. This is the sheer power of existence and may in fact give rise to novel patterns by achieving new combinations of given conditions. In *Modes of Being*, Weiss cited this spontaneity, even in its minimal form as sheer sensuosity, as the refutation of complete determinism, that which must be added to the past to get the present.[8]

In a present moment of a discursive individual there are, in addition to spontaneous essential features, essential features deriving from the past and future. That is, some of the conditions entering from the past also function essentially to determine the harmony in special ways. Those ways have to do with defining the present as a continuation of the identity of the past moment. Similarly, occasions in the future, perhaps only vaguely determined at present, can function essentially so as to be normative for the present. In nondiscursive temporally extended harmonies, the past can present conditions whose values make a claim to be recognized in the present harmony; and future opportunities also present values that should be reckoned with if the present is complex enough to anticipate them. But only in a discursive individual is a present moment essentially what it is by virtue of being continuous with past and future moments; that continuity constitutes the discursive individuality. My identity now consists in part in the fact that I secured a mortgage in the past and am obligated to satisfy it in the future. How can we understand this continuity of essential features? Paul Weiss's scheme in *Privacy* presents a suggestion.

Suppose there is a chemical conglomerate which by itself is a temporally enduring and growing harmony, but not a discursive harmony. Suppose next that it is placed in an environment to which it responds differentially and with cumulatively informed responses. One might say, then, that it has developed sensitivity, and this sensitivity grows through the deployment of a nervous system, through subtler strategies for placing itself in the environment, and so forth. Once the conglomerate has sensitivity it functions as an organism. Moreover, an essential element in any one moment's sensitive response is the deployment of previously developed sensitive structures and information, and there may be a direction of present sensitivity to anticipations of the future. Through this being's life, especially if it is a human being, the structures of sensitivity will evolve, grow, and perhaps ultimately diminish. But at any moment the available structures of sensitivity are essential to the being's response to anything.

Weiss characterizes sensibility as a readiness to appreciate certain values as good or bad, attractive or repellent. Building upon sensitivity, sensibility involves some kind of organization of the organism's own values so as to be responsive to external worths, "taste," as it will become in maturity. The structures of sensibility grow, mature, and also perhaps decline. But it is essential to the being at any time that the available structures of sensibility function essentially.

It is not necessary to review each of Weiss's epitomizations to make the point. Once developed, the epitomizing structures are essential to human life. And they are normative. That is, at any given moment, through any event, or over one's life as a whole, one can be judged by how well one embodies these structures; one's value in part as a person is how well one embodies them. And they are norms that determine failure: insensitivity to this, bad taste in that, and so forth. The peculiarly human epitomizations make the point well. Mind, for instance, is the structure according to which it is possible for people to represent themselves as representatives of thinkers who are obliged by logic; that is, one sees that there are norms for thinking that distinguish good from bad thinking, and that they apply to oneself as a representative thinker. That one refuses to admit one is a representative thinker for whom logic is normative does not mean that the norms do not apply, once it is possible that one could accept that status; one simply is a perversely illogical or alogical thinker. Responsibility is the structured epitomization in which one objectifies oneself as an agent through time, and for whom it is possible to act in the present, taking responsibility for the past and for future consequences. Once one is possibly responsible, by virtue of conceiving of the self, one is normatively responsible and under obligation. These epitomizing structures are essential to the person's identity and function as essential features in all the parts of life (although there may be some moments when they are not important, *e.g.*, taking a moral holiday).

The cumulative integrity of human life consists in being the kind of complex discursive individual harmony in which basic structures of the sort Weiss describes are the essential determinants. Each of these structures has a quasi-independent developmental career of its own, and they must all be harmonized with the changing conditions of place, associations, overall maturity, and historical circumstances.

But the person is essentially human and essentially his or her individual self by virtue of having those structures function essentially, as available, at each point in life. Since those structures are not possible individually without at least coordination and sometimes conditional support from each other, a person is a highly integrated harmony. A human being has the vast complexity of these diverse essential structures and is responsive through them to a widely diverse environment; extraordinary complexity. And yet people, at least some of the time, are able to bring all these to such integration as to make focused, conscious actions with "purity of heart," as Kierkegaard put it, with such a simple purity that all the epitomizations and all the experience conveyed through them are marshalled in the heart's intent. More complex than a dumb animal, simpler than a mighty computer, people are extraordinarily valuable. And as Weiss argued, the level of value achieved by each person in this typically human maximization of complexity and simplicity is the same for all persons, regardless of how they may differ within that level in talent and virtue.

As much as I have attempted to offer this theory of value as a beneficial adjunct to Weiss's concerns in *Privacy*, it contains nothing that presents privacy itself as a primitive interior source of action, more primitive than its specializations, which is what Weiss affirms. Weiss's position here, I believe, stems from an Aristotelian disposition to take actual enduring substances as primitive, with an interiority that thrusts outward and resists the thrusts of others.[9] On the view I have presented, harmonies are primitive, and enduring actualities are special kinds of harmonies. Is there a way of rendering Weiss's sense of privacy within the theory of value?

Only those harmonies with actual existence can be said to have an intentional interiority (numbers, for instance, lack existence and intentional interiority). Suppose there were an actual harmony that was only momentary. Its intentional interiority would consist in its subjective drive toward definite unity, in its process of integrating its conditions into a definite individual, in the existential activity of its spontaneous essential features. As even Whitehead pointed out, that subjective existential pressing toward integration within the moment is private; only the conclusion of the effort, which can be a condition for subsequent moments, is public. The privacy of a discursive individual is not only momentary. My past and my future can be objects for me, but they are also privately me. That is, as past and future participate essentially in the present through essentially human structures, my life as a whole has a privacy through which I experience and act publicly. I suggest that the existential reality of the essential features comprising the essential human structures constitutes human privacy. Without some temporally thick essential structure or other, there would be no temporal privacy, only the blind immediacy of the moment. With any of the human structures, beginning with sheer sensitivity, there is a formed, temporally thick intention to address the world.

Put in a formula, I have argued that value is the achievement of structure. This is a strong reading of Weiss's early claim that Ideality is both structure and normative value. The Aristotelian insight that things have structures needing completion or fulfillment is a subcase of the more general theory, applying to certain kinds of temporally developing harmonies. And the theory of value defends the Aristotelian insight that completeness is good against the charge of committing the naturalistic fallacy by showing that in appropriate circumstances completeness makes for better harmony. During at least some periods of his writing, Weiss would have said that this analysis reads everything through the perspective of Ideality; there are alternate perspectives of actuality, existence, God, being, and substance. Would he also say that the alternate perspectives invalidate the points made through the theory of value as harmony so as to require the separation of structure and value?

Eight

Karsten Harries

Architecture and Ontology*

Architecture is in a confused state. One only has to page through the latest issues of the leading architectural journals to get a sense that architecture has lost its way. The obvious willingness to experiment may be exhilarating, but it is accompanied by a depressing lack of direction. This confusion has spilled over into our schools of architecture and, as Norberg-Schulz remarks, has made the training of architects unsatisfactory. "The schools have shown themselves incapable of bringing forth architects able to solve the actual tasks."[1] But what are the actual tasks of architecture? Is the prevailing uncertainty not tied to an uncertainty as to how this question is to be answered? One may of course point to the obvious needs generated by our way of life and look to scientists, especially to social scientists, to state these needs with a precision that allows engineers to offer the solutions that would best meet them. But are buildings to be considered machines? Surely they should be more than that. Corbusier, to whom we owe the so often repeated determination of the house as "a machine for living in," in the same place also insists that architects be more than just engineers, that they be also artists. Should buildings, then, be works of art? Or both: machines and works of art? As Arthur Drexler remarks in *Transformations in Modern Architecture*, "We are still dealing with the conflict between art and technology that beset the nineteenth century, and which the modern movement expected to resolve."[2] The current confusion is inseparable from the disappointment of that expectation.

*The basis of this essay was a presentation at a Symposium on the Philosophy of Paul Weiss at The Catholic University of America, May 18–19, 1981. Parts of it were reworked as "The Ethical Function of Architecture" for the 1982 meeting of the Society for Phenomenology and Existential Philosophy and appeared in *Descriptions*, eds. Don Ihde and Hugh J. Silverman (Albany: State University of New York Press, 1985). Reprinted by permission of the publisher.

Confusion invites critical reflection. Not surprisingly we meet with a new receptivity to philosophy and to philosophical ideas in the architectural world. Unfortunately, much of what philosophers have had to say about architecture has proved as much a hindrance as a help in arriving at a determination of the tasks of architecture. This has to do with the way philosophers have tended to approach architecture. Traditionally, architecture has been considered one of the arts. The philosophy of architecture appears thus as part of the philosophy of art. The arts again have often been understood as granting a particular kind of pleasure, but as unable to lay claim to truth or to a revelation of reality. The latter are thought to be the proper province of science. Following Kant, I call an approach that emphasizes the pleasure granted by the beautiful "aesthetic." But can a philosophy of art that has subjected itself to the hegemony of aesthetics do justice to works of art? The question becomes particularly acute when we turn to works of architecture. I try to show that if philosophy is to make a significant contribution to the ongoing discussion of the tasks of building, it first has to free itself from the aesthetic approach.

It is one thing to assert the necessity of such liberation, it is quite another to actually achieve it. The aesthetic approach is supported by an understanding of being that has made freedom from interest and perspective the measure of what constitutes proper access to what is. To understand the aesthetic approach and its power one has to understand how it is bound up with a particular interpretation of being. We have to recognize its foundation in a particular ontology. Philosophical reflection about the problems of architecture demands ontological reflection. The aesthetic approach cannot be effectively challenged without also challenging the presupposed ontology.

One such challenge is provided by Paul Weiss's determination of the modes of being. Weiss has also rethought the essence of art, and of the particular arts, in the light of this ontology. In *Nine Basic Arts* he has thus sketched for us at least an outline of a philosophy of architecture. The following remarks grew out of something like a conversation with that chapter. I argue for a more radical break with traditional aesthetics, which leads me to a different interpretation of what architecture needs today. Presupposed is a more radical break with traditional ontology. It is, however, possible that what separates us here is more a matter of emphasis than of substance, more a matter of different vocabularies than of philosophical conviction. But more important than possible disagreements is the shared conviction that philosophy is blind without the light of ontological reflection. If philosophy today seems to matter less and less, if much of it seems quite expendable, this is because too often it retreats into metaethical, metascientific, meta-artistic investigations or, in a mistaken pursuit of relevance, ties itself too closely to the issues of the day. To be sure, philosophy has to remain open to the realities of moral behavior, of science, and of art. However, it should not just limp behind them; rather, it should point out new possibilities and light a way. That it can do so successfully only when it places ontology at its very center is one thing we can learn from Paul Weiss's many-faceted work. If this essay gives some indication that this lesson has been learned, it will be a fitting tribute to him and to what he has thought, taught, and written.

I have asserted that philosophical aesthetics has proved more of a hindrance than a help in determining the essence and the tasks of architecture. "Aesthetics" should not be taken here as simply synonymous with "the philosophy of art." If today we understand the philosophy of art first of all as aesthetics, we are the heirs of an approach to art that in the eighteenth century finally triumphed over an older approach that could not grant autonomy to the work of art, but assigned it a religious, social, or ethical function, and placed beauty in the service of the need to represent the order that assigned man his place. The establishment of aesthetics as one of the main branches of philosophy is bound up with the weakening of this older approach. The term "aesthetics" itself belongs to the eighteenth century. We owe it to Alexander Gottlieb Baumgarten's *Meditationes philosophicae de nonnullis ad poema pertinentibus* of 1735: This fact helps to remind us that the aesthetic approach to art is part of that somewhat questionable legacy left to us by the enlightenment.

A suggestive characterization of this approach is provided by one of Baumgarten's similes: a successful poem, he tells us, is like a world, more precisely like the world as described by rationalist philosophers, by Leibniz for example, who understood the cosmos as a perfectly ordered whole having its sufficient reason in God. In that best of all possible worlds nothing is superfluous nor is anything missing. The same ought to be true of a poem, and more generally of a work of art. It, too, ought to be a perfect and therefore self-sufficient whole. Its integrity should be such that to add or to subtract anything would be to weaken it. The beautiful object presents itself to us as being as it should be. Nothing is missing; nothing is superfluous. Baumgarten's simile, quite traditional in its suggestion that the artist is a second God, seems innocent enough. After all, ever since Aristotle unity has been demanded of works of art: To be sure, to demand unity is not to deny complexity, tension, incongruity, but, in the end, order should triumph. Baumgarten, too, cites the familiar definition of beauty as sensible perfection. To speak of beauty as *sensible* perfection is to insist that a work of art be "sensuous, concrete, embedded in a medium. There is no substitute for the experience of it" (*NBA*, p. 8). To speak of it as sensible *perfection* is to insist on the autonomy of the artwork. A beautiful object does not refer beyond itself. Because of this there is no point to calling it true or false; it is experienced as a self-sufficient presence. This presence is what really matters.

The self-sufficiency of the work of art demands of the spectator that he leave it as it is. In an important sense there is nothing for him to do except to open himself to its presence. Such appreciation that lets the artwork be what it is needs no justification. To the self-sufficiency of the work of art corresponds the self-sufficiency of the aesthetic experience, which, if only for a time, gives us a sense of being as we should be, lifting the burden character of time. Herein resides the magic of that disinterested satisfaction which, according to Kant, lets us judge the object that grants it beautiful. Kant's characterization of the beautiful as the object of an entirely disinterested satisfaction asserts the autonomy of the sphere of beauty, distinguishes it from that of morality, and separates it from our everyday concerns. The attitude of the aesthetic observer is determined by what later came to be called aesthetic or psychical distance. As Paul Weiss points out,

To obtain an aesthetic object we must enter into the common-sense world, with its robust and vital activities, and there, through an act of concentration detach a portion of it from the rest. The act of bounding is produced by a change in attitude. Instead of being concerned with the world of common sense, as spread out over a large area of space and time and organized by convention, tradition, and social demands, we must so attend to a portion of it that it is torn out of its context, freed from its social role, and infused with our emotions, interests, and values (*NBA*, p. 5).

There is a sense in which all aesthetic objects have been framed.

Not that Weiss finds himself here in complete agreement with Kant. While Kant speaks of the aesthetic object as object of an entirely disinterested perception, Weiss insists that it is infused with our emotions, interests, and values. This suggests that the aesthetic experience is less removed from life and richer than it is on Kant's interpretation. But on Weiss's interpretation, too, the aesthetic object is essentially dislocated. Such dislocation is a necessary condition for an appreciation of the self-sufficiency of the genuine artwork. Pure art, on such a view, brackets the concerns of the everyday. These brackets may be exclusive or inclusive. But even when they are inclusive and our concerns are preserved in the aesthetic experience, such preservation nonetheless also implies a distancing that frees us from their burden and transforms them into material for aesthetic enjoyment. Art is for art's sake.

But if art is for art's sake, it is difficult to find much architecture that can be considered art. Architecture cannot rise to the purity found in the other arts, for as Kant observes, "the suitability of a product for a certain use is the essential thing in an *architectural work*."[3] Architecture, on Kant's view, has to be both practical and beautiful, where the practical has to be given priority. Beauty appears as something added on to what necessity dictates.

That more than other artists, architects are forced to compromise their artistic vision is also noted by Weiss. Architecture "exists within a context defined by unskilled labor and such practical activities as excavation, engineering, and plumbing. It must conform to building codes written with little concern for artistic needs. No other art is so hemmed in by men, tasks, and conditions relating to nonaesthetic matters" (*NBA*, p. 68). The nonaesthetic considerations that are said by Weiss to hem in architecture also dominate the training of our architects, stifling their artistic freedom. Weiss thus concludes his chapter on architecture with a historical observation and a suggestion as to how architectural education might be improved:

It would not be amiss, though, to remark that the history of architecture does not seem to have had many great turning points. There seem to be few great adventurers among the architects, perhaps because they are so overwhelmed by judges, critics, clients, and problems relating to engineering, city planning, and scales. What architecture badly needs today are laboratories where students are not only trained and disciplined, as they now are, but also encouraged to experiment with the bounding of all sorts of space, in all sorts of ways, with all sorts of materials. They should have periods in which they do not care that their work may not interest a client or that no one may ever build it or that it may not fit in with prevailing styles. Not until they take seriously the need to explore the possibilities of bounding spaces in multiple ways will they become alert to architecture as an art, as respectable, revelatory, creative, and at least as difficult as any other (*NBA*, p. 84).

Like Kant, Weiss raises the question of the artistic respectability of architecture. What threatens this respectability is architecture's subservience to nonaesthetic considerations. And I question the hope held out in the end. Given the aesthetic approach, architecture can never become as respectable as painting or sculpture. If beauty demands aesthetic purity, it is difficult to understand how architecture can ever be beautiful in the required sense. Buildings have to be more than objects for aesthetic contemplation. The architect has to take into account the uses to which a building will be put, while those using it will not be able to keep their distance from it. To the extent that we measure buildings by the aesthetic conception of what constitutes a complete work of art, architecture has to be considered deficient and impure, a not quite respectable art.

All this would be of little importance were it only a matter of a few theoreticians arguing about the essence of architecture. But the rise of aesthetics is only an aspect of a more deeply rooted change in sensibility that in the name of reason has divorced pragmatic and aesthetic considerations and placed the architect uneasily between the two. On the one hand, the uses of architecture were emphasized; on the other, architecture was supposed to be beautiful. And who could quarrel with the demand that architecture be both practical and beautiful? Unfortunately, the hopes of functionalists notwithstanding, there is not only no assurance that an economical and efficient solution to a practical problem will also be aesthetically pleasing, but given the aesthetics of purity there is no chance that the marriage of engineer and artist in architecture will be free of tension and compromise. What passes for such marriage is usually architecture that has the look of functionality rather than being truly functional. Given the aesthetic approach, the beauty of a building has to appear as something added on to what is dictated by necessity, decoration that is given its special value precisely by its superfluity. The tensions that result from this mingling of pragmatic and aesthetic considerations are readily experienced and rule out aesthetic completeness. On these terms the conflict between art and technology cannot be resolved.

It is thus hardly surprising that with the rise of the aesthetic approach in the eighteenth century, architecture should have entered a period of uncertainty and crisis from which it has not yet emerged. To be sure, already then there were attempts to raise architecture to the status of a pure art. The prophetic designs of Ledoux offer the most obvious examples. The architect here has become an abstract artist who casts his forms, his cubes, pyramids, and spheres into the void. It is not the embodied self that expresses itself in such an absolute and pure architecture, but a purely aesthetic interest. Not surprisingly, Ledoux's most daring designs remained on paper. The pursuit of aesthetic purity has to lead the architect to utopian phantasies unlikely to be ever realized. Reality demands compromises. Aesthetic vision has to be tempered by nonaesthetic considerations. As long as the theory of architecture remains subject to the aesthetic approach, it is in no position to do justice to the essence of architecture. Thus, the nineteenth century clothed its often quite practical architecture in a veneer of borrowed ornament and placed the architect uneasily between the *école polytechnique* and the *école des beaux arts*. Architecture is caught in the tension between considerations of form and of function and it is function that finally matters, even if it cannot satisfy the demand for beauty. Given such an approach, all beauty in architecture has to be considered in a profound sense just ornament. From this perspective Venturi's so controversial call for an architecture of ornamented sheds appears as an inevitable corollary to the aesthetic approach to architecture.

I have argued that as long as the aesthetic approach guides architectural theory, architecture has to be understood an impure art; as long as this approach continues to inform architectural practice, architecture will remain caught in the conflict between art and technology. If there is to be an escape from this bind, taking a different approach must be possible. An obvious solution is to divorce art and technology. One might thus call on architecture to emancipate itself from the presumption that it should be an art. Hannes Meyer, who succeeded Gropius as head of the Bauhaus, attempted to lead architecture in this direction with his denial that building be considered in any way an "aesthetic process." According to Meyer, "Architecture as 'an emotional act of the artist' has no justification."[4] One might, on the other hand, continue to insist that architecture is indeed an art, but claim that the aesthetic conception fails to do justice to art. Weiss's philosophy of art provides the second strategy with valuable pointers. To be sure, as the quoted passages suggest, much that Weiss has to say about art argues that he, too, follows an aesthetic approach. Thus Weiss, too, characterizes the artwork as an object that can be enjoyed as a self-sufficient substance. Art "does not look to an end beyond itself" (*WA*, p. 15). Such emphasis on enjoyment and self-sufficiency helps to define the aesthetic approach. But Weiss also emphasizes the ability of the artwork to illuminate or to reveal. Art should be both beautiful and revelatory (*WA*, pp. 115, 118). Our interest in art is said to be "*ontological* in nature" (*NBA*, p. 33). "Art can provide a deep satisfaction to men because it both presents them with and reveals a reality that they must master in order to grasp who they are and what the universe promises them" (*NBA*, p. 33). It is this conviction that places Weiss in profound opposition to any merely aesthetic approach to art. Thus, when in the preface to *The World of Art* Weiss expresses his indebtedness to Susanne K. Langer's work, he also points out that his central theses constitute an explicit rejection of her view that truth and reality are the proper province of science, a view that condemns art to semblance and illusion. Art, too, serves truth. "But if truth means, as it does, the conveying of the intent of an entire situation, of its general import or meaning as well as of the structure and interrelation of its parts, then art must be said to convey truth as surely as science does. A work of art is a unified, substantial whole representing a world beyond" (*WA*, p. 56).

But how is this view of the artwork as essentially representational to be reconciled with the self-sufficiency that is also claimed for the work of art? Must such a representational art not present itself as in some sense gesturing beyond itself? Weiss himself asks, "What reason do we have for assuming that the texture of even a substantial, emotionally effective, and self-sufficient work of art reproduces the texture of a reality beyond it?" (*WA*, p. 77). He goes on to admit that "No one, so far as he is immersed only in art, clearly knows whether or not there is a reality beyond it" (*WA*, p. 77). This, it seems, has to mean that as the aesthetic approach insists, the experience of the work of art as such has no revelatory function, although it may assume such a function in subsequent reflection. But such reflection should not be confused with the aesthetic experience. Proximity to the aesthetic approach is suggested by a passage like the following:

What [the artist] makes is a better world in some respects, for it is more excellently made, and more attractive. In his work and through his work he cuts behind the randomness, the irrelevancies, the contingencies which confront him on every side, to get to the very heart of things. He masters existence by conquering a part of it and making this part represent the rest. The glory of art is that it creates a world in which men can live in a better and more satisfying way than they normally do (*WA*, p. 40).

The traditional view of the artist as a second God, of the artwork as a second world, absorbing enough to let us forget our involvement in *the* world, comes to mind. Art appears here as an appropriating conquest of existence that offers us a substitute for the all too deficient world in which we have to live. Baumgarten might have said something very much like this. He would, however, have insisted that if the work of art can be said to "represent" the rest of existence, this should not be understood to mean that it refers us beyond itself, but rather that the artwork establishes a world so complete that it lets us bracket whatever transcends it. Only this lets it become a self-sufficient aesthetic presence. And while he might have admitted that the artwork lets us exist in a better way than we normally do, better because for a time what is and what should be appear reconciled, he could have added that the price of such reconciliation is the loss of genuine interaction and thus of genuine life. Weiss does not grant the aesthetic approach quite this much. If he stresses the self-sufficiency of the work of art, he is equally insistent that art answer to an ontological interest.

Later I will examine in more detail why it is difficult—but just because of this also important—for modern man to hold on to an ontological conception of art; why the aesthetic conception is closely linked to our spiritual situation. The answer is provided by the governing understanding of reality. As long as one holds that only what can be grasped by objectifying thought deserves to be called real, one will not be able to take seriously an ontological conception of art. Weiss's ontological approach to art depends on his richer notion of being to which neither science nor philosophy can finally do full justice. Inquiry into being is also inquiry into what constitutes proper access to beings. To distinguish with Weiss different modes of being is also to argue for the importance of different kinds of access to beings. Weiss distinguishes four ultimate modes: existence, actuality, ideality, and God. Each mode is said to be grasped in a distinctive way. "The nature of actuality, as it enters into experience, is grasped most directly and with the least distortion by means of philosophical concepts. The ideal is most effectively reached through mathematics and ethics. We know God best when we worship. But existence needs the artist" (*WA*, p. 9). Art, according to Weiss, reveals the texture and import of existence. This ontological function lets it take its place beside "such other vital disciplines as mathematics, philosophy, and religion" (*NBA*, p. 8). The analysis of existence and of its three "essential dimensions," space, time, and becoming, provides Weiss with a key to the classification of the arts. To each dimension corresponds a type of art. Within each type the arts divide "depending on whether they bound, occupy, or exhaust the dimension" (*NBA*, p. 34). Architecture is understood as "the art of bounding, and thereby creating multiple spaces" (*NBA*, p. 67).

According to Weiss, the task of the artist is

to deal with space, time, and becoming in independence of the manner in which they function in daily life or in known substances. Only by exploring them in their own terms, apart from the limitations to which common-sense experience or different substances subject them, can he grasp what existence is in fact. If he portrays familiar things in his works it is only to enable him and others to locate themselves better in that deeper, more ominous, challenging world which man has a need to master (*WA*, p. 78).

Architecture, accordingly, is the bounding and thus a mastering of space. "Whoever accepts a clearing as a possible dwelling bounds it off from the rest of the world. But he who makes a dwelling not only bounds it off but produces roof, walls, windows, door, flooring, each of which itself is a newly created, tensed spatial object within a larger tensed space" (*NBA*, p. 69). Bounding space, the architect wrests place from space. Architecture answers not simply to an ontological interest but more specifically to the human need for place.

How can one understand the space that is bounded by the architect's work? Is it the space of our ordinary experiences? Or is it the boundless space of geometry or natural science? The latter is claimed by Walter Pichler and Hans Hollein in their manifesto "Absolute Architecture": "Architecture dominates space. Dominates it by shooting up into the heights; it hollows out the earth, projects and soars far above the ground, spreads in all directions. Dominates it through mass and through emptiness. Dominates space through space."[5] If he is a true artist, the architect will not worry about function. "Architecture is purposeless." Only an architecture oblivious to function can claim to be "pure" and "absolute." Ledoux's utopian designs come to mind. In its self-sufficient aesthetic presence this pure architecture breaks the meaningless silence of the universe.

Weiss has a very different conception of the architect's task. If, as artist, the architect is asked to deal with space "on its own terms," Weiss yet defines architecture as "the art of creating space through the construction of boundaries in common-sense space" (*NBA*, p. 69). Architecture, thus, appears to stand in a more intimate relationship to ordinary experience than do the other arts.

To share in a story or a dance one must turn away from (though still presupposing) the forces dominating the world of common sense. We can enter the painter's space or the sculptor's space if we can push back the space of every day. We enter the architect's created space on similar conditions, but the space of his work is also common-sensical. We truly enter his space only if while attending to his created space, we also maintain a grip on daily space (*NBA*, pp. 67–68).

I want to emphasize the last: The space created by the architect should be such that it lets us maintain a grip on daily space; it remains common-sensical. And yet it also transforms commonsense space by establishing boundaries that strengthen our sense of place. If the architect's work pushes back the space of everyday, it does so only to lead us back to it, but it returns that space to us, having transformed it.

To facilitate this return, a building may not be a self-sufficient whole. It should invite use and appropriation. Architects should resist the temptation to create self-sufficient works of art. Perhaps we can take a performance view of dwelling: A good building should be somewhat like a score that leaves a great deal of room for improvisation. But a score remains incomplete as long as it is not performed; and there is no definitive performance.[6]

To say of the architect that he creates boundaries in commonsense space is to say also that he remains bound to a particular environment and to a particular community. The architect who attempts to reject these bonds for the sake of a pure or absolute architecture will create buildings that may fascinate with their aesthetic presence, but their relationship to their environment cannot but seem accidental. Instead of strengthening our sense of place, they will have the look of transportable works of art. Mies van der Rohe's Farnsworth House looks thus essentially mobile, ready to be transported into some Museum of Modern Art. The same is true of a great many of modern architecture's most cherished achievements. But while such works may succeed as aesthetic objects, for that very reason they fail to grant that sense of place which is the greatest gift of successful architecture. Such architecture not only bounds itself off from, but binds itself to, a particular environment. "The architect must always place his environment in a setting whose nature he cannot entirely control, but that he must accept if he is to have an environment that all the rest can acknowledge in intent, work, and appreciation. It is therefore important for him to attend to the kinds of limits that are available, and to accept these as conditions that help him to define the extent and character of the environment, and the placement of his walls and other surfaces" (*NBA*, p. 75).

In this connection, Weiss refers to Vincent Scully's *The Earth, the Temples, and the Gods*. The reference is important. Scully recognizes that building is not just a matter of providing physical security. More important is its ability to grant psychical security. What stands in the way of such security is the accidental, the sense that a house just happens to be as it is, just happens to be where it is. It is, therefore, important to recognize that a temple is not just built in any place, but in response to the experienced meaning of a particular place; we can say in response to the *genius loci*.[7] Scully thus suggests that each Minoan palace makes use of the same landscape elements: "first, an enclosed valley of varying size in which the palace is set; I should like to call this the 'Natural Megaron'; second, a gently mounded or conical hill on axis with the palace to north or south; and lastly a higher, double-peaked or cleft mountain some distance beyond the hill but on the same axis."[8] Scully goes on to connect the hill with the earth's motherly form, while he ties the double-peaked mountain to the male active power. I am not concerned here with details. Important, however, is the point that landscape defines the space for architecture, which in turn helps to focus and to articulate its meaning. The example suggests that architecture should take its measure from a particular landscape. Before the architect begins to build, the place where he is to build is already experienced as a region charged with meanings. Genuine building is a response to claims presented by this region.

These claims are inseparable from the cares and concerns of those who inhabit that region. Of architecture in particular we can say what Weiss says of all art: that it is one of the primary loci of a people's "hopes, values and meaning" (*WA*, p. 26). But if the work of art is to be experienced as such a primary locus of meaning, it must gesture beyond itself and present itself as a figure of man's place and vocation. To the extent that it is experienced as a self-sufficient aesthetic whole it does not present itself as such a figure. Similarly, the artist may not understand himself as a self-sufficient creator. He must recognize that his art is bound to a prospect that belongs to the society of which he is a member more than it does to himself. As Weiss points out, "An artist's idea, even of the most commonplace thing, has a mythological base" (*WA*, p. 87). Myth provides the meaning that existence has for him and which he reveals in his work.

A myth is society's "idea"; every individual personalizes this and roots his own individual ideas in it. The artist makes a tighter union of his own ideas and society's than other men do; the prospects which he faces are always seen from the perspective of the prevailing myth. Only when he overintellectualizes his tasks does he follow the guidance of his own ideas, ignoring or rejecting part of his own being when and as he rejects the myth (*WA*, p. 86).

Although Weiss points out that more than most other arts architecture "is alert to the prevailing myths," he does not develop the point. It opens up a perspective that proves particularly illuminating when dealing with the sacred architecture of the past. Here I want to insist only that mythical content is never adequately incarnated in a particular material. Where the artist succeeds in so fusing a mythical prospect with his material that the resulting artwork is experienced as a self-sufficient whole, myth has lost its power to illuminate the whole of human existence. It has become no more than an occasion whose mythical power is effaced by the artist's mastery of his material. The rise of the aesthetic approach and the loss of the mythical dimension belong together.

I asked: what is the space that is bounded and revealed by the architect? We have seen that this space cannot be divorced from the way man dwells on the earth as member of a community. But such dwelling changes with time. So do the myths and accounts that tell man who he is and at the same time what is to count as reality. The rise of the aesthetic approach is bound up with such a change. It is this change that must be understood if we are to understand what is involved in criticizing or in submitting to the aesthetic approach.

I have asserted that the aesthetic approach belongs with a particular ontology: it may be considered a corollary of the interpretation of being as objective reality. On that interpretation, only what can be grasped by objectifying thought deserves to be called real. This interpretation rests on a twofold reduction of experience. First, we find ourselves caught up in the world. The way we encounter things is tied to the activities in which we are engaged; their mode of presentation is bound up with mood and interest. The first reduction attempts to bracket both. The self is disengaged from the world and transformed into a disinterested spectator of what is. Being becomes presence to such a subject; the world appears rather like a picture. As Schopenhauer points out, lost in this reduction is the real significance of things, that "by virtue of which these pictures or images do not march past us strange and meaningless, as they would otherwise inevitably do, but speak to us directly, are understood, and acquire an interest that engrosses our whole nature."[9]

If the first reduction distances or disengages us from the sensible, the second reduction dissociates the sensible and the real. The key to this reduction is provided by a reflection on perspective that plays a central part already in Plato's thinking: is not the way we experience things subject to a viewpoint that is ours only because of the place in which we happen to be? Our experience of things is mediated by our body and thus subject to the accident of location. To seize things as they are we have to overcome this accident. But spirit is not bound to the body; the perspective assigned to us by our location is not a prison. Not only can we move and thus gain different perspectives, in imagination we can put ourselves in other places even without moving. And we can go even further and demand descriptions that are free from all perspectival distortion, *i.e.*, objective. Truth is opposed here to perspectival appearance. Implied is the essential invisibility of reality. Whatever is real cannot in principle be seen as it is. One may object that if the eyes do not see things as they are, the spirit does so even less; indeed, it does not see at all. In its search for the truth it can do no better than replace reality with its own constructions. This must be admitted. But these constructions are more than idle creations. They are reconstructions to be tested by experience and experiment. The necessity of returning in this sense to the life-world does not, however, challenge the thesis of the essential invisibility of reality so understood.

It should be evident that once this dissociation of reality and visibility, more generally, sensibility, is accepted, it becomes difficult to take seriously art's claim to the truth, at least as long as such truth is sought in some sort of correspondence between the artwork and a reality that transcends it. Already Plato thus condemned art for being thrice removed from the truth. Essentially the same insight led Hegel to claim that "art is and remains for us, from the side of its highest vocation, something past." "We" are here those whose spiritual situation is determined by the conviction that we gain proper access to reality only to the extent that our thinking has freed itself from the tyranny of perspective. Art "from the side of its highest vocation" is art that takes seriously its ontological function. Only such an art is said to belong to the past. This cannot be said of art that resigns itself to the limits implied by the aesthetic conception. Quite the contrary: such aesthetic art belongs to the present age.[10]

We would be making it too easy for ourselves were we to think that "we" referred only to a few philosophers who by placing exaggerated trust in the power of thinking distort both the being of the self and the being of things. This would suggest that Hegel's proclamation of the death of art in its highest sense is characteristic of the sort of thing that philosophers are likely to say, given their own professional prejudice. The suggestion is thus often made that to escape their dismal conclusions, including this one about art, all that one has to do is reimmerse oneself in the life-world, in that reality that affects us with its colors and sounds, its tastes and smells. This easy opposition of the life-world to the phantastic flights of philosophers fails to do justice to the fact that the world we live in has been shaped by technology. Technology rests on science, while science presupposes the two reductions that I have sketched. Technology has carried these reductions into the world we live in. This must make every attempt to escape from the aberrations of a supposedly too Cartesian philosophy to the life-world or to the language games of the everyday questionable. Much as we may resent it, we live in the shadow of an ontology that finds its first clear articulation in Descartes' determination of the being of things as reality, of the being of nature as *res extensa*, of human being as *res cogitans.*

But in what sense does this ontology support the aesthetic approach? Why does it not simply lead to the suggestion that we no longer need art at all? The answer has to be sought in a twofold deficiency of the understanding of being that I have sketched. The first reduction robs things of what lets them speak to us and engage our interest. No longer are they infused with our emotions, interests, and values. The second reduction robs things of their sensuous presence. What we see and hear is interpreted as the mere appearance of a reality that is essentially invisible. The world is transformed into a collection of colorless, soundless facts, which just happen to be as they are. In that reality man cannot feel at home. As Nietzsche saw, so understood, the pursuit of truth must tend towards nihilism. There is something disturbingly right about Nietzsche's suggestion that "Since Copernicus man has been rolling from the center towards X." With such a truth man cannot live. This gives weight to Nietzsche's claim that "We possess *art* lest we *perish of the truth*."[11] Art offers refuge from the meaninglessness of the world.

These remarks can offer no more than pointers. But that something essential is recognized here is suggested also when we return once more to Baumgarten's establishment of aesthetics and to his understanding of beauty as sensible perfection. Presupposed by this emphasis on the sensible is what was felt to be the deficiency of clear and distinct understanding: its inability to seize the individual and concrete, what Weiss calls the texture of reality. Presupposed by the emphasis on perfection is the recognition that, although God may have created the world as an infinitely perfect whole in which nothing is unjustified, to the finite human knower the world does not present itself as such. We experience things as contingent and arbitrary; we live our life *sub specie possibilitatis*. And yet we demand to see things, including our own life, *sub specie aeternitatis*, as having to be as they present themselves. The perfection of the artwork answers this demand. But such perfection is bought at the price of truth. One may of course redefine truth and seek it in the coherence of the self-sufficient work of art. Such redefinition cannot hide the fact that, understood as the creator of self-sufficient works of art, the artist is no longer the suitor of truth, but, to quote Nietzsche once more, "only fool, only poet." Such art can only offer an escape from reality, can only cover it up. Art for art's sake and nihilism belong together. Both have their foundation in the elevation of that interpretation of being that guides science and technology into the only adequate interpretation. What is needed is a richer understanding of being that will help us to understand the legitimacy of science and technology, a legitimacy one could deny only in a romantic flight out of the modern world, and also allow us to criticize their claim to hegemony. Weiss's ontology here proves a valuable guide. But it also reminds us that ontological reflection remains ineffective as long as the ontological function of morality, religion, and art is not taken seriously, and this means taken seriously not in philosophical reflection, not by speaking of ontology, but in commitment and sacrifice, in worship, in the creation and appreciation of art, especially of architecture.

Why "especially of architecture?" Because more than sculpture or painting, architecture answers to the different dimensions of human existence and requires more than a merely aesthetic response. The very factors that tend to make architecture, on the aesthetic approach a not altogether respectable, because essentially impure art, have made it difficult for architects to sacrifice life to aesthetic experience and to subordinate the requirements of dwelling to those of aesthetic self-sufficiency. Given the aesthetic approach, attention to the requirements of life and dwelling has to appear as a deflection from what should matter to the artist in the architect. On that approach, Weiss's suggestion that what architecture needs today are laboratories where students are encouraged to explore the possibilities of bounding space without worrying too much about the demands of landscape or community is easily defended. But once that approach has been rejected and the implications of that rejection are recognized, architectural education will appear in a very different light. Far more important than giving the young architect more freedom to experiment, is making him more alert to the many dimensions of living and dwelling and that means also to the different modes of being.

Nine

Paul Grimley Kuntz

Paul Weiss:
What is a Philosophy of Sport?*

"We need a philosophy of sport."

What is a Philosophy of Sport?

In January 1966, Paul Weiss wrote the preface to *The Making of Men*. In "that pervasive and yet almost ungraspable process we call education" he singled out sport as a neglected ingredient. Surely he is right that the academic community generally has no high place for coaches and neglects the role that athletics plays in education. Scholars may tolerate teams because the few quasi- and even pre-professional players entertain alumni. Weiss comes on strong that sports should not be "the occupation of a gifted few and a spectacle for the rest." On the field and in the gymnasium, any student can become a man, developing his "sense of responsibility for doing excellently what he has committed himself to do, at the same time [acquiring] the habit of cooperating with others." The primary purpose of coaches should be to develop men, not to win games, not even to help students be healthy. What of the professed moral justification? It is often said that the virtue developed through sport is that students are "allowed to express and publicly sustain a desire for success, loyalty and distinction." Weiss is exalting a rather less Horatio-Algerish position, and it is clearly "readiness to cooperate" with others that he esteems as the virtue coaches can inculcate "more readily and happily on the field and in the gymnasium than elsewhere." Yet Weiss is unable to say which sports at which stages of a young man's growth best de-

---

*Reprinted with permission from *Philosophy Today*, Fall 1976, Carthegena Station/Celina, Ohio 45822.

velop these capacities. Out of ignorance he concludes: "We *need a philosophy of sport*" (*MM*, pp. 102–4).[1]

On February 9 Weiss writes in his philosophical diary: "I sent off my *The Making of Men* about a week ago and haven't had an idea since. I have no notion about what I want to study or write about. Last night while listening to Nathan Millstein playing Beethoven's only violin concerto . . . I returned to an idea with which I had been toying on and off. I decided then to try to give a philosophic account of sports" (*PP* 5, p. 126).

What does Weiss mean by "a philosophy of sport" or "a philosophic account of sport?" It is more than an educational philosophy, just as education itself involves all the aspects of man's life and all that man cares about. The important aspect with which Weiss begins is the problem of classifying sports, whether a division by the power of man used ("skill, speed, endurance, and contests") or the "facets of man that is being tested" (intelligence or the whole body or some specialized skill), etc. As Weiss devises a new classification he expresses a criticism that none of them is "grounded on any clearly understood principles" (*PP* 5, pp. 126–28).

Clearly then classification is only an aspect of a philosophy of sport and grounded in something else. What this is is a philosophical anthropology or a philosophy of man. This recognition does not come until a year and a half later: "A study of sport will follow something like the lead of *Man's Freedom* and *Our Public Life*, if the foregoing account is correct and if these books really do justice to their respective tasks. This would mean that a discussion of sport would have to be considered under something like the headings: 'freedom, socialization, preference, choice, will, sacrifice, love, law, authority, power, etc.'" (*PP* 5, p. 512).

But if a philosophy of sport is fundamentally a philosophy of man, the philosopher might neglect the "difference between individual and team sports, between sports for men and for women, between sports with and without instruments, etc." (*PP* 5, p. 512).

Even if a philosophy of sport does deal with profound aspects of man's destiny, "the problem of conflict and death," still it is not adequate for "it does not make room for the view that *sport is revelatory of reality* . . . " (*PP* 5, p. 512, emphasis added). A philosophy of sport, then, must deal not only with the kinds of sports, their roles in man's development, the nature of man, but with what is real.

What Weiss then means by a "philosophy of sport" is an account of sports as they reveal man's encounter with the Ideal, with Existence, with Actuality. In the four modes of being, Weiss also includes God, but God is not significantly involved as an aspect of athletics.[2]

How engaging in sport is religious without "explicit reference or more than a hint of God" is characterized by being "privately religious." This means that the athlete opens himself up to "supplementation, support, control" and in this sense puts himself in relation to "superior being" (*PP* 1, p. 709).

I think it fair to conclude that Weiss would sanction a religious philosophy of sport, which has been fairly common in XIXth- and XXth-century French Catholicism, but hardly a "theology of sport" which some contemporary German and American theologians have attempted.[3]

The important metaphysical aspects of sport are that man acts in space and time and a dynamic existence and strives towards goals. The athlete in particular not only directs his body, he should "have oriented himself in Actuality" (*PP* 5, p. 262). Sports seem to occupy "all three dimensions of Existence . . . all seem to be able to enter into any place, any time, and to involve a plurality of dynamic processes" (*PP* 5, p. 60). Weiss describes games as "series of decisive acts [which] yield a specific realization of a particularized objective." Hence there is another mode of being, for being victorious, the objective, is a "specialization of Ideality" (*S*, p. 174, *PP* 5, p. 262).

When sports are defined most generally, that is categorically and metaphysically, they are indistinguishable from the arts, more specifically the performing arts that Weiss stresses: theatre, dance, and music. The performing arts are men acting, in the space-time-causal world, and striving towards excellence. Hence, regarded metaphysically, without specifying what is specifically presented, the philosophy of sport is a specialized form of the philosophy of art. Hence there are innumerable statements of similarities such as "The athlete and craftsman are quite similar" (*PP* 5, p. 129). Yet there are also statements of the differences between a "spectator of a sport" and a "spectator in a drama" (*PP* 5, p. 128).

Consequently, if aesthetics includes an analysis of the nature of the arts, and sports are arts of special sorts, a philosophy of sport would be a special part of aesthetics. (Or is philosophy of art a specialized form of the philosophy of sport? Or are the two to be called specialized forms of a philosophy of performance? Maybe other activities such as politics, education, housekeeping are other specialized forms. The first alternative is probably to be preferred because Weiss had already developed a fully explicit philosophy of art.)

The way Weiss gets the issues of sport formulated is by relating them to the issues of aesthetics. "In *The World of Art*, I say that 'Play is self-contained activity without serious or definite purpose productive of . . . pleasure . . . and expressive use of energy . . . exhibiting a spontaneity . . . detached from any interest in what lies beyond.'" There are forms of play subject to rules, called games and sports. The question is then, how does the athlete "play," and how does the artist "play?" (*PP* 5, p. 131).

Let us reflect upon the nature of sport. "We enter the world of play for no purpose, unless it be to enjoy ourselves" (*PP* 5, p. 520). But if sports are forms of play, why did we begin our inquiry with the confident proposition that sport, as an ingredient in education, teaches us "a sense of responsibility for doing excellently what [we] have committed [ourselves] to do, at the same time [acquiring] the habit of cooperating with others?" (*MM*, p. 103).

Just as in general aesthetics we have a sharp contrast between teleological and ateleological theories, so in a philosophy of sport we have evidently radically different philosophies of sport.

The truer statement would be therefore, since we have several philosophies of sport, that "we need a true and adequate philosophy of sport."

If the play theory of art and sport is true and adequate then Weiss's metaphysics of art and sport is false. Better said, if play reveals nothing about reality, then it is gratuitous to complicate play by asking about the roles of God, Ideality, Actuality and Existence in sport!

Philosophy in Process, Volume 5, is like its four predecessors in dealing with many aspects of philosophy. I found *Philosophy in Process*, Volume 1, to be deeply revelatory of Weiss's motivation, *Philosophy in Process*, Volume 2, a climax of this lifelong religious quest. Hence came "Weiss's Search for Adequacy" and "The God We Find: The God of Abraham, The God of Anselm, and The God of Weiss."[4]

After *Philosophy in Process*, Volume 1, which covers 1955–1960, Weiss hardly mentions sport in the day by day account of Volumes 2–4, 1960–1965. This covers the period during which Weiss was thinking of education, which he analyzes in *The Making of Men*. A comparison of the two reveals that the materials of the diary are far more profound than of Weiss's book.[5]

A philosophy of sport is one theme among many in *Philosophy in*

Process, Volume 5. Others are welcome to mine this source for a valuable lode of quite diverse metals. My search of the philosophical literature on sport has uncovered nothing so valuable anywhere. Weiss's struggle for a true and adequate philosophy of sport seems to me pure gold and the best thing ever done on the complex similarities and dissimilarities between arts and sports.[6]

Sport: Pleasure in Play?

We have discovered contradictory propositions about sport. We cannot at the same time and in the same sense say that the value of sport is to educate men in responsibility and cooperation and also that sports are for themselves, without utility or value other than immediate enjoyment. Weiss at various places presses both these theories. Since he struggles between what we shall call the "Play Theory" and the "Discipline Theory," let us give his contradictory thoughts a dialectical exposition, first of play, then of discipline, followed by two further theories, therapy and agon.

" 'Sport' comes from 'disport', to divert or amuse . . . There is a delight in moving one's limbs with grace and skill; there is joy in testing oneself and one's opponent. Pleasure is rarely absent from any sport, even when one has pushed oneself to the limit of human endurance" (S, p. 133).

Probably the play theory is the best developed theory of sport, since it has had two recent exponents, on whom Weiss depends, who have devoted two brilliant books to its exposition and modification.[7] Weiss finds difficulties in the concept of play as "free activity" in the sense of being outside ordinary life and therefore not serious. Play can be both free and serious. Is play "free" in the sense that it is begun and ended with pleasure? Children are, says Weiss, sent out to play, even made to play. Play must only then be free in the sense of "carried on by the player only while he desires to engage in it. Made to play, he nevertheless plays only while he willingly does what he must" (S, p. 134).

Play has its own "boundaries" as Huizinga says, or is "separate," as Caillois says. Although cut off from the responsibilities of work where we do one thing because it serves to bring about another, play is a sphere in which we devote ourselves to what we are now doing. Hence the seriousness of play. Thus Weiss detaches the characteristic of "seriousness" from that of "usefulness." Children do not play at being firemen in order to train themselves for the life of fire fighting (S, p. 135). Although "one may play in order to refresh oneself, to be a good companion, to use up some time, and the like . . . once the step has been taken . . . all the initial reasons are left behind. He who wants to be refreshed through play must forget about refreshing himself, and just play" (S, p. 137).

There are other paradoxes of play. Play is always spontaneous and therefore the outcome is uncertain, even though the activity takes place under rules strictly adhered to. This paradox is neatly shown to be only a seeming contradiction.

No process is ever reducible to a pattern; the dynamic always adds something not expressed in any structure. Whatever we do has its element of unanticipated contingency, spontaneity, and unexpectedness. But more room is left for them in play than elsewhere. Play invites improvisation and imagination because it is serious with respect to the domain it bounds but not with respect to what is done within it (S, p. 137).

To play is to be "free of responsibilities" yet the play forms of art and sport are engaged in as work in which spontaneity is curtailed (S, pp. 139, 137–38). Art and sport are in areas removed from economic production, yet the successful achievement of unproductive achievement requires that the artist and athlete not "play around" (S, pp. 137–38). The artist and athlete might like to be "vitally unstructured," but they actually are less idle and play less than others. Although "children stop when they are tired, bored, or when they become interested in something else," the athlete "is serious about continuing the game." The game is not only bounded off from all else, but it *must* run its course (S, p. 140).

Another paradox of play is that the player like a child adopts a role and makes believe, as in a drama, that he is that dramatis persona, yet through all-absorbing play, he "goes on to learn who he is and what he can do" (S, pp. 138, 140). Weiss resolves this paradox also.

An athlete . . . finds out through his play how much of a man he is by discovering how close to the limits of human performance he can come . . . He is, therefore, free to learn in the contest or game how he meets various tests, what it is that perfection demands, and what man can bodily do and be (S, pp. 141–42).

The seriousness of play is evident in the paradox that when we divert ourselves from work, we then do not frolic, but "submit" [ourselves] to rules which often ask for effort and attention far greater than that required in daily work" (*S*, p. 142). Weiss resolves this paradox with the consideration that a man voluntarily seeks the adventure, for example, of mountain climbing. To be accepted "by the community of those who treat this as a sport" he avoids any shortcut. A sportsman must be "tested within the limits set by established rules" (*S*, p. 142). Of course in economic production the same man would make a profit by using machines, blasting a new path and getting to the peak first by some innovation not known to the competition and taking it by surprise.

Since Friedrich Schiller no theory of art or aesthetics has been without some consideration of play.

In *The World of Art*, Weiss rejected the play theory of art.

Man has an appetite for an ethical and social life; he struggles to know; he wants to worship. He loves and hates with all his being. But though art exhibits needs and makes use of powers also manifested in nonartistic activities, it nevertheless is to be sharply distinguished from all other activities. It is quite different from craftsmanship, no matter how splendid; *it is not at all a form of play*, no matter how ingenious and enjoyable this may be. Unlike these it demands a fresh and unmistakable act of creativity, terminating in the production of self-sufficient excellence (*WA*, p. 5, emphasis added).

Perhaps the play theory fits what Weiss calls "relaxed forms where there is no endeavor to produce the excellent" (*PP* 5, p. 160). Weiss's technique is to call our attention to the aspects of art and sport, as we have seen above, that simply will not fit any over-simplification. But is it only one differentia? "It is creativity that distinguishes art from work, *its intrinsic excellence that distinguishes it from play*, and its self-sufficiency that distinguishes it from the products of mere technique and craftsmanship" (*WA*, p. 11, emphasis added). Were sport motivated only by the will to win, sport would lose all relation to play and to art and, as with professionals, turn into mere work (*WA*, pp. 14–15).

The conclusion is that art (and sport presumably) are something like play in being spontaneous and self-contained, but exhibit also "the control and purposiveness of work, the value of labor, the arduousness of toil, the weariness of drudgery, the technique of the craftsman, the excellence characteristic of the liberal arts" (*WA*, p. 18).

Philosophy in Process continues the critique of the play theory. Earlier, Weiss admits, he had fixed only on spontaneity and self-containedness as the essence of play "to separate out the nature of games and sports (the one taken to be play subject to rules, the other to be games in a social context) and to isolate the factor of spontaneity in a *work* of art" (*PP* 5, p. 131).

When we turn to games and sports, the meaning of 'play' seems to be different from what it is in connection with the arts. 'To play a game' or to 'play at sports' involves a subordination of the spontaneity of play to the rules and the context. The artist has a genuine moment of free play in his working, whereas those involved in games and sports do not. We ought to distinguish 'free play,' 'playing in' a game, and 'sharing in' a sport.
It seems correct to say that a game is play subject—or more sharply, subjected—to rules. But sports seem to be more than games in a social context. There should be reference to some commitment, to the necessity for training, to the exercise of skill, to the fact that the individual is put to the test, and that he at once makes something and himself. This, it must be confessed, is a comparatively new meaning, and one which exists alongside another, almost synonymous with 'play' (*PP* 5, pp. 131–32).

As an account of the dedicated athlete, then, there is very little truth in the play theory of sport, as little truth as there is in a theory that serious art is play. The dimension of play has some validity in explaining the point of view of the spectator or the week-end player.

A number of men have told me that they are primarily interested in sports as participants for the fun of the game, and that they were interested in sports as spectators primarily for relaxation. The two contentions are related. They point up *a dimension of sports which is related to play* in that it involves a contrast with work, involves one in something which has a value in itself, and which provides not revelation, or improvement, or the satisfaction of some deep drive, but simply pleasure of an uncomplicated sort (*PP* 5, p. 518, emphasis added).

A related criticism is that "pleasure" is so vague that it can be used to explain any activity. It does not then account for the specific pleasure of sport. Since play is associated with pleasure, play would similarly be vague. Hence Weiss moves towards an examination of the specific "motivation [and] drives" of sports. Even if empirically sport provides more pleasure, or . . . provides it more readily, . . . or . . . provides it for more people," this is superficial.

Weiss moves away from play and pleasure:

We are driven to inquire into the nature of sport, and the motivation of athletes, etc., because we see sport to answer to some need in man which reflects something of his nature. Sport is not merely a source of something desirable—in which case it might be replaced by something else or be abstracted from so that we can concentrate on that which it produces—but is itself desirable. Because in sport man is enabled to identify himself with a community in a distinctive way and thereby become perfected, sport is a worthy topic for study. It is not merely a source, but an indispensable or unduplicable locus of certain values and offers *occasions for achievements central to man* (*PP* 5, p. 519, emphasis added).

Sport: Skill, Grace and Accuracy Through Discipline?

During the period of *Philosophy in Process* 5, which ends August 27, 1968, came much of the writing of *Sport*, whose Preface is dated March 1968. What is stressed as the motive in sporting activity is "Concern for Excellence" (*S*, ch. 1). Unless this theory of sport is to fall as does play (along with pleasure) to the objection that it is too vague and inadequately one-sided, it must be made clear exactly what sort of excellence is meant.

Skill is the acquired ability to accomplish an act with minimal waste and delay. Literally *it sets one apart*. Gracefulness is a quality adorning smooth, harmonious movement. It pleases. Accuracy, in contrast, is a willed arrival at a selected target. It is an achievement (*S*, p. 127, emphasis added).

A man can be accurate without having either skill or gracefulness. He might hit a target after having gone through wasteful motions, or after having jerked and twisted in the course of a preparation, aiming and moving to it. It is also possible for him to be skillful without being accurate or graceful . . . It is possible for him to be graceful without being skilled or accurate. His movements might be a delight to watch, but they may not be altogether appropriate to the task in hand, and may fail to get him where he wanted to be (*S*, pp. 127–28).

All three, accuracy, skill, and grace, can be combined in various ways and degrees. The athlete is then well coordinated . . . The ability is clearly evident in the bullfighter and the marksman. But it is always present; a good athlete is a well-coordinated one (*S*, p. 128).

Weiss is telling us that athletes may be born or develop with native strength, endurance, and speed, but other traits must be learned through discipline. Acquiring habits needs repetition.

Weiss distinguishes good judgment from skill, and he points out that the athlete may have one without the other. By "good judgment" Weiss means ability to "evaluate situations properly." To lack good judgment is to do ineffectively even what one does skillfully. "Again and again a hockey player may hit the putt [*sic* for "puck"] correctly,[8] only to have it countered by opponents whose movements he did not anticipate" (*S*, p. 90). What Weiss does not tell us is whether and how judgment also is learned, as is skill, through discipline.

Weiss invokes the name of Aristotle in calling attention to basic aptitude, without which "good judgment is beyond . . . reach" (*S*, p. 91). Similarly the whole process of athletic development is actualizing the potential. Herein lies Weiss's explanation of why young men (and we shall have to add, young women) endure the repetition, the frustration, the exhaustion (*S*, p. 48).

Discipline is the only way to make "clear what it is that men can possibly attain." The willingness to submit to discipline therefore stems from an individual's coming to recognize what can be elicited from the latent gift (*S*, p. 48).

Weiss asks more insistently than any philosopher of sport why athletes "submit themselves, often with enthusiasm, rarely with reluctance, to long periods of training." In asking the question Weiss specifies what he means by athletic discipline. Athletes do not "simply enjoy themselves." They endure fatigue, risk defeat, injury and finally failure. "Why?" (*S*, p. 18).

Weiss's answer, accounting for discipline, is complex. There are both individual and social factors, hence Weiss presents the individual explanation as a partial truth only.

Confidence and effectiveness seem to be gained when young men, under stern self-control, struggle with one another and the world beyond. Encounters which end in defeat often have a salutary effect on them: conceit is reduced, and judgment is sharpened. Although worsted, their efforts often leave them freed and purged. Young men apparently benefit from strenuous work; they seem to gain from being disciplined, and from being pushed to their limits. They must, it seems, live through tensions and crises before they can be at peace with themselves. The struggles they go through quiet their violence and structure their expressions to bring them into a vital relationship with their fellows. Athletics gives them a surplus of joy no matter what they do. Their failures and frustrations merely accentuate the inextinguishable glow that is theirs when they give themselves fully to a life of sport (*S*, p. 22).

Weiss's reservations about the "excess energy" theory are interesting. At the beginning of an athlete's career, it is true that he is restless and must "work off [his] energy in well-organized ways." It is a way to become focused. And when there is no longer this excess energy, sport occupies only spare time (*S*, p. 23).

The energy version of the discipline theory, it should be noted, appeals only to a material cause. Weiss's theory of discipline includes some final cause.

Other than the individual aspect there is the social context. Even if an athlete is not a team member, he is not an isolated individual. Weiss adduces a general desire to be with others, a need to play with others, and a competitive desire to meet the challenge of others (*S*, pp. 23–25). Exactly how men submit to discipline as a group he does not tell us.

The sharp contrast between sport that demands discipline and playing games that do not, is made clear.

He who refuses to take advice, to be redirected, or to learn special techniques, will end by 'playing at' sport instead of 'playing in' it. 'Playing at' occurs when one does not care which way things develop and end. But to 'play in' a game is to try to help determine its course and outcome. This usually requires that one first be willing to train and practice, guided by coaches who are knowledgeable and perceptive (*S*, p. 49).

Undisciplined sport may be relaxing, even when it is not excellent. "Relaxation is the art of avoiding an inclination in any particular direction." Whereas discipline demands ranking possible acts by a scale, relaxation comes when "possible acts [are] on a footing" (*S*, p. 69).

Philosophy in Process is valuable in context of the discipline theory of sport, showing how many other points were never included in *Sport*. The language of *Modes of Being* is applied to play and discipline. Just as *Sport* makes discipline the means to excellence so discipline is brought metaphysically under the Ideal.

When we try to see what such an activity as sport is trying to do we can use
. . . a kind of chart. Like every enterprise concerned with the realm of *paideia*
it is concerned with improving men, of helping them attain an excellence. It
must make him healthy (Actuality), self-disciplined, restrained (Ideal), adjusted (Existence) and organized, a man of power (Divine) (*PP* 1, pp. 466–
67).

Although discipline is man coming to terms with existence,

play is existence coming into its own rights, joining the Existence which lies
beyond, to make one cosmic in his rhythm and meaning. Taken in this way,
there is a component of play in everything we do, even toil and drudgery,
for we cannot help, when we act, meeting the rhythms of the external world
and sharing in this release (*PP* 1, p. 385).

Although discipline demands control and finishing whatever is engaged in, play allows "spontaneity and openness" (*PP* 1, p. 386).
Whereas sport leaves "a residuum in the score and in the memory
of the process," play leaves no residuum except a possible feeling of
health (*PP* 1, p. 386). Whereas sport is adjusting to existence, play is
existence but "a domain apart from the everyday world and the world
of nature." " . . . Play is the exercise of forging new connections; this
is also true of art. In work and craft and sport we get new connections
but this is not the purpose" (*PP* 1, p. 386). Weiss concludes this close-
grained analysis by calling our attention to discipline in art.

Like sport and games [art] has rules or techniques and can be pursued in
terms of an outcome desired. Like work it is arduous and occupied with
means, for the outcome is also the terminus and puts an end to the art as it
does to work. Like toil it involves much preliminary and isolated activities
of preparation—training, which is an important part of art learning, is in
good part toil. Like craftsmanship, it is occupied with having and using means
excellently (*PP* 1, p. 386).

The discipline theory of sport has direct bearing on the fascinating
problem of whether sports are arts.

If discipline is the essence of sport, then it follows that sports are
not arts, but crafts. Sports are crafts in the sense of "essentially a
technique or discipline, specifically craft in which the objective is
winning a contest . . ." (*PP* 1, p. 460). Sports are not arts in that "they
do not stress creativity, and have no way of revealing the meaning

of a world beyond" (*PP* 4, p. 459). The distinction drawn here would end the argument that the preponderant number of common characteristics shared by sports and arts bring the two families of performances under a common genus.[9]

That sport is essentially a technique is strongly defended by those who, like Weiss, observe the particular moves taught by coaches. Weiss is strongly influenced by the analogy between what coaches do and what a logician does in improving the conduct of inferential argument: break down the steps and examine each move.

Let us concentrate on the sequence of gripping, lifting, waiting, and swinging, which could be said to be the divisions that make sense in articulating what it is to swing at a ball with a bat. The pupil is first taught how to grip the bat. He is told to hold his fingers thus and so, to bend his body this way, etc. . . .

The central problem of learning something complex after we have mastered sessile moves is to turn the moves into mediators and conveyors of what one has in the beginning (*PP* 5, pp. 275–76).

Beyond this point what Weiss says about training begins to count against the discipline theory that sport is a mere craft. Artists are also taught moves. " . . . The teaching of art, music, and drama, offer close analogies of the way athletes are trained" (*PP* 5, p. 272). And what enables an athlete as an artist to do this is "a second step of learning." This is "a thrusting backward from the sessile moves to an external antecedent, 'wanting to do this excellently,' and a pointing to an end, having properly completed the act . . . " (*PP* 5, p. 277). Then sport is more than skill insofar as it is an "embodiment of the ideal in the shape of character." It is "somewhat analogous to the arts" (*PP* 5, p. 135).

A craft has immediate specific results, but an art has remote goals. To an extent training is concerned with immediately testable results, but coaches are also concerned with the heroic and noble (*PP* 3, p. 41). The excellence of the craftsman is in his work, but the excellence of the athlete is in himself: the athlete is "a maker who is a self-maker" (*PP* 5, p. 129).

Discipline with a practical aim is involved in any process of making or doing, and accounts for the craftsmanship of sport. Although discipline alone seemed initially to account for acquiring skill, some final causes, when introduced, challenge the sufficiency of the efficient cause. Discipline alone then leaves the final causes of the well-played game a total mystery. "Training-learning . . . need[s] an inten- tion. . . . " Before we pass from discipline to therapy which supplies health of body and society as ends, we can summarize the arguments Weiss supplies against the discipline theory.

1.   Although Weiss admits that he has been treating action piecemeal as a sum of moves, "it should be understood to be an organic act . . . " (*PP* 5, p. 280) of inference analogous to ath- letic moves and act. To walk is more than "a series of steps," and "requires a kind of emotional vitalization of what is occur- ring . . . " (*PP* 5, pp. 285–86).

2.   The performer in sports is not merely repeating the steps he has learned, but acting creatively in a new situation.

The traditional discipline theory neglects what is actually done: to view the sporting event as a project, which means to be "lured on" or "tensed toward the future" (*PP* 5, pp. 204–6).

3.   A third factor again makes sport closer to art than to craft. Although playing the game is "subject to the rules which define the sport," it "involves some spontaneity. . . . "

4.   A fourth factor neglected by discipline is relaxation in sport as in art.

Commitment makes one tense, relaxation makes one open, and resolution enables one to act. Manuals for sexual performance, for the making of art, for training in a sport, concentrate mainly on the different moves one must go through if the end is to be attained. But the end which calls out these moves is not that which an act, stretching over these moves, is aimed at. It is an end for being ready, or being well, or being efficient.
. . .
If one has an intent to love, or to appreciate a work of art, or to win a race, one cannot stop with the various moves . . . but must go on to engage in the act of loving, appreciating, or running as governed by the intended end. More often overlooked is the need to relax . . . One can become overanxious and not be able to perform well enough to reach the end; relaxation is an aspect of the situation out of which a well-turned act is . . . produced (*PP* 5, p. 296).

With one statement we make the transition to the next theory: "We concentrate on the mastery of moves with the implicit end [of being well] only so far as we are ill" (*PP* 5, p. 296).

Sport: Therapy of Mind-Body and of Society?

Some theorists who begin by considering a play theory conclude, as does Menninger, that "play's most important value is to relieve repressed aggressions.[10] Weiss tends to make the transition not so much from play as from training to therapy. Therapy here means "the art of correcting a disequilibrium between mind and body . . . " (S, p. 41). We may not be subsuming all of play and all of discipline under the goal of health, but health does provide an end to explain why the athlete accepts so much strenuous, fatiguing and painful discipline.

Many of the ancient Greek writers on sport were physicians, like Galen, and it seems common sense to say that one engages in sport for the sake of health.[11] Weiss goes beyond the hoary justification, "a sound mind in a sound body," by analyzing how balance is secured: either "by altering the vector [of mind], or, more usually, by adjusting the way in which the body functions until [it] follows the route that the vector provides" (S, p. 41).

To be healthy is to be at ease in oneself, in the situations in which one finds oneself, and in the work to which one has dedicated oneself. It is to be in possession of a full set of powers and agencies, to see things without distortion, and to utilize them without undue difficulty or waste (S, p. 97).

"Is not sport an instance of therapy?" (PP 1, p. 511). Other aspects of culture can also be viewed as instances of therapy, and sport then falls in place as one phase in the total development of man.

. . . To become the master of oneself one makes oneself into an instance of the Ideal; to express oneself with control, and thus to use energy one has deliberately, one practices and creates. The first leads to knowledge, the second to religion, the third to athletics, and the fourth to art (PP 5, p. 381).

Self-mastery is attractive in specific ways. Weiss recognizes a parallel between a glamorous woman and an athlete in glowing health. Both are attractive bodies. "The self-mastery is made evident in the way in which one can use the body to make it function excellently in overcoming nature, one's own insistent responses, or other men. The immediate appeal that glamorous women make to women, and sports to men "then might be summed up as strength" (PP 5, p. 259).

Weiss gives us a choice in interpreting strength: the Eastern "would insist on the primacy of non-worldly pursuits" but our Western Freudian "would surely insist on sex as more basic . . . " (*PP* 5, p. 259).

This is a very interesting line of inquiry. Great achievers of records in sport have engaged public acclaim. We have only now had documented how many times in a night Babe Ruth could score sexually.[12]

Weiss's *Sport* almost completely neglects sex, though he does canvass other attributes of good health. The athlete

presents himself, naked before the world, with his defenses down. [Although] he is readied in multiple ways . . . he is, for the moment, unprotected with respect to anything other than what he is expected to meet in the game. All energy, all alertness, he is also relaxed both as an individual and as a representative of all (*S*, p. 16).

The athlete, like Adam before the fall, is naked yet unashamed. He faces defeat with courage. "Why," asks Weiss, "do the young not turn to other things once they feel the weight of fatigue? Why are they willing to hover so long on the edge of a debilitating despair? Why do they persist once they have tasted the bile discharged by defeat?" (*S*, p. 20). The athlete is "gain[ing] in health; . . . through his participation in sport he is able to improve his overall power; he there inevitably learns how to overcome obstacles and how to meet the demands that sudden crises present" (*S*, p. 26). Weiss sees no clear evidence that the athlete "builds up a barrier against disease" or is longer lived. But he very likely has "learned the art of successfully getting on with [his] fellow man, at least with those who are on [his] team" (*S*, p. 26). Exactly how this is related to the athlete's strength, grace, assertiveness, "is not yet known. But the fact that many athletes think of themselves as being attractive seems beyond much question" (*S*, p. 26).

Other aspects of courage are the endurance and adaptability of the athlete. Is it that the athlete's "sensitivity threshold [is higher] than others?" Even if this is the case Weiss nevertheless contemplates "with awe" the heroic endurance of explorers, and others, and comments:

The winner of an endurance contest may merely have a higher sensitivity threshold than others have. He may have no pain where others suffer unspeakably . . . But we will still not be sure why it is he [who] continued in a given contest. Despite his pain, he may insist on continuing, or without pain, he may fight boredom, or fear, or even the honor of being successful, in order to be able to carry on after others have stopped (*S*, p. 120).

Adaptability marks the healthy athlete. He not merely repeats calisthenics, he uses his training more effectively in gymnastics. "A healthy man is able to be part of an endless number of situations (*S*, p. 73).

A more subtle benefit of athletic discipline is purgation of the bad emotions of despair or anger when athletes are defeated. "Encounters which end in defeat often have a salutary effect on them: conceit is reduced, and judgment is sharpened. Although worsted, their efforts often leave them freed and purged" (*S*, p. 22). The more common unfortunate emotion discussed as the object of therapy is aggression. If athletes "exhibit a native aggressiveness more evidently and effectively than" others, they are also in a situation where they are urged to kill their opponents. Does the physical expression serve as a fine outlet?" The game does not allow disastrous outcome.

What might have had serious consequences is thereby enabled, in athletics, not only to function without great injury to anyone, but with considerable benefit to him, the aggressor. Because he has allowed his aggressiveness a sublimated but full expression for a while, so the theory allows us to conclude, he emerges from his contest at once sobered and purged (*S*, p. 33).

Weiss is not happy with this theory of sport if it implies that aggression is the only dominant drive, albeit one to be purged.

Such a view does not take account of the fact that sports also involve co-operation, loyalty, and sacrifice, that they provide a test, give one a pleasure in winning, and allow for the expression of relief, joy, justice, courage, and judgment. It would be better I think to view sports as an effort to determine human limits, to find out who one is by being pitted against well-defined situations (*PP* 5, p. 135).

This is a clear move from therapy to agon, with a slight reservation that to be an athlete requires "some awareness of a benefit to the individual" (*PP* 5, p. 135).

Weiss attempts a summary of the benefits of sport to the individual. This is schematized according to the four modes of being. Sport "like every other enterprise concerned with the realm of *paideia*," helps man "attain an excellence. It must make him healthy (Actuality), self-disciplined, restrained (Ideal), adjusted (Existence) and organized, unified, a man of power (Divine)" (*PP* 1, pp. 466–67).

The problem of therapy, so stated, raises one final question about what excellence sport provides for the individual man. Does sport enable a man to be complete and integral? At different periods, different types of men are regarded as "complete." It is worth noticing that no past age, according to Weiss, has exalted the athlete. Does this mean that the future may bring an age when the athlete or sportsman is honored as the complete man?

In different periods, different types of lives were viewed as complete. The complete life for the Greek was that of the wise man; for the Romans, the political man; for the Medieval, the religious man; for the Renaissance, the artists; for the 'age of science,' the scientifically oriented man; for the Romantic, the imaginative man; for the nineteenth century, the cultured man; for today, the technically oriented man (*PP* 5, p. 166).

Could the athlete become, in some future age, what the philosopher and statesman, the saint and prophet, the creative artist, the liberally educated, and the engineer have been in these ages past? In interpreting Weiss's answer as denial, we are also saying that however therapeutic sport may be, it is no complete *Paideia*.

The only contemporary type Weiss considers a candidate is "the ethical man . . . if he could engage in acts of heroic proportions in multiple situations, and in such a way that the virtues of other kinds of lives would be captured or replaced" (*PP* 5, p. 167).

Surely Weiss is right that the coach is more concerned than is the ordinary teacher "with the heroic and the noble" (*PP* 3, p. 41).

In that disciplining he must now subjugate the heroic values which appealed to him before, make them have a new role inside a larger and richer world. And he must also take account of the seriousness of the role he assumes. No longer does he have it all under his control as the child does through fancy; no longer does he make it merely dramatic; he takes it seriously as actually involving him and his destiny (*PP* 3, pp. 41–42).

So far, we might try to make a case for the athlete as great, the complete man, in the sense of "the ethical man." But the athlete acts only within the restrictions of the game and not in "multiple situations." "To be sure, he lives in a limited artificial world of games . . . ."

The athlete is then a hero only for a period, and in the competitive situation in which he has status (*PP* 3, p. 42).

There "is always the ideal of becoming complete men." Yet for athletes this ideal is a qualified one: "complete men who have reached the limits of physical achievement." Yet we might pause to ask whether the meaning a "complete man" is not one who has reached the limits of achievement? (*S*, p. 141).

If Weiss qualifies the completeness of the athlete's life, does Weiss then conclude that the athlete "lives only a partial life?" It would seem to follow logically and also to fit what Weiss means by "a partial life." The world of sport is one of the "law-abiding occurrences" within which we play a game.

If we play a game, there are rules that determine what must be done after what. Despite the passivity of the individual who fits, he is not entirely subject to the conditions; instead he allows himself to be *governed only in part, leaving the rest of him uncommitted*, out of gear. He then *lives only a partial life* as one who is *accepting some role*, as a policeman or a waiter might, keeping the rest of himself in abeyance (*PP* 5, p. 200, emphasis added).

The athlete "fits some condition" and is therefore "partial," yet because he is purposive rather than merely passive, he "adopts that condition [and] makes it his own." He may then not merely allow part of himself "not to become involved" he "may alter the condition so that it becomes the very structure of his activity" (*PP* 5, p. 200).

How is it possible for the athlete to be himself and not a mere puppet or pawn? Weiss's answer is that the athlete is so "involved with the rules" that he is "himself over against everything else" (*PP* 5, p. 398). If it is generally true that "we express what we are in and through our bodies," this must be most true of performances designed to express a life-style or a self (*PP* 5, p. 147).

The athlete unites body and mind in all the common ways, through control, through will, through emotions, and through such virtues as courage and temperance, through habituation manifested in efficiency, grace, and craftsmanship. Weiss clearly thinks of the perfect athlete as the modern illustration of the Platonic and Aristotelian ideal (*PP* 5, pp. 156–57).

The athlete is, produces, and expresses all these forms of union. But his primary stress is on the conjunction of control with skill, and thus with the unification of mind and body through an imposition of mind and a submission of the body. He is Plato's state writ small, and thus, in Aristotle's terms, the embodiment of justice and temperance, the virtues where each part does its proper task, and the body is willed to be and is willingly subordinate to the mind—once we free the virtue of temperance from the Aristotelian association of it with pleasure of some kind (PP 5, p. 157).

Perhaps few athletes know the "project in back of the mind of the trainer" and this therapeutic goal is "an exteriorly defined project for the athletes" (PP 5, p. 218).

The coach is somewhat like a psychiatrist. This must be true if sport is a kind of therapy, comparable in this respect to the cure of souls (PP 5, pp. 242–44).

Psychiatrists and coaches have a somewhat common method. They try to combine firmness with kindness, direction with an encouragement to be free, sympathy with criticism. The coaches, however, have three advantages: their clients come to them confident rather than in despair; the objective to be attained is fairly clear; and there are well-defined tests to determine whether progress has been made (PP 5, p. 242).

The coach wants his charges to achieve a degree of excellence, and perhaps to win in some contest. He learns whether or not they have achieved the excellence by making them face objective tests, often in competition with others . . . The coach [in contrast to the therapist] does not inquire into the question of the degree of comfort which his charges may feel . . . (PP 5, pp. 242–43).

Coaches [again unlike therapists who may prepare clients for undesirable societies] prepare their charges . . . for contests which the vast body of mankind would approve, and in any case which are approved by those who belong to other political and social wholes (PP 5, p. 243).

We have then two stages of help: there is the help to get men to function in the normal ways . . . and there is the help to get them to function in ways which perfect themselves and others. Coaches get men who come for the second stage, whereas psychotherapists get them to come for the first stage. But is the first stage different in principle from the second? I think not (PP 5, p. 243).

In respect to sport as therapy, as with sport as play and sport as discipline, Weiss is a dialectician. He makes out the best persuasive case in the face of difficulties. One of the difficulties is that sport is a testing of human limits and in providing tests gives the pleasure of winning. We are moved dialectically to examine agon.

Sport: Agon or Contest in Which Men Test Themselves?

Sport is essentially men testing themselves and usually it is a contest or men testing themselves against one another. The first aspect is individual and the second, with the stress on "con," with, is social (*S*, pp. 25, 100).

Is agon the clue to the desire and dedication of the athlete? Is it this specific kind of excellence that explains the phenomena of sport? Is this fourth theory demonstrably superior, if we pit theory against theory, to play, discipline, and therapy?

We have already seen argued against the play theory that there is no necessary place in it for the athlete, one who strives for the prize of victory. Recreation, yes, but dedication, no. And if therapy is considered, if the body and mind can be harmonized without the stress under which men may break, why should men run the risk of disintegration? Discipline comes closer, but training in a skill is not preparation for contest. "The craftsman . . . does not as a rule face crises" (*PP* 5, p. 129). Yet men train, and accept discipline for some purpose never stated in a theory of learning skill, grace, and accuracy. The answer must lie in agon.

Men test themselves in many particular sports which fall under agon. In the "game" as well as the "contest" unqualified, there is "The Urge to Win." Chapter 11 of *Sport* explains why the Greek background induces us to say of athletes, following the ancient language, that they strive for a prize, the "athlon."

There are three moments in the analysis of sport as agon: for the individual there is the discovery of his *limits*, socially there is the *challenge* between contestants, and for humanity in the context of the modes of being there is *tragedy*. By developing agon in this way we can grasp why the metaphysician Weiss gives the place of honor among theories to agon. It is as agon that sport is closest to dramatic art, and as art is at least semi-religious and also accordingly "revelatory of reality" (*PP* 5, p. 512).

1.   *Limits*. It is because sport is agonistic that it contributes valuable kinds of knowledge to the individual who puts himself to the test. Not only does the athlete discover whether he can break some record, but also comes to know his limits (*PP* 5, p. 135).

2.   *Challenge*. One of the finest features of Weiss's theory of

agon is the analysis of the thirty kinds of challenge, with the suggestion that each sport includes different factors to different degrees (*PP* 5, pp. 375–76).

"Challenge" is so general a category that all aspects of culture fall under it (*PP* 5, pp. 151–52).

Hence sport is a limited mode of challenge.

The *athlete seems to take account only of the challenges of body, sex, and nature*, and then primarily as obstacles or conditions defining what he is to do in order to test himself maximally. The *rebel sees society as a challenge*, and the religious thinker, and perhaps the artist and the philosopher, sees mankind as a challenge. *Mankind is also a challenge for the mystic* and the Eastern religious thinker (*PP* 5, p. 152).

3.   *Tragedy*. "Sports are tragic (in something like the classical sense applied to drama) because they involve a basic challenge to be met seriously." This is an aspect of the agon theory, quite the opposite to play theory. "Entertainment is comic in something like the classical sense, for it seeks to please" (*PP* 5, p. 140). We might ask how discipline and therapy fit into the modes of drama. Perhaps discipline is serious, but without the drama of challenge, and the chance of loss or defeat. Perhaps therapy is pleasing in its kindliness and steadiness, but without the drama of reversals it cannot compare with agon.

The agon theory alone brings out the tragic character of sport. It is only when there is an athletic contest with the possibility of victory for one side that there must be defeat for the other.

. . . Defeat [is] debilitating [and] humiliating . . . Yet something good comes out of it. A game is, after all, in between a drama and a common event. It has the artificiality, the conventionality, the detached separated nature of a drama, but it has the vital struggle, the actual effort to bring about some unpredictable result, which is characteristic of ordinary affairs. *A defeat is in between the tragedies which are to be found in both.*

The tragedy in a drama is self-induced, it portrays what it means for a vital value to be lost, but it itself does not exhibit such a loss of value. A tragedy in real life is open-ended; it involves a real loss of value, but in a setting filled with irrelevant details. The drama highlights the loss, but does not exhibit it; in real life we exhibit it, but rarely in a focused way. In the game, on the other hand, value is lost, as in daily life, but in a context where irrelevancies are excluded (*PP* 5, pp. 267–68, emphasis added).

The same point is made specific in the case of bullfighting, with stress on the marks of art in sport:

Bull-fighting is so *cut away from play, is so serious in its import and so big with ominous, adumbrated meaning* that it seems to be an art. Is it perhaps the case that all sports have a kind of make-believe about them, so that one does *not really struggle with nature but only makes preliminary* stabs at it under conditions which preclude her full activity? (*PP* 1, p. 467).

Conclusion: Weiss's Achievement

Has Weiss achieved a philosophy of sport? One might conclude that he has done better than give us a philosophy of sport, by providing us four philosophies of sport. We owe much to Weiss for having expounded play, discipline, therapy and agon as well as the proponents of each of these four theories. Yet what Weiss achieves is more than an overview of types, for he stresses not only the advantages but the defects of each theory. By exploring the perspectives together, we get then from Weiss a dialectical survey of possible philosophies. This is a unique contribution and surpasses by far his predecessors.

Each of the four theories might be broken down into subtheories, for there are types of types, as we referred under therapy to Jungian, Freudian, etc., each of which might reveal interesting aspects of sport that might otherwise go unnoticed. Nor would it be correct to claim, however much four fits in well with Weiss's fourfold metaphysics, that there are only four general types. What we have done is typical of theories of culture and religion, namely to stress individual motivation. Weiss is well aware of social relations and refers to men "who are exceptional in interaction, and others who are excellent team-players." Men are not merely "individuals who function well by themselves" (*PP* 5, p. 522). Weiss is sensitive also to the relations between performers and spectators. Whether we can reduce whatever needs saying about sport as social to play, discipline, therapy and agon must remain problematic until we have made further inquiry.

Within the dialectical development of Weiss's writings in *Philosophy in Process* is there any advance beyond *Sport?* Has Weiss his own distinctive philosophy of sport with which we can conclude? Although Weiss's writings on art and his *Sport* failed to resolve the issue of whether the sports are performing arts, and left us with thesis and antithesis, it seems that we can present from *Philosophy in Process* a positive synthesis. Not that Weiss has presented his position formally. Rather it could be formalized from his specific case of bullfighting.

Since we have seen in detail what Weiss says of the bullfight (above, "Tragedy") we need here only make explicit why this is important.

Are there aspects of play in the bullfight? Yes, there are rituals from the start to finish, the procession, the salute to the governor, the final award of the tail, etc., and these Weiss calls "artificial" and "conventional." We are delighted to watch them when they have been well learned and performed with grace. If these were all, we should be merely entertained. But there is the kind of seriousness that goes beyond mere play, so we cannot wholly subsume the bullfight under play.

Are there aspects of discipline in the bullfight? Certainly the judgment of the matador and his skill in executing movements are slowly acquired by submitting the first clumsy jerks to judgment and re-learning. But it is not the whole of bullfighting, for there is the inner courage that evokes our sympathetic identification with the bullfighter.

Are there aspects of therapy in the bullfight? Again, we must respond that the meaning of the fight, man facing death, would not be complete without courage. As in all sport that involves agon, there is victory and must be defeat. As Weiss says of all athletes, "the possibility of defeat . . . does not defeat them" (above, from *PP* 5, pp. 267–68).

Are there aspects of agon in the bullfight? Surely this theory is more adequate to the essence of man facing the bull in the ring in which there is struggle for victory. But is there something more, as we found with the play, discipline and therapy theories?

What is more than all four of the theories found in the bullfight? The two elements are transcendence and sublime grace, the very aspects that make sport religious and artistic. Sometimes Weiss qualifies the transcendent and artistic qualities of sport generally but

we find in the bull-fight . . . that, despite its cushioned or civilized setting, there is a transcendence of these limits in the very fact that death is being met. To meet only the demands of nature, to see what one can do with its material is one thing; to deal with her as the very locus of death . . . seems to force sport into another dimension. Or should we say that it is *necessary for an art to have the ominous* only within a controlled make-believe, and that a sport either A] does not have the ominous at all which is the case when it is artificial, and B] *does not remain within the realm of the make-believe but struggles with fundamental realities* and is so far like work?

Is it not the case that we can escape from work in two directions? *We can enhance it through gracefulness, in the mastery of a craft,* and *we can ennoble it by focusing on the greatness of the problem or the nobility of its struggle.* The bull-fight combines these two. Though its result does have something of the ominous within it, it is not yet an art. An art requires the ominous in a result, which is in itself good in and of itself, and not because of the magnitude of what is being confronted (*PP* 1, p. 467, emphasis added).

Weiss clarifies his judgment of the superiority of art to sport, at least when we consider the absorption in play, one aspect of sport, and the absorption in art. In the case of art there is the "work itself as a kind of icon for a reality beyond itself which it enables us to iconize, just so far as it is enjoyed by itself. In the case of play we have merely a withdrawal from the world which allows us to be open to what else there be. Play then is not revelatory in the way art is; it is revelatory in the sense in which faith is—the absorption in the content makes evident that there is something transcendent, without telling us the nature of that transcendent reality" (*PP* 5, p. 550).

Sport could be revelatory, if not of existence, then of human actuality. " . . . The player competes with nature, either directly or indirectly, and cannot so far be said to represent it. But he could be said to represent the Being of Actuality, which he then tries to exhibit as the Being which makes all men equal and which places them over against the rest of the space-time world" (*PP* 5, p. 310).

Then, although Weiss sometimes qualifies sport as only quasi-religious or quasi-artistic, he has found in sport the exhibition of some transcendence, albeit human, but akin to "exhibiting an excellence that transcends them" (*PP* 5, p. 308).

Although generally the excellence of sport is only the limited kind Weiss calls "style," and this is merely skill exhibited "in and through his bodily functions under the influence of good judgment and knowledge," this is only one first stage (*PP* 5, pp. 568–69, 514). A game or event may go through three further stages. The fourth of these is marked by "the achievement of a union with the spectators to constitute for a moment a single totality having a semireligious tonality, where this is understood to involve an increase in intimacy" (*PP* 5, p. 514).

Let this be the last point about transcendence discovered through sport. Although the situation of opposing teams is one of "antagonisms, chaos, conflicts, and even acts of destruction and violence" yet it is "one in which all are enriched by becoming more intimately and sympathetically united with one another" (*PP* 5, p. 515) and in this quality Weiss reminds us of the union of man and woman in love, of great leaders who raise their institutions to a new and high level of expectation, as Pope John became a great leader of the church (*PP* 5, p. 207).

Ten

Robert Castiglione

The Metaphysics of Name and Address: Weiss's Answer to Kant and Frege

This essay focuses on "What is naming and what is the logical status of singular statements employed in naming?" In the twentieth century, the issue has captured the attention of philosopher-logicians including Frege, Peirce, Russell, Whitehead, Carnap, Weiss, Moore, Austin, Searle, Hintikka, Sellars, Prior, and Strawson. The contention of this inquiry is threefold: (1) Weiss's conception of names and the notion of evidence on which it is based clarify the problems that have arisen in the past century; (2) his reflections allow us to position the work of Frege within the larger context of logical investigation; and (3) his analysis of the kinds of proper names ultimately resolves the Kantian dilemma regarding metaphysical speculation.[1]

Kant's Dictum and Frege's Dilemma

Kant's statement in the *Critique of Pure Reason* regarding the manner in which logicians have treated singular judgments and his explanation of that treatment lay the base for much of the confusion that has permeated logical investigations since that time. He states that, although the character of singular judgments (naming statements) differs epistemically from general judgments, they can be treated, from the logician's standpoint, as if they were general judgments. His reasons for accepting this practice of logicians are clear and at first sight convincing. First, since such judgments have "no extension at all," the predicates of su h judgments apply to the whole of the subject, not "to part only of that which is contained in the concept of the subject." Second, this relation of predicate to subject in singular judgments makes them conformable, from a logician's standpoint, to

188

analysis as universal propositions; "the predicate [of such singular judgments] is valid of that concept, without any exception, just as if it were a general concept and had an extension to the whole of which the predicate applied."[2]

Having subsumed singular judgments under the rules for general judgments, Kant makes it possible for later philosophers to apply his conceptions of analytic and synthetic necessity to singular judgments. According to Kant, a predicate stands in relation to the subject in one of two ways: "Either the predicate B belongs to the subject A, as something which is (covertly) contained in the concept A; or B lies outside the concept A, although it does indeed stand in connection with it."[3]

Kant's claims in this regard are of concern not only to those philosophers interested in the history of metaphysical speculation and critical analysis, but also to those whose own work is rooted in the generation and understanding of the powerful tools of logical analysis found in Frege's work. Frege accepted the results that follow from Kant's claim. His work, "On Sense and Nominatum,"[4] which has had such a decisive influence upon nonmathematical philosophy in the twentieth century, turns upon Kant's distinction between analytic and synthetic judgments. In that essay, Frege claims—following Kant— that we can never be sure if an expression that has sense, has any designation in fact; often although there is a sense to an expression, there is no corresponding nominatum, *e.g.*, the case of "the heavenly body which has greatest distance from the earth." In order to resolve this issue of the existence of nominata, Frege makes two moves: one, he identifies the nominatum of sentences with "truth-value" (the circumstance of its being true or false); two, he distinguishes between direct positing of nominata and indirect references to nominata. This notion of the indirect nominata, which for Frege is a direct reference to the customary meanings of words, circumvents the problem of whether or not all references to individuals have an existential valence.

To this point, nothing in Frege's analysis is problematic, if his proposals and distinctions are considered merely in terms of the light that they throw upon the world and the behavior of the beings within it. Even his claim that the identification of nominatum and truth-value entails that "all true sentences have the same nominatum, and likewise all false ones" is easily recognized to be not a warranted metaphysical claim but a stipulation that "the True" (and likewise "the False") prescind from any explicit designation of domains within the world. That prescinding has not been defended by Frege in his essay, but if it is only a strategy of inquiry, it does not have to be defended. However, a related problem emerges from Frege's analysis.

The problem arises when Frege maintains that language does what it ought not to do. Language allows us to suppose the existence of entities whose being is connected with the being of other entities, but language does not provide us with evidences that are detachable from the judgments forming the bases of the propositions, detachable asserta that Frege believes we need:

It is to be demanded that in a logically perfect language (logical symbolism) every expression constructed as a proper name in a grammatically correct manner out of already introduced symbols, in fact designate an object; and that no symbol be introduced as a proper name without assurance that it have a nominatum . . . then it will be seen that whether a proper name has a nominatum can never depend upon the truth of a proposition.[5]

If no detachable asserta are found within a proposition, then the truth conditions necessary for a judgment to be made are incapable of further analysis. An extensional logic reaches a point beyond which it cannot go. However, if nominata are yoked to other nominata within the propositions of our language—as there most certainly are—that language is not a satisfactory instrument for investigating or even declaring what exists within the world around us. Frege wants assurance that the language he uses will not allow him to misconstrue the world which the names in that language make available to him. He does not want a naming-language that allows him to make judgments about the world without also showing him the isolate, individual warrants for those judgments. The assurance of a nominatum, whether the True or the False, is the guarantee that the content from which one infers contains no conjectural elements; first, no indeterminate designators from which two inconsistent propositions might be inferred and second, no noninstantiated content masquerading under a simple or complex name.

The path of twentieth-century philosophy originates in Frege's concern with the assurance of a nominatum, which is for Frege a prerequisite to the warranted acceptance of the truths of propositions because in certain cases—cases where the meaning of a description in a subordinate clause adheres to the assertion of a nominatum, or where two descriptions are yoked or infect each other—the asserta cannot be detached from a tissue of propositions. Where the inter-changeability of truth-values is an issue, these adherent, or yoked, or infectious meanings render the nature of the designation in propositions problematic. The rules for extensional logics, as Frege and those following his analysis presume, demand that the meanings be detachable in order that the designations can be verified in the world independent of the use of that language.

Quine's notion of the bound variable and his own prescriptions regarding language are drawn from one such interpretation of Frege:

The use of alleged names is no criterion, for we can repudiate their namehood at the drop of a hat, unless the assumption of a corresponding entity can be spotted in the things we affirm in terms of bound variables. Names are, in fact, altogether immaterial to the ontological issue, for I have shown in connection with "Pegasus" and "pegasize," that names can be converted to descriptions, and Russell has shown that descriptions can be eliminated.[6]

The problem with Quine's interpretation of the functioning of names lies in the fact that he presumes that the activity of naming relates one domain (that of signs) to a presumably alien domain (that of physical individuals or parts of individuals).[7] The existence of physical individuals is obviously not dependent on language, but the presumed naming relation between names and physical individuals is not the only appropriate relationship between a name and its designation. On Frege's view (and by extension, on Quine's) language must be so syntactically controlled that only certain detachable designators would fulfill a semantic function. However, on this view language is construed as a valve that operates in as exclusive fashion either fully open (existentially) or fully closed (hypothetically). It would be more appropriate to consider language as functioning like a membrane, opening out on the world that surrounds, and allowing the world to permeate it.

This is the exact situation in which Kant left logicians when he prescinded from the epistemic import of singular judgments in order to subsume them under the category of general judgments. Neither Frege nor Quine can get back from singular judgments what they eliminated in their first precisions; for, as Kant recognized, a singular judgment (a naming-statement) "not only according to its own inner validity, but as knowledge in general, according to its quantity in comparison with other knowledge, is certainly different from general judgments."[8] We must go beyond both Frege and Kant in order to understand why each leaves us where he does.

With Weiss, in opposition to Frege, we must recognize that some expressions, as they are used in discourse, do not function simply as signs that point "to some external but independent reality as [their] counterpart" (*BAA*, pp. 92–93), but function also as symbols that "are involved with what they symbolize, not because they organize these, or produce them, or control them, but because they are appearances, rooted in what they symbolize" (*BAA*, p. 92). Designation alone is insufficient to enable us to understand how a living language functions, not only in poetry and daily human commerce, but also in our attempts to communicate our appreciation of the importance of logic, mathematics, and science. The symbolic import of these investigations cannot be understood apart from a language that participates in the reality of the world which these investigations illuminate.

We must also go beyond Kant and affirm with Weiss that in those situations where we are provoked to search beneath the appearances of the individuals that surround us in our world, we reach toward a depth where we cannot point to an other, but must look to the whole to give us a perspective upon the part. Where we are concerned with the purpose of birth and death, of health and illness, of friendship and loneliness, we use names quite differently than in our commerce with the world of actualities. When we speak of final things, the "outcome of the use of such proper names is verified, not by looking to an alien world to see if what was in mind somehow had a duplicate there, but by noting how the name gains intensive meaning, depth, and emotional weight when it is in fact used" (*BAA*, p. 120). For Weiss we can both name what we know and know what we name, without presuming that either activity can do without an active, imaginative penetration of the world that surrounds and permeates our existence.

Weiss's Conception of Names and of Evidence

Weiss distinguishes himself from the majority of contemporary logicians when he denies that the principle of substitutivity and the detachable asserta of extensional logical analysis are the bases from which a proper understanding of inferences and of names derive. In a sustained attempt to respond both to the Kantian critique of metaphysics and to the Fregean reduction of logic to one of its branches, Weiss claims that

a precise logical notation will distinguish φ -a, which is an intensional expression, brooking no divisions and no generalizations, from φ a (*i.e.*, a is φ 'd) to which it refers and which allows for generalization and substitutions, and from (φ a), the unitary entity that allows us to confront an object, φ a (*FC*, p. 78).

Weiss offers four conceptions where contemporary logicians, following Frege, offer one explicitly and conflate two implicitly. Both Frege and Weiss recognize that φ a allows for generalization and substitutions and that *a* is an individual entity stripped of its predicates and liable to substitution by a variable *x* . Weiss also recognizes, following Peirce, that φ may be construed as a variable, where the individual entity is viewed as the constant and the predicates applied to it are construed as variables.[9] This difference between Weiss and Frege remains insignificant as long as the functions and variables secured by abstraction are conceived as detachable from each other, *i.e.*, where the subject(s) and predicate(s) are construed simply extensionally. However, when the possibility of a predicational class is interpreted intensionally, *i.e.*, as adhering to a given individual, then the differences between Weiss's view and Frege's become most evident.

Frege distinguished between the entities to which judgments were referred and the nominata designated in sentences; as soon as he had distinguished between the objects of judgments and defined nominata as the conditions under which sentences are true or false, however, he conflated these two: " . . . in every judgment—no matter how obvious—a step is made from the level of propositions to the level of the nominata (the objective facts)."[10] Weiss, however, proposes to maintain the distinction between "nominata," that is, the object of the proposition φ a (the object as it appears to us, where appearance is construed in a wide sense to include not only sensory qualities but also the meanings that are used in the articulation of the presence of entities) and the unitary entity (φ a) that allows us to confront the object. That unitary entity (φ a) includes not only those we address when we speak (our listeners), but also what we are speaking about to our listeners; it is also not subject to the distinction of subject and predicate as detachable elements that we offer in the formulation of our propositions in extensional logic. The unitary entities form the tissue of the world to which our discourse ordinarily refers, but Frege's

logic provides no index of the differences between the separable functions and values within a logic and the organic interconnection of
functions within such unitary entities. Where the organic interconnection of functions within unitary entities is the focus of our discourse, we speak intensionally, and the connection of predicate and
subject, between "function" and "value," is an intimate one "brooking no divisions and generalizations" (*FC*, p. 78).

Allowing the reader to suppose that Frege was not aware of these
intensional expressions that allowed no divisions or generalizations
would be unfair. These are precisely the cases where Frege believed
that language was deficient, where language allowed for the articulation of yoked assertions, where the designations of clauses within
propositions (or of multiple propositions) could not be shorn from
one another without loss of the meanings of those propositions. The
proposition beginning with the phrase "he who," which resisted
Frege's analysis into separable nominata because it contained designations that were adhesively related in ordinary discourse, *e.g.*, "He
who discovered the elliptical shape of the planetary orbits, died in
misery," is on Weiss's view an intensional expression that ought not
to be interpreted in terms of a bare subject, *i.e.*, as an "it" to which
the predicates "discovered the elliptical shape of the planetary orbits"
and "died in misery" could be applied. The proposition is in fact a
name, an adherent name, that refers to a historical object that we
come to know about in a variety of ways (each extensionally analyz-
able into φ a's), but which ways are rooted in a unitary entity, *i.e.*,
the man Kepler. When we use an expression such as "he who," it is
not the indeterminate character of our address that is at issue but the
pregnant possibilities of a language that allows its use as evidence of
the existence of such unitary entities. According to Frege, " . . . it is
a defect of languages that expressions are possible within them, which,
in their grammatical form, seemingly determined to designate an
object, nevertheless do not fulfill this condition in special cases; because this depends on the truth of the sentence."[11] Frege recognizes
that the two senses, *i.e.*, "discoverer of the elliptical shape of the
planetary orbits" and "one who died in misery," are yoked in a way
that does not allow us to tear them apart without loss. He would not
have been content with the maneuver of adding an identity operator
in the formulation to make up the difference because it was precisely
the issue of "identity" that his analysis of sense and nominata (both
direct and indirect) was to explicate. To accept the addition of an

identity operator as an explication of the notion of identity is to ignore the issue rather than to resolve it.

Weiss recognizes that such a proposition cannot be explicated in this way. Instead of ignoring the issue, he proposes that where such adherent names are operative, the nature of the individual, who is the subject of such yoked claims, can be explicated in terms of names that are drawn from our knowledge of the possibilities that are available to individuals of certain kinds. We must conceive of the range of qualities that are available to individuals of differing kinds and of the tissue of interconnections that relate certain domains of qualities to others. In Weiss's terms, to explicate the proposition that caused Frege difficulty, we must first recognize (as Frege does) the domains of individuals to which both "dying in misery" (mortality) and "discovering elliptical orbits" (mathematical mentality) are appropriate. These predicates are for Weiss "honorific names." Obviously chimpanzees are liable to both mortality and mentality but not to "mathematical mentality" of the sort required in this instance. Yet to proceed only this far is to have fallen too far short of the goal of explicating the sense of the "he who" proposition. What is needed is a way of investigating the overlapping domains of "mortality" and "mathematical mentality," i.e., of proceeding within those portions of the world where human beings die in misery and think abstractly.

We do this not simply by considering "meanings" shorn of their existential import but by asking ourselves who dies in misery and who thinks abstractly. We scour our memories for instances in life and literature where both "meanings" have been instanced, but we do not reject the possibility for lack of an instance. Instead, we conceive of the interconnections that exist among such meanings in the lives of our contemporaries and our predecessors. We consider that such a name as "discoverer of elliptical orbits who died in misery" was realized by some one human being at some time. Such consideration entails the use of evidence, i.e., reflecting upon historical events and following the connections within human life. But the evidence we use is not that which flows from the predicates we believe appropriate to human subjects; we have to go from a knowledge of "discover," of "elliptical orbits," of "death," and of "misery" as possibilities separable from one another, to the real possibility of their actualization—their convergence—in one or more than one entity. That convergence Weiss calls the use of a quasi-honorific name: a name drawn from the recognition that powers operative within the spatiotemporal world are liable to intersection within the activities of various kinds of individuals.

In the example at hand, the "he who" proposition functions as a hypothesis, a question put to the world; whether there could be one being that had a body, a sensitivity liable to the specter of loneliness, the social station that left him uncared for, and a mind capable of formulating the inferences entailed by spherical trigonometry. Each of these is a real possibility, a body, a sensitivity, a social role, and a mind; whether there ever was or would be a being who instanced all four of these possibilities is a question that only investigation could answer. But the explication of their interconnection within the world is accomplished every day and cannot be left without an appropriate theoretical base, an intensional logic which recognizes how these meanings are yoked. According to Weiss, when we examine a proposition in its unity, we are led to replace the "intensions" we find there by "quasi-honorific names." Each name designates an object as "a bounded portion of an indefinitely large domain of truths or knowledge . . ." (*FC*, p. 78). These domains are specified by who I am, by how familiar I am with the investigations of other men and women, by what I have experienced and remember, by what I imagine and consider possible or probable. Each specification operates under the aegis of an ideal that I consider pertinent to the situation at hand. Were it not for that ideal, *e.g.*, my conception of the kind of person who knows spherical trigonometry, I would have no way to connect the "facts" that I review in my attempt to determine whether the being who understands elliptical orbits of planets can die in misery; and when confronted with evidence for the existence of such mentality, I would have no way to connect it with such sensitivity and social station. Those connections are made "privately," but they are operative in the common world. Unlike the individual objects that too often form the base for the examination of "naming"—objects that are both public and common—the entities that are essential in the formulation of an intensional logic are common yet private; they are the entities that are operative values in the commerce of individuals and they function under the aegis of the ideals that yoke them in the activities we call inferences.

Inferences and Infectious Designation

A second quite significant domain where Frege finds that the detachable warrants for the presence of a nominatum are not available lies in conditional sentences that, according to Frege, contain more basic propositions than sentences. In such a case the sentence must be translated into an inferential structure in which the constituent propositions of the inferential pattern contain designators yoked infectiously to one another. Frege considers the case of the causal conditional proposition, "Since ice is specifically lighter than water, it floats on water."[12] He analyzes it into three propositions, which, as he notes, "do not correspond one-to-one to the clauses":

1. Ice is specifically lighter than water;
2. If something is specifically lighter than water, it floats on water; and
3. Ice floats on water.

It is to Frege's credit as a philosopher that he admits that his translation of the causal conditional into this inference pattern does not correspond in any clear-cut manner to the original claim, and, consequently, that his stipulations regarding nominata—that their warrants be derived from detachable asserta within a compound proposition and not from the truth of the compound as a whole—do not hold in this case. Inferential activity, as classically explained, is rooted in this difficulty—that I, following Weiss's usage, have called "infectious designation": " . . . the sense of a part of the clause may simultaneously be a constituent of another proposition which, together with the sense expressed in the dependent clause, amounts to the total sense of the main and the dependent clause."[13]

What Frege discovered was the dependence of extensional logical propositions, e.g., in the argument sketched above, upon senses derived from intensional expressions, i.e., the causal conditional. He could not handle this because he did not construe the "since-clause" of the sentence as the explanans in a process of discovery. If he had, he would have recognized it as a meaningful conclusion of an evidencing activity that exhibited an inferential pattern. He presumed that the proposition "Ice is specifically lighter than water" was the premise of the inferential structure implied in the causal conditional "Since ice is specifically lighter than water, it floats on water," and he drew from that causal conditional the leading principle "If something is specifically lighter than water, it floats on water." But this is to mistake completely the very meaning of "since" in this sentence; here "since" means "because" and, when so interpreted, the inferential pattern can be recognized as precisely the reverse of that proposed by Frege.

The premise of the evidencing process is "Ice floats on water." The principle that one looks for is derived from an investigation that utilizes the fact indicated in this proposition as evidence and searches for what is being evidenced; that principle will form the answer to the question, "If ice floats on water, then what is the relation between ice and water which accounts for this behavior?" The questioning in this case is itself evidence of the belief of the investigator, *viz*, that such behavior of ice is part of an encompassing pattern, or of rules operative not only between ice and water, but also between wood and water, pumice and water, seaweed and water, and dead fish and water. In Weiss's terms, the investigation of the evidence is based upon the belief that the "exhibitions of actualities are subject to an all-embracing Context with which they consitute a single set of appearances" (*FC*, p. 74).

Without presuming to narrate the actual course of the discovery of the notion of specific gravity, it is still possible to recognize that the inferential process (as a whole and to hindsight) took the form:

1. Ice floats on water;
2. If something floats on water, it is specifically lighter than water; and
3. Ice is specifically lighter than water.

When interpreted in this way, the actual discovery of the causal condition is distorted. The rule at (2) was discovered and not, as the form of the inferential pattern might lead us to believe, given beforehand. It results from a tissue of empirical generalizations on buoyancy united in a theory of density of fluids. But as the pattern is exemplified here, it does *not* prescind from the evidencing relation that exists between (a) "floating on water" and (b) "having a specific gravity lighter than water." The evidence is (a) and (b) is what is evidenced.

Frege's prescinding from the activity of evidencing and his attempt to translate the conditional proposition in terms of detachable asserta made it impossible for him to recognize that there was a very significant nominatum elucidated in the explanatory proposition, "Since ice is specifically lighter than water, it floats on water." For Weiss, the use of the evidence contained in a claim like the one "Ice floats on water" presumes that the evidence is freed from an involvement with one type of reality and recognized as already involved with another type of reality (*FC*, p. 79). To begin to discover the conception of "specific gravity" within the interlocked appearances of ice and water, "floating" must be focused upon and "floating" occurs not only on the water but also on a wide variety of other kinds of fluid media. We take up what had served as a predicate and use it as a name for what is evidenced—knowing that it is not enough simply to speak of a power or capacity that some media have to "hold up" others (*FC*, p. 75). We have to work to move from the domain of floating objects and their media to what is common to all of these objects and media. We must move from "floating" to "density." (This conceptual move is much easier to make after a creative mind has disclosed their connection.) To dislodge "floating" in this way is to name "the manner in which actualities are objectively connected," while at the same time interconnecting "the names of those actualities, hopefully in a concurrent way" (*FC*, p. 74).

When we have done this, we have moved beyond a consideration of isolate nominata and detachable asserta and have begun to explore the tissue of the context within which the individuals in our experience, and those not experienced by us, must move and have their being. We have begun, in Weiss's terms, to explore the final things that are implicated in the ways we name the world around us and address it. Logical entailment is not a causal process; just so, no logic is a substitute for the process of investigation, the use of evidence. However, there are ways of construing the logical relationships that distort those processes more than is necessary. To restrict ourselves to such extensional logics, while denying a place to the intensional logics that they presuppose, is to misconstrue and distort the world. Weiss's conception of "names" and of their functioning as evidence serves as a helpful corrective to that distortion.

Eleven

Richard J. Bernstein

Human Beings:
Plurality and Togetherness*

Heidegger tells us "to think is to confine yourself to a single thought that one day stands still like a star in the world's sky."[1] This is a theme to which Heidegger keeps returning in his late writings when he searches for various "pathways" that will enable us to elicit and disclose thinking in its purity. It is the mark of genuine thinkers to possess and be possessed by a single thought that shines like a star and radiates throughout their work and the pathways they pursue. Paul Weiss is such a thinker. Or to put the issue slightly differently, from his earliest work until his most recent book, there is a theme and variations that pervade all his speculative thinking. With nuanced subtlety he has persistently pursued the theme of the one and the many. Explicitly or implicitly, it is evident in everything he has written and is manifested in the entire range of his concerns whether they deal with the most speculative metaphysical and ontological issues or the most intimate aspects of human life.

There is something curious about the theme or the "problem" of the one and the many. It is at once the most abstract and concrete of philosophical issues. It is abstract because immediately one asks what are we talking about, what is the one that is intended, what type of many are we referring to? But it is the most concrete of issues because it turns up everywhere, in every aspect of philosophic or reflective inquiry.

The theme of the one and the many is the oldest and most persistent theme in Western philosophy and seems no less central to Eastern thought. It is already evident in the fragments of Parmenides and Heraclitus, and emerges as absolutely central for Plato and the tra-

*This essay first appeared in *Review of Metaphysics* 35 (December 1981): 349–66. Copyright © 1981 by the Review of Metaphysics. Reprinted with permission from the *Review of Metaphysics*.

dition he initiates. Despite the claims of the great thinkers to solve the "problem" (or cluster of "problems") once and for all, to demystify, or deconstruct, or dissolve the "problem"—like Proteus—it takes an indefinite variety of forms. It is the basis for asking the most critical questions that can be raised about any philosophic scheme. It has, for example, plagued the discussion of mind and body ever since Descartes so "clearly and distinctly" distinguished these two types of substance. Even those philosophers who pride themselves on overcoming metaphysics and ontology have had to struggle with how we can reconcile what seems to be mental and what seems to be physical—how we are to understand their apparent togetherness. Whatever our assessment of Kant's critical philosophy, we cannot avoid recognizing that the thorniest problems for Kant concern how we are to understand the type of unity that the noumenal and the phenomenal can have—how, for example, we are to make sense of human agents that are at once noumenal and phenomenal selves. My references to Parmenides, Heraclitus, Plato, Descartes, and Kant are illustrative. Some version and some solution (or dissolution) of the "problem" of the one and the many stands at the center of every significant philosophy. Perhaps the greatest modern thinker to struggle with the one and the many in its many variations was Hegel—or at the very least one can claim that Hegel self-consciously brings it into the very foreground of speculative thinking in his dominant concern with the identity of identity and difference. When I turn to the way in which Weiss grapples with the relevant issues, I want to show how close he is to Hegel, and yet how different Weiss is from Hegel.

But lest one think that the problem of the one and the many is only a concern of speculative thinking, metaphysics, or ontology, let us not forget the ways in which it is central for every ethical, social and political philosophy. The stand we take on the one and the many has the utmost practical significance. Thus, for example, if we think of human beings as discrete and separable—as basic atoms—having inalienable rights, then the range of positions that we take on the nature of society and the *polis* is already set for us, and will differ significantly if we think that an individual can only be properly understood of an aspect of, and internally related to, a larger, more fundamental social reality, community, or *Geist*.

It is an illusion to think that the newer philosophic movements of the twentieth century are any less concerned with variations on the one and the many. It is central to Husserl and appears as soon as we ask whether there is a plurality of transcendental egos—or even whether or not it makes sense to ask this question. It is evident in Heidegger in his own struggles to clarify identity and difference. It appears in a new form in Derrida's playful variations of *différence* and *différance.* We do not escape the problem by speaking with Wittgenstein of "family resemblances," for this itself is intended to be a proposed dissolution of the problem that is not without its own difficulties. It lies close to the surface in the fashionable talk about incommensurable paradigms, forms of life, language games, or the fusion of horizons.

What is at once so clear and extremely perplexing about the one and the many is that we all know what traps and temptations are to be avoided—we might even call this "Plato's lesson." For we know that every doctrine is doomed to failure and paradox that commits one of the three closely related errors: the doctrine so emphasizes unity and oneness that it cannot do justice to manifest diversity and plurality; that it becomes so obsessed with the integrity and independence of what is different that it cannot make sense of the unity among these different "entities"; or, it so insists on dualities—whether these be ontological, epistemological, or linguistic—that it cannot make intelligible how these dualities can be interrelated or even conceived of as *dualities.* But while we know what counts as failure, it is much more difficult to know what would be an adequate solution, resolution, or dissolution of the one and the many—that does justice to both the unity and diversity of what we encounter.

Paul Weiss has thought deeply and subtly about the problems provoked by the one and the many. To say that he has confined himself to a "single thought" is to say nothing less than that he has been thinking and probing the thought that is at the center of philosophy from its earliest origins to its latest developments. It is already evident in his first book, *Reality,* the title of which I think is properly understood as an ironical and critical comment on the *magnum opus* of his teacher, A. N. Whitehead's *Process and Reality.* For Weiss, who sometimes seems to have an almost infallible sense of the Achilles' heel of any position, argues that Whitehead's main failure and the failure of all process philosophies is satisfactorily to come to grips with the one and the many. Or rather, one might say that in the emphasis on process, duration, and the creative and dynamic aspects of reality there was a tendency to undermine the integrity, persistence and sustaining of those actualities that are capable of being creative, dynamic and free. Being the master dialectician that he is, Weiss also showed that such a dialectical extremity has the unintended consequence of undermining the very intelligibility of process and duration itself. It is important to realize that it was not only Whitehead but the variety of process philosophies which were articulated in the early part of the twentieth century that Weiss was criticizing and attempting to reconstruct—for he detected the same tendency to dissolve the integrity of actualities into a single all encompassing dynamic process in the thought of Bergson, Dewey and James. William James has poignantly recorded how his own struggles with a version of the one and the many became the focus of an intellectual and personal crisis. In *A Pluralistic Universe* he tells us: "Sincerely, and patiently as I could, I struggled with the problem for years, covering hundreds of sheets of paper with notes and memoranda and discussions with myself over the difficulty. How can many consciousnesses be at the same time one consciousness? How can one and the same identical fact experience itself so diversely? The struggle was vain; I found myself in an *impasse*."[2]

It is not my intention to survey the many ways in which Weiss has grappled with the one and the many. Rather I want to probe how this "single thought" is manifested in his most recent book, *You, I, and the Others*, especially in the first part, entitled "Encountering Persons." A primary test of a philosopher's reflections on the one and the many is the way he or she treats human beings. The reason for this should be evident. For whatever we have to say about this "problem" when dealing with the cosmos or with all those dimensions of reality that exclude human beings, there are extraordinary complexities when we deal with human beings. If we are to do justice to the phenomena or "save the appearances," we must realize that human beings are the only creatures that we know that master language, discourse, communication, and conversation in which there is the use of first, second, and third person talk. This is not a "mere" linguistic fact. If we are to understand fully the complex ways in which I, you, we, and others use the variety of pronouns, we must face the issue of what we are talking about, what we are referring to when we engage in this type of linguistic activity. We must not only try to gain a clear view of the uses and roles of "I," "me," "you," "we," "they," etc. but also what *is* the I, me, my, you, we, they, etc. Think of the complexities this introduces concerning the one and the many. Even if we limit ourselves to a single individual, we want to know who and what is the I that is speaking, how this is related to the me, what is the relation of the I and the me to what I call mine—whether it be my body, my rights, or my community. How am I to distinguish the I, me, and mine? How am I to understand how this many does or does not form a unity? If one thinks that this is *merely* verbal play, think of the problems that arise when we question Descartes's "I think therefore I am," and ask ourselves who and what is this I and whether the first and second mention of "I" refer to the same thing. Or think of the difficulties raised when we ask Hume who and what is the I and myself when he tells us, "For my part, when I enter most intimately into what I call myself, I always stumble on some particular perception or other. . . . " Or again, what unity is there among Kant's discriminations of an empirical, transcendental, and noumenal ego.

After outlining the main points of Weiss's treatment of the key issues, I want to raise questions and problems that are left unresolved. Weiss begins *You, I, and the Others* with a systematic analysis of you, and moves through an analysis of me, the self, and I. The following are some of the primary claims Weiss makes about you. "You are confrontable." "You have a dense depth." "You have a public and a private status." "You persist." "You have a temporal span." "You are a free causal agent." "You have value." "You have a predominantly bodily role" (*YIO*, "Recapitulation," pp. 397 ff.). Now a key motif that helps to make sense of, and unify these (and closely related) claims is that of privacy and publicness. For while I can encounter, perceive, and know you in scientific and other ways, you are never exhausted by *what* I perceive, encounter, and know. This does not mean that there is a hidden, veiled you that somehow stands behind and beyond the you that I encounter, perceive and know, and which is *totally inaccessible* to me or even to you. For this would entail that there is an unbridgeable ontological and epistemological gap—something like a duplication of you into a public you and a private you which have no connection with each other. Nor is it the case that when I encounter, perceive, and know you that I am encountering, perceiving, and knowing something which is *totally* different each time, for this would mean that at best you are only a many—a many in which the elements have no relation to each other. Indeed, it is not even clear that it would any longer make sense to speak of a you which is made up of the manys that I encounter, perceive or know— for the very intelligibility of a single you consisting of these manys has been called into question. "You are confronted in public," but "when I attend to you, I attend directly to what is presented from a privacy which remains continuous with it" (*YIO*, p. 5). Every you has both a public and a private dimension which are continuous, although distinguishable from each other. It does not follow that my knowledge of you is limited to the public you. I can come to know and penetrate your privacy. We must be careful not to distort what this means. For it does not mean that I can *fully* penetrate your privacy. If I could, it would mean that this is not a "true privacy" (*YIO*, p. 6). For what is the most fundamental fact about you is that you have a "dense depth," "root ontological privacy" that can never be fully penetrated or violated. But although I cannot fully and exhaustively penetrate your root ontological privacy, I can penetrate you beyond what is confrontable. When, for example, "I confront you in sympathy, hate, fear, or love" I do not merely encounter you at those times, "I move into you" (*YIO*, p. 6).

Having an intrinsic public and private status is not unique to human beings. In a manner that is reminiscent of Aristotle, Weiss is always comparing and contrasting human beings with animals and things in order to show what they share in common with other beings as well as to highlight the subtle ways in which they differ. Thus while there is also a privacy of animals and things, and it is also true that we cannot fully penetrate their privacies, there are crucial differences between humans and other beings. "Privately, animals and things are incipiently public; privately, men have dense distinguished unities with many divisions, engaged in many different acts, many of which are not directed toward the public world" (*YIO*, p. 7). Furthermore, human beings "maintain their privacies in contradistinction to what they make public . . ." (*YIO*, p. 9).

The you that I encounter is both spatial and temporal, but even here there is a public and private dimension. Some of Weiss's most illuminating analysis is revealed in the way in which he explores the human lived body. To think of the body simply as a public physically extended entity is to do violence to what the body is. The body is, of course, a physical entity, and it can be studied in the ways in which other physical entities are studied by the natural sciences. But to think that this is all there is to the body would be a classic instance of mistaking the part for the whole. You are more than the parts that make up your body and more than the body itself which has its own distinctive nature. "You have a privacy, only part of which is bodily expressed. Because of that privacy, it is possible for you to know yourself as a me" (*YIO*, p. 95).

Before we pass on to the me, and the ways in which Weiss's dialectical pathway ineluctably leads us to the distinctive character of the me, I want to pause and reflect upon the significance of what Weiss is showing us. Although I have not mentioned right, value, and dignity, it is not difficult to see how this flows out of Weiss's inquiry. At the center of his vision of human beings is a profound appreciation of the radical plurality of human beings. By "radical plurality" I do not mean mere otherness—there are other entities and persons in the world that obstruct or thwart my desires, intentions, and actions, or are simply there as the termini of acts of knowing and perceiving. Rather every actuality has a "root ontological privacy." Comparing humans with animals and things, we can say that it is only humans who are capable of distinguishing "what they are privately and what they are as present in a public world." A human being's privacy is both continuous with and distinguishable—by himself or herself and by others—from what he or she is publicly. Other human beings are not simply duplicates of what every human being is—although, of course, there is a common nature and common conditions that affect all human beings. Nor is it true that what distinguishes one human being from another is some collection of *accidental* attributes. A human being simply would not be a human being unless he or she possessed a distinctive and unique ontological privacy. This is what human beings *essentially* are. And to possess a root ontological privacy which is capable of both being and not being expressed in a public world means that every human being is unique and distinctive. Each and every human being has intrinsic value, inalienable rights and dignity. This is what I mean when I say that Weiss's understanding of human beings is one that underscores the radical, nonreducible plurality and singularity of human beings. His concern is not just with humanity or Man in general but with human beings in their *essential* radical plurality. But to insist upon this is not to claim that each of us is so unique and so distinctive that we do not share a great deal in common with our fellow human beings and the other actualities in the world. Unless there were real (and not just nominal) common conditions and characters, it would not make sense to even speak of *human* beings or a *common* species. More strongly, an adequate description and understanding of the public you that I encounter forces me to recognize your ontological privacy which I can never fully penetrate. I can also categorically say that unless you were capable of expressing (although not exhaustively) your privacy in a public world then it would not make any sense to ascribe such a privacy to you. To paraphrase Wittgenstein—and in *this* respect Weiss agrees with him— we are on the very brink of misunderstanding if we think that acknowledging the privacy of a human being means that we are acknowledging an entity or a realm that is so completely cut off from a public world that it cannot be known, understood, or referred to by anyone else but me. If we think of privacy as something like Wittgenstein's "beetle in a box" where we supposed that everyone had a box with something in it, but where "no one can look into anyone's else's box, and everyone says he knows what a beetle is only by looking at *his* beetle," then I think Wittgenstein is right in suggesting that "the thing in the box has no place in the language-game at all."[3] But even when we tease out the full consequences of what Wittgenstein is questioning and can purge ourselves of false pictures and conceptions of privacy, I think that Weiss is right when he argues that we must go on to deal with the ways in which privacy *is* known and linguistically expressed by you and me—and we must deal with the richness of privacy that involves much more than so-called "private sensations."

The fertility of Weiss's analysis can be seen when examined from another perspective. There is still a widespread bias that to think seriously about ethical, social, and political issues, we can dispense with ontology and metaphysics. And there is an equally pervasive bias that the results of a metaphysical and ontological analysis are neutral in regard to ethical, social, and political issues. Weiss has persistently challenged both these biases. Furthermore, there are strong practical consequences of his understanding of human beings. The radical plurality of human beings where each human being possesses its own essential ontological privacy leads directly to a radical egalitarianism. Of course, we must be careful to clarify what is meant by egalitarianism and the ways in which human beings are not equal. Clearly it is false to think that all human beings are equal in strength, talent, intelligence and ability. But every human being possesses a distinctive ontological privacy, is a free causal agent, and not only has value but a value which is at once absolutized and individuated. Consequently any ethical, social or political theory that neglects or distorts this type of equality does violence to what we truly are—to what is *essential* to our very being.

Earlier I indicated that in pursuing the analysis of you, we are ineluctably and dialectically led to the analysis of the *me*. The point is stated emphatically by Weiss when he tells us "As just a you, you cannot act or even be acted on, for a you is not a distinct reality. But since you are privately possessed, you are enabled to act, and can be present for others to act on" (*YIO*, pp. 74–75). The crucial point here—and it is one that Weiss has emphasized over and over again since *Reality*—is that when I know, encounter, or perceive anything, I am aware that there is more to *what* I am knowing, encountering, and perceiving than what I immediately confront.[4] I am aware that things, animals, and humans have a depth and a privacy that is not exhausted in my encounters. This is a theme that Weiss shares deeply with phenomenologists and which has been so carefully and extensively illustrated in Merleau-Ponty's *Phenomenology of Perception*. This generic point about all encounters becomes specific in my encounters with you, because when I fully appreciate that the recognition of you requires a recognition of the private dimension of you, then I can come to appreciate that "because of that privacy, it is possible for you to know yourself as a me."

While "me" and me are distinguishable from "you" and you, and consequently all four items require careful discrimination—the me itself is continuous with the you. Indeed "a me faces in two directions" (*YIO*, p. 99). "You, as reached from the standpoint of another, may give way to your me . . . " (*YIO*, p. 99). But your me can also be "attended to only by yourself" (*YIO*, p. 99). Or to switch to the first person, I can say that while you can know me—the me which is expressed in a public setting—I can attend to my me in ways in which you or any other person cannot. This does not mean that I can attain complete self-knowledge or self-transparency, or even that what I know about myself is always beyond your knowledge. On the contrary, you can know something about me that I myself do not know. "Though I am never directly and entirely known by myself or by another, I do provide evidence of who I am by what I *express*. There is no item that is necessarily and forever hidden, but there is also no knowing which exhaustively captures all that is" (*YIO*, p. 98). This is not due simply to human ignorance, weakness, or fallibility—as if it were possible to conceive of an omniscient being who would not be subject to this limitation. "Even an omniscient being must stop short of the inward being of what he knows, for his knowledge too is distinct from what is known" (*YIO*, p. 98). This is one of the many reasons why I think Weiss is at once so close and so distant from Hegel. Like Hegel, Weiss argues that there is no item that is necessarily and forever hidden, there is nothing that is knowable in principle that cannot be known. Consequently Hegel is right in his dialectical assaults on Kant's *Ding-an-sich*, especially when Kant suggests that there is a *Ding-an-sich* which is in principle knowable—or at least that an omniscient being might grasp it by intellectual intuition—but is not knowable by human beings. But where Weiss sharply departs from Hegel is when Hegel claims that there is an *identity* of thought and being. For according to Weiss while we can think and know everything that is thinkable and knowable, this does not mean that knowing—not even God's knowing—"exhaustively captures all that is." When we apply this to human beings, we can say "If it is men who are known, they will insistently live in depth what he or others grasp as grounded you's, and which the men themselves grasp as grounded me's. The grounding in both cases is beyond the reach of an approach through either. Both the fact that it occurs and the nature it has can be known speculatively, by reflecting on what must be if there are to be you's and me's" (*YIO*, p. 98).

Weiss's analysis of me flows directly out of his analysis of you—and this is true in a double sense. Not only does my encounter with and knowing you lead to a recognition of *your* me but this dialectical path is itself revelatory of the ontological fact that every you is also a me. Not only does Weiss attempt to do justice to what is distinctive about a me, how it is continuous with a you, and what is unique about the ways in which I refer to *my* me, he seeks to clarify the complex interrelations and togetherness of the I, me, and self—each of which he carefully distinguishes from the others so that we can grasp at once the internal unity and diversity of the I, me, and self. Once again the task is to clarify the distinctive character of each of these moments and at the same time to demonstrate their unity and togetherness. The I, me, and self are distinguishable but not separable. They are *essentially together*, each mutually requiring the other. Every I "possesses" a me, and the I itself is what Weiss calls "one of a number of condensations of the self" (*YIO*, p. 191). There are other "epitomizing condensations of the self." Thus, according to Weiss, the mind is one of the condensations of the self.

Action itself—indeed the very action that I am aware of when I encounter you—originates in the I and not in the you or the me. This, of course, is just as true and just as fundamental for your I as it is for my I. Strictly speaking, "neither you nor me originates acts" (*YIO*, p. 165). "You and me are origins to which manifestations, expressions, and actions can be traced, but you and me are not their causes; you and me have no power, are not able to do anything. Were it not that you and me continue in depth into more powerful, free privacies, what occurs would have to be credited to the action of an impersonal, cosmic force rearranging the ways in which you's and me's are related to one another and other items. . . . Though neither a you nor a me originates acts, neither just modifies the manner in which a cosmic force is being exhibited. Actions pass through both the you and me, carrying the burden of preferences, choices, and wills, and therefore also of the thoughts, aims, purposes, ideals, and dedications which are involved in preferring, choosing, and willing" (*YIO*, p. 165). Here, too, we witness a deepening of Weiss's version of radical pluralism, for ultimately it is each and every I that freely acts, and is the cause of its expressions. It is because each individual is in this sense an end in him or herself that we can ascribe responsibility to each and every human being.

In order to clarify what Weiss is telling us about the distinctive character and the essential unity of the I, me, and self, it is helpful to compare what he is saying with Hegel and Sartre. Using Weiss's terms, we can say that for Hegel there is not only an essential togetherness of the I, me, and self but that there is an identity, an identity that is realized when all forms of self-alienation are overcome, when the for-itself becomes the in-itself and the in-itself becomes the for-itself—an achievement that is realized only in and through the dynamic concrete actualization of *Geist*. Against Hegel, Sartre protests—and this is the basic theme in *L'être et néant*—that this grand synthesis is a grand illusion. The for-itself (*pour-soi*) can never become identical with the in-itself (*en-soi*) although this type of identification haunts human beings. There is always an irreducible fissure in existence. This is at once the condition for anxiety and human freedom. I always transcend myself (except in death). Weiss is clearly on the side of Sartre against Hegel in insisting on the ontological difference and nonidentity of the I and the me—the two are not and can never become identical. But against Sartre, Weiss in effect shows why Sartre's position is so paradoxical and unstable—because Sartre can never tell us what the I really *is*. Indeed the I must—on Sartre's grounds—lack any determinate character, for to possess a determinate character would turn the I into a me. The I then becomes "a nothing," and to claim that it is a creative nothing or source of nihilation is only a dodge. Here I think Weiss would echo the way in which Hegel would certainly respond to Sartre—that if we pursue this dialectic rigorously, then ultimately we cannot even claim that there is an I or for-itself that is the source of, or is identical with, human freedom. Against both Hegel and Sartre, we must recognize that there is an I and a me each possessing a distinctive character, each continuous with and requiring the other, and each never wholly identical with the other. There cannot be a you which is not grounded in a me; there cannot be a me that is not grounded in an I. Finally, the I itself presupposes a self—a self which is "single, accumulative, and persistent, forever private, beyond the reach of external observation."

It is the mark of the genuine thinker that his single thought radiates in all directions. Just as the you leads to the me, I, and self, so too Weiss shows how this dialectical web of concepts leads on to the we and the they. I cannot adequately explore what Weiss says about the we and the they, although in my judgment his analysis is not nearly as thorough, illuminating, or persuasive as is his discussion of you, me, and I. Let me briefly indicate what he says about the we, and I will return to this in my critical comments. The referent of "we" is, of course, different from the referent of "I." We has its own integrity, complexity, and character. " 'We' may have any one of three referents: it may refer to a *simple we*, a condition for a number of men; to a *factual we*, an interlinkage of men; or to a *complex we*, a combination of the simple and the factual" (*YIO*, p. 270). Each of these referents can in itself be divided into a variety of subtypes. Here Weiss touches on the cluster of issues that have become focal for many contemporary philosophers—for he touches upon what is sometimes called the problem of intersubjectivity or community. Formally, it is clear what Weiss wants to say, that an I presupposes a we, and a we presupposes a plurality of I's—that neither the integrity of the I nor of the we dissolves into the other. But if we ask what concretely this means and how a plurality of I's is not only affected by the appropriate we but *constituted* by a we, how the very nature of an I is determined by a relevant community without losing its integrity and how a community is constituted in and through individual I's, Weiss does not sufficiently complement his formal dialectical analysis with a concrete phenomenological description.

The power, incisiveness, and comprehensiveness of Weiss's pursuit of the one and the many as it pertains to human beings should now be clear (even though I have only dealt with some of the highlights of an analysis that he pursues in enormous detail and with sustained verve). I want to conclude, however, with suggesting two lines of criticism. Let me begin my critical remarks with an observation that may seem quite peripheral but will take us to the heart of the matter. In an age that prides itself in its sensitivity to language, we have not fully explored the significance, *enabling power* and fertility of figurative and metaphorical language. There is still—although it is now under attack—the myth that we can clearly distinguish the literal from the metaphorical and that serious science and philosophy ought to dispense with metaphors. This myth is now being exploded and we are coming to realize how vital and central metaphors and models are for the fertility of scientific inquiry and philosophy.

Nevertheless we must recognize that what is also required to gain philosophic insight is the appropriate *commentary* on those figures of speech which can prove so powerful and seductive in philosophy—otherwise there is a danger of diffuseness and only the illusion of understanding and clarity. It is certainly not a criticism of Weiss (or any speculative philosophy) to note how much depends on tropes. But there is something very revealing about Weiss's *use* of language. Despite his "official" stance which claims to do justice to the spatiality and temporality of the various dimensions of human beings, his own language is heavily weighted to the spatial and the physical. He speaks of *"dense* depth," of *"dense* distinguished unities," of *"penetrating* your privacy," of *"moving* into you," and of a representative or epitomizing *"condensation"* of a self. But precisely how are we to understand the underscored physicalistic expressions which pervade his entire discussion of the you, I, me, and self? They are not to be understood in a physicalistic sense. But once this negative point is made, it is never entirely clear how they are to be taken—what is the appropriate commentary which enables us to understand the nonphysicalistic meaning of these crucial expressions which are supposed to clarify the nature of privacy and publicness. According to Weiss, however much a self may express or manifest itself in a public spatial world, it is *not* itself spatial or merely physical, it is "forever private, beyond the reach of external observations." Bergson noted how deeply our language is affected and infected by spatial or physical expressions, even and especially when we talk about time and temporality. This certainly seems to be a dominant characteristic of Weiss's speculative language. One wonders whether it is really an "advance" from the tangled problems that Descartes faces (or rather avoids) in explaining how a nonspatial and nonextended mind acts through or affects a spatial and extended body, when we switch to Weiss's claims about how a self (which is private and nonspatial) manifests or expresses itself in a spatial and extended world. What concretely does it mean to *penetrate* or *move* into your privacy? (This cannot be answered simply by telling us what it *does not* mean.) Can we *measure* the "dense depth" of an individual's ontological privacy? Can we discriminate comparative *densities* of "*dense* distinguished unities" as we can of different physical objects? If these are the wrong questions to ask, if we are somehow making a category mistake, then we want to know what precisely is wrong here, and what are the right questions to ask. Indeed, it begins to look as if Weiss *may* be accused of making something like a category mistake by constantly applying physicalistic predicates to what is essentially not physical.

The type of difficulty that I am locating is especially evident in Weiss's discussion of the "condensations" of the self. For here we touch on the vital nerve of the one and the many as it pertains to the self. Clearly it is not sufficient to understand what is meant by "condensation" by appealing to how this concept is used in characterizing the condensation of a mass, or even the condensation of a novel. But what precisely does Weiss mean when he uses the expressions of a "representative or epitomizing condensation"? How does such "condensation" take place? Is condensation itself a process? How many condensations are there of the self? What are the relations of these specific condensations to the *generic* self? What are the criteria for distinguishing the several condensations of the self? I do not want to suggest that language has gone on a holiday here and is, therefore, *necessarily* misleading or defective. However, it is important to realize that Weiss speaks of "condensation" in a context which is radically different from the normal ways in which we speak of "condensation," and he has not sufficiently characterized the "rules of this game"—what counts as a right and wrong move, and what are the criteria for knowing this. This is not a minor aberration or something that is dispensable from the substance of Weiss's views. For it is precisely this (unexplained) concept of condensation that is supposed to "solve" the problem of the one and the many in regard to human beings. Presumably we can (or are supposed to understand) that the one—the self—can also be a many, *e.g.*, an I, me, mind, etc.—for these are *condensations* of the self. Unless Weiss can clarify this concept of condensation—and avoid an explanation *obscurum per obscurius*—there is a real danger that his entire analysis will collapse.

The other line of criticism that I want to press has to do with temporality, or more precisely with that form of temporality that has been called "historicity." Since the expression "historicity" is one that is itself frequently abused, or conjures up a specific style of philo-sophizing, let me explain what I mean. I think it is fair to claim that whatever role history and historical developmental processes played for philosophers prior to Hegel (and we are discovering how complex this has been) there was nevertheless a dominant bias that history was only of incidental importance for genuine philosophic problems. In the grand tradition of philosophy from the Greeks on, the aim of the true philosopher was noetically to comprehend the cosmos *sub specie aeternitatis*—to transcend historical context and limitations. Cer-tainly after Descartes, who explicitly denigrates the study of history as necessary for genuine *knowledge*, many philosophers have shared this bias. In the main currents of Anglo-American analytic philosophy (as well as in Husserl's transcendental phenomenology) this bias has asserted itself with a vengence. We are told it is one thing "to do philosophy" and an entirely different enterprise to study the history of philosophy. Analytic philosophers have frequently been not only indifferent but *hostile* to historical studies (except when this is viewed as a means for solving ahistorical philosophic problems). One con-sequence of logical positivism and empiricism has been to reinforce the prejudice that history at its best is an empirical discipline having as much or as little relevance to philosophy as any other empirical discipline.

One of the most significant contributions of Hegel was to challenge this bias, to argue—and perhaps even more importantly—to *show* the intimate or internal relation between history and philosophy. Even if we reject Hegel's more grandiose claims, this central insight still stands. Curiously there are even developments in analytic philosophy—es-pecially in the philosophy of science—which are coming to appreciate the intimate dialectical relation between history and philosophy. He-gel never falls into the trap of the type of historicism and relativism that has become so fashionable where it is asserted that different historical periods are so different and alien to each other that they do not share anything in common. Returning to the theme of the one and the many, we can say that Hegel "discovered"—or at least em-phasized a new dimension of this "problem"—that the task of philosophy is not only to comprehend or interpret the world *sub specie aeternitatis* but it must understand the dialectical unfolding of the *Begriff* or *Geist*. Or to put the point in a stricter Hegelian context, we can *only* achieve genuine comprehension and *sophia* if we understand how that which is eternal *also* historically and temporally actualizes itself in history. Now it is not my intention to play Hegel off against Weiss, but rather to *use* Hegel in order to highlight a weakness and deficiency in Weiss's approach to you, I, and the others. Hegel is most brilliant in *showing* the significance of dialectical developmental processes in studying those *very concepts* that are central for Weiss. Hegel traces for us the stages of the dialectical *unfolding* of I, you, me, and especially we (*Geist*). Both philosophers would agree that the complex of concepts that are isolated by Weiss (all of which are needed to understand intersubjectivity) are *internally* and dialectically related. But what Hegel emphasizes (rightly, I believe) and Weiss tends to slight is that the way in which these concepts unfold and change in history is *essential* to understand their distinctiveness—here, too, we must at once grasp unity and temporal or developmental differences. Thus for Hegel, if we concentrate on the we, or that form of the we that is distinctive of communities, then one must understand how the very notion or concept of community itself has changed in the course of history. If it is true—as both Weiss and Hegel assert—that the concrete expression of a *we* is dialectically related to the *references* of the range of first, second, and third person pronouns, then, as the very *nature* of the we changes, so also does the *nature* of all the other referents.

I have used Hegel to highlight a deficiency in Weiss because Weiss shares so much in common with Hegel. Whatever one's assessment of speculative philosophy, no one could accuse Hegel (or Weiss) of compromising the idea of a speculative philosophy which aspires to comprehend *sub specie aeternitatis*. This is not the issue. Rather, the primary issue is whether *what* we study from the perspective of speculative philosophy—and in particular the rich terrain of "intersubjectivity"—itself has a *historical ontological* dimension. It is this dimension—this aspect of diversity and difference—that Weiss tends to slight.

The main point that I want to make can be made without any reference to Hegel. Whether we limit ourselves to the history of philosophy, or extend our vision over the entire range of anthropological, cultural, and historical studies, we are coming to an increasing realization of the significant *differences* of what is being talked about when different communities—whether they be different historical communities of "primitive" societies—use expressions which we *translate* as "I," "you," "me," and "others." The problems and questions this raises are not just *theoretical* but have enormous *practical* significance. For many thinkers have sought to analyze the malaise of contemporary society by isolating the ways in which we have lost or distorted a sense of community, *i.e.*, the subtle and complex ways in which what we mean by I, me, you, and we are undergoing a transformation. Whatever continuities there are in the use of "I," "me," "you," "we"— there are also essential (and not just accidental or empirical) differences which must be highlighted in any proper philosophic reflection. It is here that Weiss fails us.

Weiss's response to what I am saying might take the following form. However much one needs to be sensitive to historical, temporal, developmental differences, there is something common to these differences which underlies them and makes them intelligible. After all the Greeks as well as nineteenth-century Germans or twentieth-century Americans use the range of pronouns and are referring to or talking about something when they do so. Of course, there is a need to be sensitive to manifoldness and differences but *not* at the expense of what is common and what unifies a manifold. He might add that what the speculative philosopher must do is aim for a level of discourse in which he can do justice to both the unity and differences of the you, I, me, we, etc.

But such a reply does not really meet my criticism. I am *not* here challenging the idea of speculative philosophy but rather Weiss's understanding of its *character* and *task*. Here again references to Hegel may be helpful. Hegel tells us that *Geist* is at once eternally the same (and consequently one) and always changing (and consequently many). The issue is not one of doing justice to historical change, transformation, and difference *at the expense* of continuity and unity. The issue is rather seeking to synthesize *both* of these perspectives in an integral, comprehensive, coherent scheme. A speculative philosophy may be judged not only by what it highlights and brings into focus but also by what remains out of focus or is relegated to the background.

My essential objection here is that although Weiss clearly acknowledges that there are changes in the uses of the personal pronouns and changes in what they refer to, I do not think he has taken us very far in comprehending what is involved in such changes and transformations—why they occur, what challenges and dangers they present. In this respect, there is a major aspect of the problem of the one and the many—where the many consists of historical transformations—that Weiss has failed to penetrate in depth. Despite Weiss's dialectical dexterity and concrete phenomenological insight, an adequate solution (or dissolution) of the problem of the one and the many still eludes us.

Twelve

Antonio S. Cua

Queries and Replies: Correspondence of Antonio S. Cua and Paul Weiss

Foreword

The following letters pertain to three of Professor Weiss's later works: First Considerations *(1977),* You, I, and the Others *(1980), and* Privacy *(1983). Professor Weiss has kindly consented to their publication without knowing that they will appear in this volume. My own letters have been edited without affecting their style and substance. I am indebted to Professor Daniel Dahlstrom for his valuable assistance in preparing the letters for publication.*

❧

September 18, 1977

Dear Paul,

I am deeply appreciative to receive your *First Considerations*—an insightful contribution to systematic philosophy. Together with *Beyond All Appearances*, much of my earlier skeptical response to ontological theories has largely disappeared. I must admit that your grand efforts have been unjustly neglected and these works, at least, should be an excellent beginning for metaphysical aspirants in seeing clearly the pivotal issues involved in doing systematic philosophy. For its clarity of exposition and "inferential moves," I find *Beyond* a better work. *First* is an awfully difficult book to read, a breathtaking effort for my part, but it does resolve some queries I had with *Beyond* and is definitely much more compelling in the articulation of your metaphysical vision in relating actualities and finalities. Particularly attractive to me is the sustained argument against monism of either idealistic and

218

nonidealistic versions. You have preserved the insights of a metaphysics of substance within a dynamic cosmos. If I understand correctly, a neo-Confucian conception of *li* (reason, principle, pattern, unity) parallels your effort. This should not be surprising given the crucial problem of the One and Many. Ching I's (1033–1107) remark that *"Li* is one but its manifestations many" may be of interest to you. On your account (I find congenial), the one is provided by an actuality: "The position from which one can have all five finalities distinct but yet together is provided by an actuality" (p. 171). I should like to talk with you more on this.

As I am sympathetic with your conception of the philosophic enterprise, I am struck at the outset of my reading on a key issue that seems to be buried throughout the book: What are the basic *presuppositions* implicit in your work? This query runs through my reading of the first one-third of your book. At one point, I put your book aside and asked myself this question: Would it be more profitable to ask another question, an old question—What sort of a "picture" of the relation between man and the world does Weiss find compelling? By "picture" I mean a model that is operative in many systematic works. Perhaps I should follow Pepper and ask about your "root-metaphor," but this sort of question should come later. Let me here record an initial response to my question (a bit facetious, but seriously entertained): You have given me the impression of a picture of a "model" much like that of Greek mythology with "gods" and "goddesses" possessing *powers* that affect man in his knowledge and action. A Berkeley could very quickly and unjustly remark that you are dealing with "ghosts of the departed entities." This initial impression of a picture is no doubt a serious misunderstanding, a caricature of the depth of the issues with which you dealt. However, my initial naivete leads me to a formulation of your *operative* model throughout the work: The *model of agency*, or better, a conception of agents as possessing powers that "condition, control, affect" (p. 236, etc.) actualities. In effect, and if I am not mistaken, this model of "efficient causation" is a profoundly original feature of your metaphysics. One danger of this model, as Shimony wants to accuse you, lies in its anthropomorphic character. Your reply is an adequate one (p. 195), but I believe it needs to

be amplified. One can fully accept this model and be
vindicated in doing so, as long as the grounds to be
traversed are open to any inquiry. However, one must
admit that the model does carry assumptions that need to
be acknowledged explicitly. *One* evidence I have for
attributing the model to you particularly pertains to your
discussion of finalities and insistence that our claims to
knowledge need to be accepted, accommodated, or altered
(or rejected) by the finality at issue (*e.g.*, pp. 104–5), and
also a finality in "a source must help a man yield what he
had produced" (p. 105). Am I not right then in my
attribution? As a linguistic observation, note how
pervasive are such terms as "power," "accept," and
"affect" throughout the book. To borrow the terms of
Reid, your picture of the world is heavily populated by
"active and intellectual powers" (your finalities), so also
actualities. This is not meant to be a destructive criticism.
For me this model is viable, but the assumptions need to
be articulated with care, for some of these assumptions
about agency may turn out, in the course of inquiry, to be
nothing but unwarranted presumptions.

Let me raise here one of my major difficulties relative
to the crucial phase of your book. The model of agency I
find operative in your *doctrine of evidence*—certainly the
most original theory in epistemology, but one I find also
the most puzzling. I am sure I misunderstand your points!
(This relates also to your queer doctrine of proper names.)
My puzzle here in part echoes Reck's (pp. 238–39) and
your answers did not seem to address the basic issue. This
issue is: What sorts of inferential moves enable us to go
from the evidence to the evidenced? You mention that
these are constitutive speculative "principles." You
suggest that one begins with a withdrawal and forms an
epistemic pair that "presupposes an ontological pairing." I
am puzzled when you also said that the latter is known
through "the use of evidence" (p. 85). The point here
appears *circular*. I wonder how you extricate yourself from
the charge. Of course, the circle may be a *virtuous* rather
than a vicious one. But this has to be shown. More
importantly, my question deals with the question of
identifying the evidence and the evidenced. Obviously
when such an identification is possible, there is no need
for an inferential move of the sort you required, but still
there must be "rules" or "principles" with which one

must comply in inference. If such speculative principles exist, don't they in part reflect certain built-in conceptual categories? And when these principles are taken as constitutive rather than as regulative principles in the Kantian sense, don't we need separate credentials and arguments to show them to be such? Of course you may reply that the match of our epistemic pairing with the ontologic pairing depends on whether the reality at issue "accepts" or "rejects" it, but how can one avoid here falling into skepticism unless we have principles for matching and these principles in part reflect the assumptions implicit in the agency model, how can one be sure? My questions here are intended to provoke you to clarify and rectify my misunderstandings and erroneous conceptions. If there are speculative inferences, the governing principles are basically epistemic. (You yourself incisively said on p. 66: "Evidence is like a question open to its answers.") And note your agency model: "No one could return to that source unless aided by the source itself." But "it is only through the *agency* of the evidenced that the evidence takes one to the source of both" (p. 67, my italics.). The operative framework, however, involves man as an inquirer with concepts that govern its course. This does not mean that there is no independent reality, but it does focus on the interlocking character of concepts and reality. Perhaps what is at issue is my unclarity on your explanation of "speculative errors."

I like your distinction between adherent and exalted names. Contrary to Reck, I find your view exciting, though not as an account of proper names in the traditional sense, but of the uses of names within speculative philosophy. Your view reminds me of the Confucian doctrine of rectifying names (terms). I am almost tempted to call it the Weissian doctrine of rectifying names. This doctrine can be misleading. "Proper names" may suggest unwanted interpretations (see Reck). Perhaps what you have in mind may be the Chinese notion of *ming* (commonly rendered as "names") or terms which may function either as names or descriptive labels. Proper names are a subclass of *ming* or names in the broad sense. One can talk also of the "names" of titles of persons, occupants of roles or positions as well as identifying labels of particular individuals. Just as names (proper) can denote individuals, they can also be used in a more

interesting way as "exalted names," which quite rightly
are inseparable from deep emotions (Reck missed this
point). I do not think that it is helpful, as you did in reply
to Reck, to appeal to the distinction between signs and
symbols. Your insight is quite independent of the Peircean
semiotics. In prayer, "God" is more of a term of address
with emotive tone. As a term, it encapsulates both the
emotive and descriptive features of the situation. An
emotivist interpretation, like that of Hobbes, only partially
accounts for this religious situation. Your "arresting
names" are particularly interesting and call for more
extensive discussion.

I am aware that even in the midst of my excitement
with the doctrine of names one can easily *object* that the
doctrine, as a semantical doctrine, is faulty in confusing
meaning of terms and the associated complex in the use of
terms. One may find unsatisfactory in particular that
"semantics has a practical, emotionally toned dimension
utilized by proper names" (p. 246). This remark is
defensible on one interpretation, but dubious as a general
characterization of semantics. Obviously formal
semanticists (like Martin and Carnap) would reject it, so
also Austinian speech act theory or Chomskyan. But let
me offer here a distinction implicit in your discussion:
meaning of terms and its *import* for the users. We
sometimes use "meaning" in the latter sense, though the
sense is typically excluded in philosophy of language.
Some of your "honorific names" like "saint" or "genius,"
and all your "arresting names" have built-in *import*. (You
used that term on the same page, p. 246.) I agree with
you, then, we need a larger or broader sense of semantics
that directs attention to the relation or connection of terms
with meaning and import. Of course, one may simply
relegate it to *pragmatics*, but what you want and need is a
fuller doctrine of the ontologic import of terms. I hope you
will write on this topic. I am fully in agreement with the
aim, though I am still fumbling. Intuitively I feel that a
doctrine of this sort will help clarify the mind/body
problem. I understand you have a forthcoming book on
this. I am eagerly awaiting the publication.

I have many more comments regarding details which I
am sure can mostly be cleared up by rereading *Beyond* and
First. But I do have one query on your ontologic vision, in

particular "Unity and unity." Like Reck and Martin, I am a bit at a loss, but for different reasons. I have no problem with unities, but Unity as a separate finality. In your reply to Reck (p. 250) and to Martin (pp. 259–60), I sense that the term you want is really "Harmony." This is suggested by your remark: "However it may be termed, there is surely a finality which encompasses and reconciles various limited, partly diversified unities." You may quite rightly respond that "Harmony" carries excessive ambiguities throughout the history of philosophy, but I think the associated meanings could be pruned away by a nonhierarchic or nonlinear conception of Harmony, which I have been recently exploring in Chinese ethics. I see that you are groping for a *nonlinear* conception like *Tao* (on my construal), which can be reconstructed both as a moral and ontological vision. With your agency model, Harmony in the nonlinear sense, seems a guiding motivation and ideal. Coherence in a speculative system is more than just a system of connected propositions, but also an articulation of a deep vision of man and the universe. In this light, Harmony is not just another finality but what renders (ideally) diversified unities in harmonious equilibrium. I would have said "reflective equilibrium" if the terms were not used by Rawls. If I am right, you are closer to the inchoate Chinese conception. (I have a forthcoming paper on this.) Unity lies in your vision of Harmony. If it be a finality, it is the finality of your speculative system and not a constitutive feature of reality. I am almost tempted to say that it embodies a regulative principle for the operation of your agency model. I have no fear that the regulative principle affects your insights (ontological). I wonder whether your inferential moves from the evidence to the evidenced are free from the implicit deployment of this principle (regulative). In saying this, I am not ascribing to you a Kantian position, but simply employing a Kantian distinction without however construing it as a dichotomy.

In closing, let me express my gratitude to you for our friendship and for much that I learned from you these past eight years. I hope you find my comments, however metaphysically naive, useful to developing your ideal. I am also attaching here an outline of *First Considerations* which you may correct and revise and may find useful for

224 Antonio S. Cua

students in your metaphysics seminar. I wrote the outline
(and a number of notes) before embarking upon this long
letter. Take care.

With respect and affection,

Tony

≈

Figure 12.1 An Interpretive Outline*

A. S. Cua

Ontology: A Theory of Reality

Appearances	**Actualities** (cosmos)	**Finalities**	
subjective	substances ————————▶	Substance	(S)
objective	beings ————————▶	Being	(B)
	natures ————————▶	Possibility	(P)
	existents ————————▶	Existence	(E)
	unity ————————▶	Unity	(U)

Explanatory notes:

1. "→" for direction of both explanatory and inferential "moves"
from appearances to reality.

2. Scope of the ontology—the range of issues raised and discussed with a focus on finalities.

S—accounts for the unity of parts within an actuality and its

*Paul Weiss, *First Considerations* (Carbondale: Southern Illinois University Press, 1977)

contrast and interaction with other actualities (p. 229). It focuses on the intelligibility of connections or affinities of actualities and their independent persistent integrity (no. 86, p. 120).

B—accounts for the ontic status of actualities.

P—accounts for the structures and relations between actualities; in particular, the nomic necessities inherent in actualities.

E—accounts for the operative domain of actualities in terms of space, time, and dynamics.

U—accounts for the evaluative harmony of unities in actualities.

Epistemology: A Theory of Speculative Knowledge

1.   A detachment of the pairing of evidence and the evidenced.

2.   Correctness depends on *matching* the epistemic pairing with the ontologic pairing.

3.   An inferential movement, by way of *speculative* principles, from one to the other—the development of speculative inferences.

4.   Success in speculative inference ultimately depends on "acceptance" of either actualities or finalities. (Epistemic claims depend on ontological acceptance by the realities at issue.)

5.   Speculative epistemology, in light of (4), represents a venture in ontological probings. Its adequacy depends on inquirer's self-criticism and criticisms of competing views. Speculative philosophy has no *a priori* closure. Philosophy, in systematic issues, is an open adventure in search of scope and precision that does justice to both reality and human experience.

ﾞﾞ

September 22, 1977

Dear Tony:

No author could want a better response to his work than that which you have made to my *First Considerations*. It is thoughtful, perceptive, careful, critical yet sympathetic, and it leaves me pondering many questions I

might have passed over too lightly. I have one basic
reservation. Knowing your native courtesy and natural
kindness and gentleness, I wonder whether you have
expressed your doubts and objections in full force. For the
moment, I have to be content with trying to give them as
much weight as I can. My reply will take days, for I have
distinguished some twenty distinct, important issues:

1. I am interested in what you say of *Li*, though it is
not yet clear to me just to what extent the idea coincides
with my view of the One and the Many. You remark that
I take each actuality to be a one for all the finalities; but it
is also true that each finality is a one for all the actualities.
Is this, too, intended by *Li*? (My extended discussion of
the One and the Many is in *Modes of Being*.) Though it is
true that what is a one has many manifestations, it is more
basic to remark that the one is for an independent many.

2. You ask what the basic presuppositions are; what
my "root-metaphor" or "picture" is. You suggest that it is
the idea of agency. But this surely is only one of a number
of equally basic notions. I also call attention to: a search
for adequacy; the inseparability of fixed positions from
thrusts beyond them; the denial of final resting places; the
centrality of penetrative intensive moves; the inseparability
of the dense from the thin, ground from surface. I am not
convinced that there must be only one "root-metaphor"
for each philosophic view, or that, if there be a number,
the view is incomplete or unsystematic. But, of course,
there is no reason why someone might not bundle
together the whole set of them and call this "the root-
metaphor." I don't think anything much would be learned
by doing this.

3. You remark on the importance of efficient
causation in my view. But constitutive causation also plays
an important role. Indeed, it warrants the (reverse) move
to actualities and to finalities, and from these to the
appearances.

4. You rightly remark that there is a danger of
anthropomorphism in the idea of agency. But my warrant
for holding the account of causation that I present is based
on an analysis, not of agency, but of the temporal distance
between an efficient cause and its effect. It does not
depend on making analogies with the way humans act. Of

course what I say needs amplification. An extended treatment of efficient causation is in my *Nature and Man*.

5.   It is not clear to me why the idea of agency is associated by you with the finalities. To say that our knowledge must be "accepted," etc., by the finalities, does not mean that they are attentive, that they act voluntarily. One could just as well say that they are receptive of the evidenced, absorb it, or allow a place for it.

6.   You ask that the assumptions behind the use of terms referring to "active and intellectual powers" "be articulated with care." I thought I did this when I observed, again and again, that the conditions operating on distinct actualities and appearances, enabling these to be together and to function thereupon in various constrained ways, transmit powers which can be traced back to the finalities. Conditions are expressions of finalities; like all expressions, they have unitary sources which are able to diversify themselves insistently by means of those expressions.

7.   You say that I have a "queer" doctrine of proper names, but do not indicate in what sense it is "queer" or whether it is sound.

8.   You have trouble in knowing what "sorts of inferential moves" take one from evidence to evidenced. You also ask how an ontological pairing (which I say is presupposed by the epistemic) can be noncircularly known, since I also say that it is known through the use of evidence. As I see it, evidencing is at once formal, positive, negative, and eminent, epistemic, and ontologic. It is not a movement from predicates to something else, but from finalities in a limited guise to them in depth. When I come to the finalities at the end of an evidencing I know them to sustain the evidenced with which I end and to be the sources of the evidences with which I started. I can therefore say without circularity that my evidencing is in consonance with (but not identical with) what is done by the finalities as they hold together what they themselves have expressed. There are 'virtuous' and 'vicious' circles, differing in that the one is all-comprehensive and the other not, but I don't think the difference is pertinent here, for I see no circle at all. I proceed from evidence to evidenced without regard for

and without presupposing the way in which the finalities relate the two; but when I come to know the finalities I can see that what I do is in accord with and presupposes what they do.

9.   You say that when we identify the evidence and the evidenced, there is no need for an inferential move. But the evidenced is known only through such a move. Were you presented with the evidenced without the evidence and the process of evidencing, you would not have justified or accounted for the evidenced. In any case, the evidence serves as the beginning of an effort to get the evidenced. Perhaps it is here you could raise the question of circularity, for the direction one moves in order to use evidence properly is dictated by the evidenced—and yet it is that at which one tries to arrive. The difficulty, common to all teleological moves, and inescapable even in the most elementary inference (since any premiss formally allows for an infinite number of conclusions and arrives at only one because this has a status denied to the other entailed conclusions) is overcome, I think, by distinguishing the evidenced as a possible from it as an actual conclusion. The one guides the other; the latter instances the former.

10.   These last problems arise for you, I think, because you do not allow (?), see (?), or understand (?) that the possible exerts constraints, guiding, limiting, governing that which makes it be realized. My view here is not too alien to Aristotle's contention that actuality precedes potentially—except that what is not yet realized, though having controlling power over the potential, and even over the activity by which this is expressed, is not identified by me with the actual. Aristotle was too much of a formalist (though less of one than the rationalists and logicians who followed); he therefore failed to allow for an adequate distinction between the essence as present (even as apart from the matter in which it was embodied) and the essence as luring, governing, constraining, but still only possible.

11.   It is through the agency of the evidenced that one gets to the source both of it and the evidence. You seem to think there is a difficulty here. But note: the evidenced at which one arrives is a finality in a limited guise.

12.   You say that you are unclear about "speculative errors." The move to the evidenced from the evidence is precarious; the evidenced is continuous with the finalities, but it may be at any one of an endless number of positions on the continuum, depending on its degree of consonance with the finality in itself. Only if the evidenced does not require serious modification to be accommodated, do we know the finalities as the evidenced in intensified forms. However, all evidenced content, no matter how unsatisfactory, tells us something about the finalities. We always know the finalities, for the evidenced, no matter how distortive or overlaid, is a version of the finalities. But that is also true of the evidence. We are in touch with the finalities from the moment we attend to the evidence, but we do not then know the finalities with the precision, completeness, or at a depth we want to achieve.

13.   You say you like my view of proper names within the confines of speculative philosophy; you apparently reject it as pertinent elsewhere. But what warrant is there for separating what is daily said and known from what is speculatively reached? There are different names used for actualities and for finalities; but those names also have a use in daily life.

14.   I am happy to be thought the author of a doctrine of rectifying names. Though I don't agree with Confucius that once we start by rectifying names, we can proceed step by step to the correct ordering of a kingdom, it does seem true that rectifying names does help one see a little more clearly what is the cause.

15.   When I appealed to the difference between signs and symbols I did not use Peirce's distinction, but had in mind what was said in *Beyond All Appearances*, where symbols are taken to be penetrative, and signs are held to have external referents.

16.   You object to my saying that "semantics had a practical, emotionally toned dimension utilized by proper names"; you also contended that it is "dubious as a general characterization of semantics." Of course, it is not compatible with "formal" semantics. But such a semantics is hard to distinguish from a formal syntax, since it is unable to relate language to what is external to it. You

could have referred to Quine as well as to the other "semanticists," for his "commitment" to the world is just a private matter, and it does not enable him to make contact with what is beyond his words.

17.   You say I need "a fuller doctrine of the ontologic import of terms." But this is exactly what I tried to provide in the account of symbols, in the references to penetration, intensive inferences and intensive references, acceptance of the evidenced, adherence, and adumbration. In different ways, all bring out the point that we are always involved beyond our terms with that to which our terms are about. The scholastics "posit" the view that the copula not only relates terms but orients them in what has them objectively united, and my references to accompanying emotions, and particularly to sympathy and love, make the same point. Yes, all the arresting names have a built-in import, as you acutely remark; that is inevitable, since they are not merely empty sounds somehow attached to what is indifferent to them, but condensations of what is already discerned of the object which they name. Peirce says that nouns are used in place of pronouns; he is right I think at least with respect to "I," "me," "you," and "we." These are not mere denotatives; all adhere and are grounded in their referents. Substitutes for these in the form of ordinary proper names do not entirely abstract from the penetrativeness of that for which they substitute.

18.   I have tried to deal with the mind/body problem in an article in the *Review of Metaphysics* a little while back; it is also dealt with in *Philosophy in Process*, and in one of the books I am now rewriting in mss. I do not see as yet that the theory of names is particularly pertinent to this problem, unless it be in the sense that the union of mind and body is emotional, and that proper names are always used emotionally to take us to what is the unity of mind and body.

19.   "Harmony" is not too alien to what I intend by Unity. But (a) it allows too much room for a plurality within it; and (b) it is dependent for content on what is beyond it. Unity acts on multiple actualities, but it has its own singularity, depth, and reality. Harmony does not.

20.   You seem to say opposite things about Harmony.

You say it is not one among the finalities, that it is not a constitutive feature of the world, that it is a finality only for my system, and that it is regulative principle. But your references to Reck and Martin seem to show that you also hold that Unity is a finality, superior to all the others. A regulative principle needs justification; if harmony is not constitutive it cannot unite the finalities; it cannot be a primal One without being denied a Many, and without raising the question of the unity of it with the Many, and so on without end. Unity is one of a number of finalities.

21.   Nothing is so terrible for an author as to be neglected. It is joyous to be read by a perceptive, careful thinker. I am grateful to you for the time and thought you have taken. If there are difficulties which I have slighted or misconstrued, I hope you will remark on them forcefully, and I will try to deal with them. In the meantime, I am much in your debt.

Appreciatively,

Paul

ॐ

September 25, 1977

Dear Tony:

The outline needs to be corrected, as follows:

1.   We proceed to both actualities and the finalities from objective appearance. We also can proceed directly from individual actualities, and from the actualities together. Actualities are together in the cosmos.

2. S does not account for the interaction of actualities, but for the condition that makes it possible for them to be relevant to one another. It does not focus on "intelligibility" but on affinities.

3. B accounts for the equality of actualities.

4. P does not account for the nomic necessities which the actualities themselves provide from within.

5. U accounts not only for the harmony of unities in

actualities but also for the ordering of the actualities in a valuational hierarchy.

6.   *S, B, P, E,* and *U* also account for the contexts in which the expressions of all the actualities are together.

7.   We must first detach evidence before we can pair it with the evidenced.

8.   Not all inferences are governed by speculative principles.

9.   Correctness of an inference to finalities is determined by the consonance of the evidenced with the finalities.

10.   Your 5 is excellent. It needs supplementation, though, by a reference to ontology as grounding what one knows.

I hope this helps.

Appreciatively,

Paul

❧

March 1, 1980

Dear Paul,

Again I feel greatly honored and privileged to receive your new book *You, I, and the Others.* This is certainly an important work that deserves wide attention. My experience in reading it has not been a smooth and easy one, largely owing to the deceptive simplicity of your style of writing. But in going through my notes, I now feel more confident about what I learned, though not without some queries. Let me remark on the importance of this work for me as an ethicist. For two decades, there is a discernible tendency in Anglo-American moral philosophy to broaden its subject matter. While perhaps still dominated by a conception of ethics as an autonomous enterprise, there is now a clear concern with the relevance of philosophical explorations in philosophy of mind (*e.g.*, Anscombe and Hampshire, more recently Brandt and Gewirth) and in metaphysics (*e.g.*, Iris Murdoch and Dorothy Emmet). My own concern has greater affinity to the latter and to Melden and A. E. Murphy. In retrospect, my recent book and the Chinese studies were preoccupied with the relation of ethics to philosophy of mind and metaphysics or what I like to call philosophy of vision or moral ideals. Your book offers a comprehensive approach to this problem. In what follows, I am merely offering a partial response to the first part in your book. I need more time to work on the second part. No doubt, there will be misreadings and mistakes which I hope you will rectify. My queries represent initial responses only, for I hope to reconsider them in light of more work on the second part.

Let me begin by remarking on your distinctive approach to understanding and/or encountering other human beings, *i.e.*, by way of *you*. This is an incisive approach for a number of reasons. First, it avoids the classic Cartesian difficulty of privileged access and avoids it by focusing on another human being as a subject of confrontation or encounter. Though not fully knowable because of privacy, a presentation of *you* by another is a subject for cognition in terms of space, time, causality, affiliation, and value. However, your insistence on a privacy that cannot be penetrated lays no claim to privileged access. If I understand it correctly, privacy is the domain of the self that has a variety of "epitomizations." (I shall comment on this point later.)

Second, your treatment of "you" as a term of address is significant. The point quite clearly suggests another as a being with value (1.32) and thus to be respected. Confrontation with another human being is *in* this sense a confrontation with a value. "You" as an addressing term (1.5) is a *value-term*. The ethical significance of this is clear. To confront a *you* is to respond to a subject (human) in a normative way. What marks a human being is a capacity to respond to another of like kind with a value-attitude. Although animals and other things can also become subjects of our normative focus, their value-status is in some sense derivative from the value-encounter among men. If this is a correct interpretation of your general thesis, then one can quite readily appreciate the insight that being and value are interconnected concepts. I see this point as crucial to understanding your successive treatment of "me," "self," "I," and "persons." More on this later.

Third, the focus on affiliation, on perception at a distance (which involves judgment), on intelligibility, in addition to the value-integrity of a *you*, is quite illuminating (1.20–1.38). For even if I cannot, by any device (scientific or otherwise) intensively move into *your* being or privacy with total success, I can still know you in these ways. Quite naturally affiliation-recognition leads to a *we* (or *they* or the other when I fail to probe affiliatively). And in these moves, however unsuccessful, into *your* privacy, I also know the constraining conditions that govern the I and all that is *yours* in terms of space, time, and causality.

Fourth, for me as an ethicist, the most incisive point relates to your distinction between *accountability* and *responsibility*, though some may not like your terms. For accountability, it is important to focus on your body as a point of origin (1.14–1.16), regardless of your desires and intention, or even your deeds or misdeeds. Accountability merely raises the question of justification but does not settle it. Only when we can "prove" responsibility can we properly praise or blame another human, though we can reward or punish him solely on the basis of accountability. Observe here that your distinction has close affinity with the more usual distinction between behavior (which is accountable) and action (for which a human is responsible). We can control behavior by rewards and punishment, but not action. And in this sense, action requires a free agent, or at least in the sense of a privacy of a *you* who prefers, chooses, and wills (1.29). Thus, the public and the private cannot be separated, though they are distinct. Behavior is human only when seen as a display of an inaccessible privacy which is responsible. But accountability and responsibility are connected, for "the attribution of accountability is a responsible act" (1.16).

The preceding four points do give rise to a query on your approach. Does not your approach utilize a predominantly *normative* model grounded in an ontology of privacy? This query stays with me throughout the book but receives gradual clarification as I move to the second and the third chapter. The *move* from *you* to *me* is a move

to my private being via my public status (2.16), but it is
also a move to my moral being (2.6). The *me*, however, "is
sustained by the I at the very same time that I refers to it
by means of 'me' " (2.4). "The me is sustained at the point
where I responsibly assume accountability" (2.4). Since I
have no question on the *me* that is worthy of your
concern, let me go on to the I and the self, the most
exciting chapter that displays quite clearly your normative-
ontological model. It is also this chapter that gives rise to
my main criticism of your book. For the way the model is
deployed makes use of a highly questionable assumption,
i.e., a hierarchy of values. But let me first address some
insights on the I and the self with some queries.

    For you, the *self* and *I* are distinct but connected. If I
understand it correctly, the *self* is a domain of privacy of
which the *I* is a primary representative epitomization or
"condensation." According to a lexical guide, "an
epitome" is "one that is consummately representative of
an entire class." This seems to be your point too (3.10).
There are other epitomizations like mind, decision (3.10),
and I suspect, volition too, though I miss a detailed
discussion of these. You attribute to the *I* a normative
status as that which "provides a measure in terms of
which all else can be assessed" (3.20), and an absolute and
relative import (3.23). In 3.28, you explicitly said: "I am an
evaluative base of all evaluations" (also 3.47). It seems
evident that *I*, if it were an epitomization of the self,
would be a *nuclear* epitomization. But in view of the *I*,
which provides a measure for all assessments of other
epitomizations, can I not simply regard the *I* as a *self-in-
action*, for after all, the other so-called epitomizations
appear to be nothing but my mental acts. The *I* is my self
in its unitary point of active reference and intelligibility.
The self *qua* self is still the privacy "undiversified" (3.19).
Put in another way, the *I* is the *pivotal and active* normative
center of my mental acts (the other epitomizations); the
self is the normative center of privacy—a *state* rather than
an activity in which all epitomizations are held in
equilibrium. This point is suggested in particular by your
remark that the self is "its own center of gravity,
prompting compensatory occurrences when someone of its
epitomizations achieves too great a dominance" (3.13); and
that it is "an insistent point of equilibrium" (3.19).

    If you accept the foregoing characterization of your

view, then it appears to be very close to the Confucian doctrine of central harmony, or equilibrium and harmony in *The Doctrine of the Mean*, except that the Confucians center their concern on the psychology of emotions (just one epitomization of the self). Your view makes sense of the notion of the self and the I as both normative centers, distinct but in effect complementary. In later neo-Confucian language, the self is the "substance" and the I the function. But just as "substance," *i.e.*, the intrinsic nature of a thing, cannot be understood apart from its function (*i.e.*, the intrinsic import for activity), so also function without substance is unintelligible. My activities are after all *rooted* in my privacy as normative, they point to a normative center of equilibrium to which I cannot have access except via *me*, and then only an *appreciation*, but no knowledge, of my self. If I am right then, both *self* and *I* are normative notions, as are *you, me, we,* and *they*.

Let me now turn to my uneasiness with your normative-ontological model. I fully agree that human beings are subject to constraining conditions, as are nonhuman things. Your *finalities* recur throughout the book. But of special relevance to the problem of the relation between ethics and metaphysics, your model, while allowing us a perspective to view our mental life, seemed deployed with *one* assumption, that of a notion of an objective hierarchy of values. This notion appears quite early in 1.32 (p. 84). (I note its appearance on the following pages: 251–57, 215–16, 258, 389, 307, 371–72, and 384.) I am not convinced by your appeal to unity as a finality (p. 84), for I am unable to see the force of your statement that "were there no such hierarchy, we would have to be content with taking value to rest on the questionable supposition that because men find something to be good, it is good" (p. 84). Consider, for example, the different values men may have, say, with respect to moral excellence. One value may, of course, be regarded as superior to another. Courage may be said to be better than temperance. But saying this does not entail that our judgment, if sound, *must* be based on some notion of objective hierarchy called Unity.

To rank x as better than y, of course, presupposes a scale of values, but such a scale need not be one of hierarchy but rather a temporary or occasional comparative judgment governed by a context and a point of view. The context is governed by our view of the nature of circumstance, and the point of view may well just be a perspective deemed relevant to the context. Vary the context and the perspective, we vary our comparative judgment. x, which is judged to be superior to y in context C_1, with a perspective P_1, may turn out to be inferior to y in context C_2 with a perspective P_2. Comparative value-judgments are thus context-perspective dependent; and these judgments need not be subjective, for they are amenable to argumentation (reasonable). An appeal to a hierarchy of values may even be unreasonable when it ignores the context and relevant perspective of judgments.

In 5.20, p. 372, you insist on Unity in a comprehensive sense. But it remains unclear how this Unity can yield an understanding of our value-perplexities. Even on sheer ontological grounds, you yourself recognize that "the demands and satisfactions of one condition sometimes conflict with those of another. . . . The ideal, unrealizable in fact and unenvisageable in detail, is to have each demand fully satisfied, and all harmonized without loss" (4.17, p. 333). If this is so, the hierarchical conception of value is a *mere* ideal that has no practical import in human experience. Even as a grand perspective, it is likely to distort the nature of value experience. A more viable ideal is what I call an ideal theme—a kind of coherent vision of the harmony of values in terms of complementarity of excellences. Though in a concrete situation, some of these excellences admit of ranking, they remain equal in import. In Kantian terms, it is a regulative idea and not a constitutive principle of reality. Perhaps you need the hierarchical concept of value to sustain your normative model, but I feel that the insight of this model is best gained without such a conception.

There are still many points you made which are not clear in my mind. I find your treatment of *persons* in terms of rights very puzzling and its status not very clear except with reference to *you* and *I*. But is it an epitomization of the self, or simply a *me* that coincides with the you in juridical contexts? Rights as claims to entitlements are best viewed as claims to the preconditions for the effective epitomizations of the self, centrally exemplified in "I am a person" (3.37). I hope in your next work you will tell us more about the other epitomizations, particularly volition (also desire?), intention (?), purposes (?), and emotions (?).

These quick references to your book, I hope are useful to you. They conceal much that I learn from you. For the first time, I appreciate the importance of the notions of time and space to a systematic reflection on the "primary dimensions of man." Let me end with a minor point on your comment on *Tao* (2.20, p. 136) in relation to "the final affiliating power" as "too insistent to be equated with Tao." This applies only to classical Taoism, not to Confucian *Tao* whose insistence is expressed in *jen* (or the ideal of humanity), which is an ideal of coherence without hierarchy, an affiliation without value-subsumption. I have a paper on the contrasting views of Confucianism and Taoism on *Tao* to be published this month (?) in *Journal of Chinese Philosophy*. I'll send you a copy.

With respect and affection,

Tony

ॐ

March 4, 1980

Dear Paul,

I have thought about the second part of your book. I am afraid what I have to respond now is even less reliable than the rather hasty notes I sent you on part one. I write with much less confidence because your treatment of the *we* and *they* and *the Others* are highly "metaphysical" and less empirically intelligible. This is my own failing I am sure, for I am not always sensitive to the ontological issues that preoccupy you. The little that I understand, perhaps nil, is incisive. My queries have thus to be taken as questions from an eager student rather than from a destructive critic.

The distinction crucial to your discussion of *we* in Chapter 4 is an important distinction between the varying types of interrelationship between men independently of the conditions they were subject to. You point out quite incisively the five functions of simple *we* that enter into the complex affiliated *we*. The social one, or later, associative *we* for me represents merely a condition of togetherness that makes sense of what it is to be a *community* rather than a mere collective or aggregate of *me's*. Significantly, as you point out, *tradition* is part of being a social *we* (4.4), but unlike you, I regard this social *we* not so much as prescriptive but rather a condition that renders intelligible men's relationships as personal relationships. It is a condition that renders intelligible the force of communal prescriptions. It itself is not prescriptive. As to the second function, the equitable or coordinative *we* (4.17), it appears to be the principle of impartiality. Here we have a prescriptive condition commonly recognized by moral philosophers. It is a normative, substantive, and not a formal principle as you will grant. The organization or structuralizing use is for me formal in character. A community, if it is viable, requires a social structure. And organization constitutes a way in which social order can be specified in a formal way, though in actual function, it is hardly detached from substantive import. The distributive *we* in terms of time, space, and causality is an incisive way to deal with the problem of social change. The assessive or evaluational *we* is plausibly here a hierarchy, for in a social setting some notion of authority and its ranking import has to be recognized. My previous notes expressed unhappiness over the individual import of the hierarchical conception. At any rate, I still feel that there need be no objective hierarchy, since different societies can have different ways of ordering their relations. Much of this difference has nothing to do with ontology, but with actual circumstances and varying traditions. The intelligibility of this diversity of value-scales does not seem to depend on an ontological theory.

I find the last chapter the most difficult one to grasp and, at the same time, perhaps the most difficult problem to tackle, *e.g.*, the problem of negation. You have exhibited the complex considerations involved in negation that cannot be reduced to propositions governed by the logical law of double negation. I would like to work hard on this. My difficulty has to do with the highly abstract way you deal with this problem. I hope a more detailed discussion can be given with "human" negations, the different imports of not being so-and-so. I agree that a negative always involves an assessment in a human context (5.12), and this may result in a contrastive, attributive, or completive terminus (5.6–5.8). A *they* sustains the others. And I think it is most perceptive of

you to point out that "to move from they to others is to
move from definiteness to indefiniteness, from specific
value to a general . . ." (5.12). Naturally, the question
arises: Why make this move? Is this because that *they* is
one of identifiable import, or is it because the others *can*
be a subject of our discourse without the concern we
express for a *they*. More likely both. We care directly for a
they and indirectly for the others. Perhaps it is less
misleading to say that *they* are accepted as subjects of
concern, and the others as *potential* subjects of concern. A
potential subject of concern is, of course, not mere
potentiality, but what you in the *Modes* call an ingredient
possibility. Am I right here?

One further comment relates to your treatment of a
human being as a lived body. Why does this occur at the
end of the book rather than at the beginning? A real
puzzle for me.

Affectionately,

Tony

2▲

March 6, 1980

Dear Tony,

As is usual, you make acute observations within the
frame of a sympathetic and perceptive understanding. I
will indeed be fortunate if the reviewers will read *You, I,
and the Others* in the same spirit and with the same insight.

I

As my references to responsibility and accountability
show, I share with you a concern with ethical issues, and
take this work to provide a foundation for it—as well as
for other enterprises focused on man, such as art, science,
and politics.

I agree that humans have values and that there are
value attitudes. But this is only one aspect of the problem
of value. You tend to take human value and attitude as

alone or to be most basic. No less basic are the substantiality, being, nature, and existence of entities. Nor do I see any warrant for your supposition that the value status of a man is derivative from a value encounter among men. Were it a derivative, one would like to know what it was derived from—is the encounter itself without value?

You have correctly interpreted my views on accountability and responsibility, except that you seem to neglect the fact that I can be held accountable for what does not originate with me or at my body. A society might find it just as convenient to reward or punish me even for what I never did. Generals, for example, are rewarded for battles won by subordinates; men are held accountable for some of the things their children and servants do.

It is not altogether correct to say that privacy is "inaccessible"; it is accessible but not fully penetrated. It can be understood but not lived through by another. You ask whether I have a normative model founded in an ontology of privacy. No and yes: privacy is not separable from a body, but together they provide a normative model for understanding what an actual being is.

You have a fine grasp of what I understand by the self and I, but not of other epitomizations of the privacy. These are not all "mental," and they have an affect on the I. Volition, as you remark, is one of the epitomizations of privacy. It was dealt with by me at some length in *Man's Freedom*, and it will be attended to again in the work in progress.

I think I have knowledge of my self. Otherwise I could not know that it was being appreciated, that it was epitomized, that it could effectively act on its epitomizations, etc.

You are most troubled by the idea of an hierarchy of values. You say that a scale of values could be "[just?] . . . governed by context and viewpoint." But then we would have no basis for judging different contexts and viewpoints as better and worse. Surely one can be superior to others. You would not equate Confucius's with Hitler's. Comparative judgments of course are to be made, but the contexts in which they are made are themselves not value free. If they were, there would be no judging all men, and we would be caught in an irreducible relativity, which itself would have to be justified.

You think that a mere ideal has no practical import in human experience. But surely ideals of absolute beauty, virtue, truth are at once unattainable and have great practical import, dictating where and how one should strive, and enabling one to distinguish the careless from the dedicated, the worse from the better.

You ask whether a person is an epitomization of the self. I am sorry that I was not clearer. Like the self, "person" is an epitomization of a constant privacy. Unlike the self it has both a public and a private side, and is present as soon as there is a human. You anticipate what I am now working on—the examination of the various epitomizations of privacy, particularly responsibility, resolution, mind, desire, and sensitivity. I am glad to learn about the distinction between classical and Confucian Taoism, and to find that I am in some accord with the latter.

II

Yes, the social *we* is a condition for communication, but conditions are prescriptive, limiting what they affect, dictating to it what can and cannot be done. The conditions are of various kinds. One is intelligible, but the intelligible is also prescriptive.

The coordinative *we*, as you remark, provides a base for impartiality, and the organizational *we* is primarily formal.

The concrete application of the ideas contained in the discussion of negation is provided by the remainder of the chapter.

I like both your question and answer about why we move from the they to the others. I don't think, though, that a "potential object of concern" is equatable with an ingredient possibility. The former is relative to someone who can be concerned; the latter is present whether or not one is or might be interested in it.

There is a warrant for beginning with the lived body. Indeed, in the work in progress I begin somewhere near this. It is also true that the proper ending of a philosophic book is with what the beginning presupposes. In the book in process I end somewhere near the "I."

Thank you for the thought and time you have spent on the book, and for your comments. The strong affirmative tone of my answers should not deceive you. Both apart from your comments and because of them they are on the surface of a basic hesitancy, doubt, and perplexity.

As ever,

Paul

ﻬ

April 17, 1983

Dear Paul,

Again I feel honored and greatly privileged to be among the first to receive your new book on *Privacy*. This work, together with *Beyond All Appearances, First Considerations*, and *You, I, and the Others*, indubitably displays the incisive power of a speculative mind in dealing with a wide range of philosophical problems. It has become clearer to me why it is not possible to be a specialist in a branch of philosophy without probing the deeper connections among so-called branches of philosophy. *Privacy*, in particular, exemplifies the interconnection between philosophy of mind, ethics and value theory, and metaphysics and ontology. I want to bring forth a number of questions, for the sake of further clarification rather than for the sake of rational criticism. These queries are best preceded by some remarks of my general understanding of your efforts in terms of my own exposition of the significance of the problems that beset you.

Privacy concerns an adequate theory of the nature of man, the primary dimensions of man and the ways in which they affect and modify one another. There are two *generic* dimensions: "person" and "self"; each may be viewed as an epitomization of privacy in a generic sense. They represent two "primary powers," though you reserve this for the idios. Put differently, if one is to understand the nature of man, one must attend to two different sorts of "powers" (much in the sense in which Reid talks of active and intellectual powers). Person, however, differs from self in that it is a repertoire of first-

order powers that are normally expressed in connection
with one's lived body. Self, on the other hand, is a generic
power of the second-order pertaining to the power to
exercise or reject the first-order powers of the person. I
find this general view congenial, though your manner of
exposition is not always free from doubt. I will first attend
to "epitomizations of person" and "epitomizations of the
self," and indicate the respect in which your
reconstructions are affected by some of these difficulties,
which I must say are due perhaps to my
misunderstanding. But my aim is to bring to light what I
believe are your profound insights in bringing closer the
enterprise of ethics and philosophy of mind to an
overarching metaphysical system.

Person and Its Epitomization

A reader may be puzzled at the outset. For if person
in your sense is an epitomization, how can an
epitomization admit of further epitomizations? This
difficulty is spurious, since person is a generic concept
that requires specifications in context. It may be viewed as
a generic term for the repertoire of first-order powers. I
believe that this lies in your use of "specialization,"
though at times you seem to have something else in mind.
With the terminology cleared, one can appreciate your
account of the epitomizations of person, for these are the
specifications of a generic power of a man. Thus,
sensitivity, sensibility, need, desire, orientation, society,
mind, and resolution represent the range of our first-order
powers. I find much of these discussions quite instructive,
except on desire, mind, and resolutions. On desire, it is
indeed very strange to claim that they are species-
oriented. In the same context, one missed a discussion of
other desires and their relation to emotions in general.
Your conception of mind is much too narrow. Why restrict
its function to inference? One would expect that what is
relevant to the exercise of the generic power is one of
reflection. Moreover, "mind" is commonly used also to
refer not only to thinking but also to volition and choice,
which you discussed under resolutions. Incidentally, if
"mind" is used in the broad sense, it can be properly

viewed as a second-order rather than as a first-order power. In general, your discussion of resolutions would be more incisive if it were given in connection with the self rather than in the context of persons.

The most incisive discussion pertains to choice, though your use of the term may cause some difficulties for the reader. I see it, for example, as a special kind of choice that attempts, as you have profoundly pointed out, to link the past with the present by way of rectifying the errors in the past, *i.e.*, "compensating losses" in past choices. It is a "restorative" or rectificatory act (p. 153)—a point consistently ignored by all major moral philosophers. It is commonly taken to be axiomatic that all choices are forward, rather than backward, looking. Of course, saying that choice can be retrospective does not preclude a concern with its present and prospective significance (p. 157). (This incidentally is a pervasive theme in Confucius.)

The Self and Its Epitomizations

If I am right about person, then the self is also a generic concept of the second-order powers (I mean such a repertoire). Thus autonomy, responsibility, and the I. A reader, like myself, is bound to encounter the following difficulties. First, your account of responsibility contains a serious ambivalence with respect to the supreme or ultimate good. On the one hand, like in *Beyond* and *You*, you want to espouse a conception of absolute good, a hierarchically ordered state of excellence. On the other hand, but more plausibly, you want to insist that the final good is an indeterminate ideal. If you consistently adhere to the latter view, one cannot maintain that there can be an assessment of actions in terms of what is absolutely right or wrong (p. 184). But how can this absolute assessment be possible when, as you say, there is no pre-established harmony? It is at least unclear how an ideal, while indeterminate, can serve as an absolute measure of concrete actions. This is the heart of my own distinction between ideal themes and ideal norms. The two sorts of ideals are distinct, but of course, not unconnected. Perhaps the latter is a systematic way of articulating the significance of the former, though I doubt whether it can fully exhaust its significance. Note also that your notion of choice would support the notion of indeterminate final good and not the absolute norm. I hope you can clear up this puzzle for me.

One may also question whether the epitomizations of the self are in themselves ethically significant. As I see your view, they depend in large part on idios as "a primary power," which is part of your "Reconstructions." Another puzzle pertains to the "I" as "representing the self." Why not reserve this role to the discussion of the idios, which provides a basic grounding and a way for dealing with conflicting epitomizations of both the self and the person?

Reconstructions

Let me now turn to the part entitled "Reconstructions." Forgive me for saying that I find the whole part too diffused, particularly the last two chapters, which also interest me the most. Chapter 3 is clear about the problems: (1) to show the connection of privacy and lived body, and (2) to exemplify the interplay and grounding of the epitomizations in "finalities." I do not find the exposition pertaining to (1) problematic. But I believe it is because I have some acquaintance with your previous works. (This remark also applies to "idios" in Chapter 4.) As for (2), perhaps due to my own failing, I am disappointed for not seeing an account of the interplay. When I started reading this chapter, I said to myself, "At last, I am going to learn of the way in which each epitomization acts on (affects) and modifies one another." At the end of the chapter, I comprehend their "final grounds" but hardly anything about their mutual interplay.

Chapter 4 on the Idios is for me the best and most incisive one in Part II. Let me articulate my response to your insights. The epitomizations of the self and person do sometimes conflict. For the resolution, there *must* be a "primary power," playing heed to "finalities," to provide a unifying and harmonious expression of all epitomizations. The idios, if I may put it in my preferred

terminology, is a *third-order* power. Its successful
governance in fivefold manner (self-sufficiency, self-
mastery, etc.) exemplifies your ideal of a "mature man."
But there is no assurance that the idios can deal with
conflict with total success. It is the "I" that ultimately
provides a concrete foothold for the exercise of the idios.
And it is in terms of the *I*'s concern with conflicting
epitomizations, "grounded" in the idios, that remedies
and cures are attended to.

   And this in Chapter 5: What is not clear in this
chapter is how such a task can be performed at all unless
one holds on to some vision of the "good will"
(reminiscent of Kant's); and, moreover, such a good will,
even with the support of the *I* and the idios can encounter
the "perverse will." In Chapter 5, I miss a fuller
discussion of the final good and its relation to the good
and bad wills. The title "human excellence" seems
misleading, though I fully agree with you on the insidious
problem of moral perversity. Is human excellence simply a
matter of "full health?" If so, we need a more detailed
account of this notion.

   The last chapter on rights is for me the most obscure,
and perhaps the weakest in the whole book. The thesis is
clear, and not commonly accepted, that there are native
rights that do not depend on public or state recognition.
More particularly, rights are claims of privacy (pp. 299,
305). I am most puzzled about the *claim* that each
epitomization implies a right against other persons. But
this conception is more a tautology in view of your
conception of person as a locus of rights. Strictly,
according to your definition of "person" (also Kant's),
rights pertain to persons. But you also seem to want to
say that the self has rights. And here, my general
statement on your distinction at the beginning, seems to
fail to do justice to your view. Of course, self can have
rights by an extension of this term. But also, it is by virtue
of the "I" that claims of privacy are made. Is there a
distinction between "claims of persons" and "claims of
privacy?" I am very confused about this whole discussion.
My basic difficulty is that you seem to neglect the
distinction between "claims" and "valid claims"
(Feinberg). All claims equally deserve attention, but some
may fail in justification. The epitomizations of privacy may
well have claims, but whether they are justified remains a

separate issue that cannot, I believe, be resolved on metaphysical grounds.

The foregoing observations on *Privacy* are hasty responses after a first, and not always close, reading. But at least, what I think to be your profound insights into "man as an active being" (Hume) are not misrepresentations of your thought. Also, these observations, particularly in the form of critical queries, are designed to seek your enlightenment.

I look forward to your next work, and sincerely hope that the current one is as widely read as it should be. I have refrained from commenting on many good points concerning the distinction between man and animals, man and machines, and the governing role of finalities, etc.

With respect and affection,

Tony

ঽ৯

4/24/83

Dear Tony:

It would be hard to exaggerate how grateful I am to you for your thoughtful, penetrating, honest examination of *Privacy*. I wish I had shown you the manuscript before I sent it off. I am going to revise my current manuscript in the light of your comments, and will want you to look at it before I send it to a press.

1. "First-order" and "second-order" have an epistemological or methodological connotation, do they not? If so, they do not do justice to an ontological distinction which I think distinguishes person and self. But if it does help, I certainly have no objection to having the two distinguished in this way.

2. Why may not an epitomization have epitomizations of its own? Let it be supposed that I epitomize "man"; I can still have epitomizations. There would be a difficulty if there were no independent action possible to an epitomization. You say that the difficulty is spurious, but nevertheless seem to believe that it will cause difficulty. It should be momentary, should it not?

3.   I was troubled again and again by my use of "desire"; it is, though, the way psychologists and biologists seem to use the term, I think.

4.   As you know, Descartes had two accounts of mind—one relating to what just thinks, the other to what also wills, believes, etc. Those who speak of minds as computers or with Hobbes as calculators, I thought dominated the discussions, and so I went along with them in using the term in that way. You know the literature in a way I do not. I should have asked you about the normative use today.

5.   If resolution were dealt with under the self, it would not be possible to take preference to be a type of resolution, or we would have to deny that a child can exercise a preference before it has a distinct self.

6.   The problem about the proper terminology which you find in connection with desire, mind, and resolution, apparently also arises in connection with choice. I suppose all attempts to break new ground are up against this kind of problem. I now can hope only that my usages are not too *outré*.

7.   It would not be amiss to speak of person and self as "generic" provided that this was not supposed to refer to what is merely general, that it was recognized to have power and activity.

8.   If the good is an ideal it is so far indeterminate, lacking the details that actualizations provide. Such internal indeterminancy does not, I think, preclude being a measure of what is absolutely right and wrong. I think now, in the light of what you say, I should distinguish between an indeterminate "rule" or "right," which is illustrated in specific ways, and an indeterminate objective, which is realized in specific shapes. Would this take care of the problem you see?

9.   I thought of *I* as the locus of identity. The idios could not represent the self, I think, since its function is to reconcile it with the person, and its epitomizations with one another and those of the person.

10.   I am sorry that you did not care for the last two chapters of Part II. I agree that the last was too brief, and

perhaps should have been omitted, but I still think that something important is being said about remedies and cures. You are right in finding the discussion of the interplay of epitomizations and finalities skimpy. I was trying (perhaps foolishly) to avoid references to the finalities as much as I could, making a reference to them only for the content with which the private idios would interplay. But I do hope that what I say about the connection between privacy and lived body can be understood by those who know nothing of my other works.

11.   It never occurred to me to inquire into the various ways in which the various epitomizations affect and modify one another. That perhaps is a serious mistake.

12.   Since the idios is the boldest idea of the book, I am glad to hear from you that the chapter on it is the best and most incisive one in Part II.

13.   I agree that there is no assurance of complete success by the idios. And I have been using "healthy" not to refer to bodily well-being; I have been using the term in some consonance with its philology to refer to "wholeness" or "sound." That is why I am thinking of calling my next book "Toward a Commonhealth."

14.   I don't understand the difficulty you are raising in connection with the "good will." But I do see that I did not make evident how one could be an ethical being.

15.   The native claims are essential claims and are all valid. The self has rights, but expresses them through the person. Privacy as such makes no claims; it is its epitomizations which do.

The foregoing tried to provide the clarifications you seek. I am sure they do not meet all your difficulties, but that is in part because I am not sure I have understood them—not because you are unclear but because I haven't seen the issue clearly enough. I would like to try to clarify what you think still remains painfully obscure. Most important, I hope that you and I can now discuss the problems which divide us, and clarify those on which we agree.

I cherish our friendship. And once I am able to get

beyond your unfailing courtesy, I find that you face me with problems whose full nature I had not discerned, and that you have insights into the nature of man and the life he is to lead which open up whole areas of thought and truth. I do hope that you will return to these issues and that we will be able to discuss them at length. My own evaluation is that I was more interested in providing a taxonomy than in indicating what a good life is and how it is to be led, having thought, perhaps mistakenly, that I had done this in *Man's Freedom* and in *The Making of Men*. You are making evident to me that I still have an ethics to write. Is that correct?

Gratefully,

Paul

Thirteen

Irwin C. Lieb

Being and Becoming

This essay is about being and becoming, about their meaning and opposition, and about a resolution of the opposition between them. In describing these notions I will occasionally refer to some historically important formulations of them. I will also provide examples of their use. I hope the references and examples will make more accessible the abstractions in which the opposition is described and then discussed.

Ontology has, from its beginning, tried to settle which reality is more fundamental, being or that which is, or becoming, occurrence, happening, coming to be, and passing away.

The terms "being" and "becoming" have been used mainly in two ways: First, they have been used as the names for what is fundamentally real. So, being is what is most real; becoming, what is most basic. (There are almost inescapable redundancies in the use of the words "is" and "being," and there are near contradictions in expressions like "becoming is . . . .") This is the way Parmenides and Heraclitus used the terms. The terms have also been used to stand for kinds of conceptions or for kinds of fundamental entities: conceptions of platonic forms are, for example, conceptions of being, and conceptions of events are conceptions of becoming. I will use the terms in both these ways; I hope the references will be clear.

What is the opposition between being and becoming? It is that only one of them can be fundamental, that the other cannot be derived from the fundamental one, and that one of the two, then, is less real than the other, perhaps being only apparent or abstract. There can be no saving case, where the two are equally basic, equally real.

The two exclude one another because of being's not becoming and because of becoming's not having the same complete fullness as being. Nothing of the one is in the other; nothing can ever come to be there—

so that if only one reality can be fundamental, it has to be either being or becoming.

Were either fundamental, however, there could be no derivation of the other. Being does nothing; it would be incomplete or otherwise imperfect if it had to become anything else or even it if had to create a becoming. The opposite is true the other way around, and there is the quandary then how one or the other of them can be real if it is not derived from the fundamental reality.

Nor is there sense in the idea of their being equally real. If they were equally real, would the two be described as being? Or would their being together be a kind of becoming for which no being is a correlate? Or is there some other sort of being or becoming which the classical notions divide, so that neither is fundamental after all? These questions leave us unsettled and unsure, and the abstractness of the formulations may even make us wonder about the sense of being and becoming themselves.

Still, the notions have played an important part in the history of Western thought, and they are important for us now—and not only historically. It is not currently in fashion to discuss being and becoming, but these notions, or notions very close to them, are prominent in present thought, in conceptions of experience; self and person; agent and action; material or physical object; and occurrence, event, and happening. Contemporary formulations of these last notions have received extensive and technical development. But all of them, I think, show strains of the opposition between being and becoming. I hope, then, that it will be a contribution to contemporary discussion to look again at the opposition, to see how it occurs in some of our current notions and to consider whether the opposition can be resolved.

Let me look at the opposition again, referring now explicitly to time. Which is fundamental? Being or becoming? That which is, is— and it neither comes nor ceases to be. Were either of these last the case, being would be, but only for a time. It would therefore not be the basic reality. It would be derivative, dependent on what caused it to come to be or caused its dissolution. Becoming, by contrast, is or is *in* or is *through* its own becoming. There is no *before* in it, nor is there an *after* it. If becoming is fundamentally real, nothing is before or after it. It is not a becoming of being; it would not wholly be becoming if that were so.

These references to time, to what must or can or cannot occur in it, provide general characterizations of being and becoming. Those who, like Parmenides, contend that being alone is real, suggest that the transiency or passing of things is not finally real; its only being is the derived being of appearances. Those, on the other hand, like Heraclitus, who point to becoming as the fundamental reality argue that there is no eternity. They acknowledge, however, that the constancy of becoming sometimes appears to be the becoming of becoming or to be a sort of law.

If there is being, then, in the classical opposition, becoming is not equally real; and the other way around as well. Being does not cause a spread of transiency or come into or pass out of it; it excludes becoming of any kind. On its side, again, becoming is thorough transiency. There are no parts of it that are not becoming. It is not a transformation either of being into becoming or a transformation into being. Becoming, in its own way, excludes being, providing no place for it. The contention between being and becoming is direct and complete. Neither allows for the other. But it does not satisfy us to have only one of them as fundamentally real while the other is not real or real enough.

Many of us, despite the opposition between being and becoming, have nevertheless tried to say that both can be or that both can become together. Can there be a coherent joining of the two? Can both be in a becoming, or can both become in a being? The answer, I think, is "no." In any of these combinations, a joining of being and becoming is or becomes unstably ambiguous. Either side, being or becoming, spreads through the joining and excludes the other, or the two otherwise never really join.

Take, for example, the horizontal line in Plato's image of the divided line (or the two sides of Kant's form of time). The line is not a third thing, distinct from the being and becoming it divides. It shares in each of them, so that it has an upper side, which is the form of time that mathematics explores. It also has an underside, which is the transience of the flux that has somehow to be informed. The division between upper and lower, however, is not firm or stable. There seems to be no bottom for the upper part of the line and no upper limit for the lower part; each side spreads through the other. This trivial illustration shows, I think, that Plato never brought being and becoming together; the join, even the connection between them, cannot be made clear.

This is also shown, in a deeper way, in Plato's doctrine of participation. For though the flux or what is in it participates in forms, the forms themselves do not enter the flux. There is no transport of their being. Forms and flux stand apart from one another. Again, the platonic conceptions of being and becoming do not really join. The lesson of their separation is that we cannot think of being and becoming as together without extensively changing the platonic conceptions of them. This is true of other historically important conceptions as well.

For example, what juncture is there in Aristotle between a directed matter and the unmoved mover that enables it to sustain its forms? Or, has Aristotle an account of how the forms of substances form their matter? Do we understand—now taking examples at random—the difference in Leibniz between a possible and an actual world? Do we understand the communion between a Spinozistic being and its manifestations, between phenomena and noumena, or between the Kantian categories and the sensuous manifold they organize? Finally, in more recent thought, have we a sound conception in Whitehead of how eternal objects are given for actualization in occasions?

These citations are examples of claims that being and becoming can be or become together, either of themselves or in kinds of entities or processes. It seems to me, however, that in each of them the opposition between being and becoming remains unreconciled. Being and becoming are irreconcilably opposed in classical thought. They are redefined or partly so in modern thought. But they have not been changed enough. We should feel an incoherence, comparable to the classical opposition, in conceptions of the entities and activities in which something like classical being and becoming have been parceled out.

There is no obvious or easy resolution to the contentions I have described. Still, the issues might be turned because of another difference between being and becoming, or between our conceptions of them. The difference is that our conception of being is simple, but our conception of becoming, so far as we have a conception of it, is complex. There have always been difficulties in forming definite conceptions of becoming—we remember Aristotle's exasperation with Heraclitians during the defense of the law of noncontradiction. But the complexity of becoming does not seem owed to the requirements for there being conceptions; nor do the requirements subordinate becoming to being. The complexity seems to be in becoming itself, in having it be a *one* and be a *one* in a different way than being is. The importance of the complexity in turning the issues is that the complexity of becoming can be explained. In turn, the explanation will show that becoming is a derivative reality, though not, of course, a derivative of the being to which it is opposed.

Acknowledging a complexity in what had been thought to be a fundamental reality, elucidating it and then constructing its explanation is an important method in the philosophy of Paul Weiss. Its use is especially prominent in *Modes of Being* and in *First Considerations*. One might even say that Weiss came to think of *the* modes of being because he saw, not that the fundamental philosophical conceptions of others are not comprehensive, but that the complexities in them obscure their meanings and strain their use in explanations. It is as if he thought the conceptions should be *divided* and that new affiliations should be arranged for the divisions. Where others had thought of one or two or perhaps three modes of being, in *Modes of Being*, Weiss came to think that there are four. Later, reflecting on what seemed to him compressions in his earlier thought, in *First Considerations*, he came to think that there are even more.

I think that Weiss's method of division is sound. It is directed to philosophy's aspiration for the highest and, therefore, widest generality. It sees, though with suppositions and formalities of its own, that whenever our conceptions of realities are in a certain way complex, they are not yet conceptions of what is fundamentally real. I also think that this method, which I learned from Paul Weiss, will help remove the opposition between being and becoming in a way that will remind readers of some themes in Weiss's work.

The difference between being and becoming that signals their simplicity and complexity has, again, to do with time. Whatever is, is altogether and all at the same time. The time of being is eternity. Such unity as becoming has or had or comes to have, such continuity as it has, is never all at once. Becoming continues itself, and the completeness that is required for a conception of it is that it always or continually continues. The complexity is that, for becoming to be endlessly, there has to be transience in any *now* and the *nows* have to be continuing. Endlessness is not the same as eternity. There is no "ever the same" in eternity. But in becoming there is "ever a difference." In the conception of becoming, then, we have to distinguish what there are differences *in* and what makes for there continually being such differences.

The complexity of becoming suggests that becoming is derived. Since being and becoming are opposed (as we think that there can be only a single fundamental reality), a derivation of becoming will suppose instead that there are at least two fundamental modes or kinds of being. This notion will have sense only if our conceptions of the proposed kinds of beings are coherent and only if they do not reinstate the opposition between being and becoming. I think that these coherent and innocent characterizations can be provided. They will enable us to develop the idea that becoming is a joining of two fundamental beings or beings of two fundamental kinds.

How should we characterize the sorts of beings which, together, account for the complexity of becoming? There can be no separate and independent description of them. When being and becoming are considered separately they exclude one another. If we are not to repeat their opposition, we have to characterize the beings which constitute becoming as they are together. Indeed, that will characterize their being. They are, and they are by being, *in* one another in different ways. Were we to think of them as separate, we would have to think of still another entity, the field that separates and connects them and makes it possible for them to come together to be joined. It is therefore more sound to say that the being of the basic kinds of things is *in* their being in one another in certain ways.

Suppose, then, that there are beings of two modes or kinds. Let me consider the kinds first only formally, and without fine detail. How can beings of several kinds be *in* one another so as together to be becoming? If becoming is a derivative, if it is a combination of beings of different kinds, then what must those beings do *to* and *for* and *in* one another to constitute the becoming? The answer to these questions, feeling now for the complexity in becoming, is that there can be becoming only if one being or one sort of being provides duration or temporal extension for the other, while the second provides for there continually being new moments of transiency.

Let me try to say why this is so. Becoming has to be long enough to be becoming, and such duration as it has must be owed to one of the kinds of beings that constitute it and from which it derives. Time does not, as Newton thought, pass of itself; even if it did, it would not pass in dimensioned packets. Something has to dimension becoming. It seems therefore that extension, as one of the marks or major divisions of becoming, has to be owed to one of the kinds of beings from which, without having it itself become, becoming derives.

It is also a serious issue for those who remark on the reality of becoming to explain its continuity. The flux is only now, matter has its vitalities only in a moment; energy, forces, and causes are effective only momentarily and they then define the present time. What is it that makes for continuous becomings? The assurance of the continuity of becoming must, I think, be provided by something whose being is not itself a becoming. That, still formally considered, will be the second sort of being I have in mind.

This formal view, turning on a division of the characters of becoming, is that there are beings of two sorts, that these are and have to be *in* one another, that they are *in* each other in different ways, and that one of their ways of being *in* one another is a moment of becoming in becoming as a whole. Becoming, then, or this becoming, is not opposed to being. It is the being together of beings of different kinds, one of which dimensions the other while the other, in turn, conditions agitations in the first.

What are the kinds of beings that constitute becoming? Let me try to render their conceptions less formally. It seems to me that one of the required conceptions is provided by that being and then by those beings that we think of as substantial, material, actual, particular, or individual— though it is not part of our conception that their being is always in singularities.

The other sort of reality is, it seems to me, like what Plato called the *flux*, or what Aristotle meant by *matter*; it is perhaps the same as whatever in Leibniz's thought makes for the difference between what is possible and actual, and like Schopenhauer's *will*, Bergson's *élan*, Whitehead's notion of *creativity*, and Weiss's *existence*. I have, in another presentation, called this being Time, to emphasize its affiliation with Newton's thought and with contemporary conceptions in the sciences. The notion is that this reality, whatever is a suitable name for it, does not pass of itself, though our words almost make us express ourselves as if this were the case. Instead, it is made to pass by the singular realities and it is dimensioned by them.

These, then—entities that are like individuals and a being like existence or creativity or time—are the sorts of beings from which becoming derives. The becoming they constitute can, therefore, be looked at from two sides, from the sides of both the beings that constitute it. Becoming is action, when it is looked at from the side of individuals; individuals act and becoming is the action *in* which they are. Looked at from the side of temporality—looked at in the way Whitehead describes occasions— becoming is an event or an occurrence. As between the perspectives, there is no ground for preference. Individuals and time are equally real, and we have to refer to both of them in describing the transiency of things. Individuals without temporality could not act; they would be nontemporal entities that could not affect anything. Existence, creativity, or time, conversely, would not pass without individuals; there would be nothing to make it pass and nothing to account for its regularity.

There are, of course, a number of critical questions to be raised about these conceptions, and there should also be reflection on their underlying suppositions. I have space to explore only one of the questions; then I will turn to the suppositions that are most likely to be troubling.

The question is why, if these two sorts of beings constitute becoming, there are only moments of becoming? Is it that they do not suffuse one another but join only at a point which is a *now*, and that they otherwise hold themselves apart from one another? Were they to suffuse one another and be altogether *in* one another, would not an extended and whole becoming exist for which no measure and no contrast is found?

I am not certain of the answer to this important issue. The following speculation, however, seems the most appropriate. The kinds of being that constitute becoming do not hold themselves away from one another, nor are they *in* one another only at a single part or place. If they did, if they were, there would never be more than a moment, or else the beings that constitute becoming would have themselves to move and to become. The two, therefore, are *in* one another through and through. Still, while they suffuse one another, one or another of them is more prominent through the different portions of their joined being—so that, through a part of their suffused being, one of them dominates the other while through the other part the other is dominant, and the area in which individuals and time contend for dominance is the area of the present and of activity. If the past is real, for example, it is the reality in which temporality has overridden singularities and transformed individuals into a connected tissue of fact. So far as the future has direction and shape, it has it, not of itself, but because of the reach into it of shaped and charactered individuals.

The answer to the question, then, is that becoming consists of these two sorts being *being in* one another: the two sorts of beings suffuse one another entirely, but there are areas of domination in their union, now by one, now by the other, and the arena of contending beings is their issue in the present moment. Becoming is a whole of being while its occurrences are momentary.

These last remarks suggest serious questions about the suppositions in these conceptions. There are two suppositions that should be especially examined. The first is about becoming's being complex and about elucidating its complexity, either as I have suggested or in some other way. But why this supposition? Is it because we are set against becoming by our understanding, so that we think of it as complex by thinking that it has to become before our eyes and then be contrasted to a stable nothing and a steady but expectant mind? Why not simply construct a countersupposition—that being is complex and that its complexity is owed to the several becomings that constitute or sustain it?

This is an issue of importance, and several observations suggest the complexity about which to ask. There are kinds of beings. But if there are kinds of beings and if each of the kinds is fundamental, why is not there simply a complexity in being? Why is not there only one being after all? Why, following a doctrine of Peirce's, are there not compound but still indecomposable kinds of being, so that not all complexes are derived?

It is difficult to be sure how these interesting observations can be shown to be unconvincing. Let me take Peirce's expression of the issue to be representative. He claims, as you know, that in addition to monadic conceptions, which are obviously indecomposable, there are indecomposable dyadic and triadic conceptions; he claims, comparably, that there are kinds of being that are complex. There are beings which are what they are in themselves; others that must always relate to a second; still others that must relate triadically.

This is a brilliant insight and a compelling criticism of the early empiricists' doctrine of ideas. But it does not tell us what the beings are and it does not show us that they are complex. It shows instead that several sorts of being are always in one or another sort of relation. It shows that the beings are located in a complex, not that they are complex themselves. In this essay, individuals and time are always *in* one another. Yet they are two, distinguished by what they do to and for one another. The inseparable connection of one sort of being with another does not make them an indecomposable complex being. We find complexity, not in beings, but in their being combined. Being is single, both for thought and in reality.

Perhaps the most challenging supposition in the conceptions of individuals and time is whether there is not something like becoming in them—so that it is no advance to take becoming to be a complex that is owed to the two of them. Is there something, then, near to the character of classical becoming in either of the two sorts of beings I have so formally described?

I do not think there is. The prominent characters of becoming are not found in either of the two beings from which becoming is derived. The characters of becoming derive, really derive, from the two together. It is in the two of them as the two are together, as they are *in* one another in a certain way. The togetherness of the whole of the two does not come about. What does come about, becoming, is *inside* of them as they are together. So far, then, as the two beings can be conceived separately, abstractly, there is no becoming in either one of them. But, as they are together, they in part contend, and that contention, making for the present, shows that there are two of them and is the becoming which derives from both of them. If one wanted a still further showing that the beings that constitute becoming are two in number and more fundamental than becoming, we could perhaps also show that, in addition to constituting becoming, the beings are connected with other basic realities. Becoming is one consequence of basic realities, and perhaps not the only one.

In summary, to recompose what seemed otherwise an irreconcilable opposition in classical renditions of being and becoming, this essay claims that individuals or individuality and time are fundamentally real and that becoming derives from them; it is in the two of them together. Perhaps, though, these conceptions will not be considered conceptions of being at all, but conceptions of some amalgam of what used to be thought of as being and becoming. Even that, I think, would be an advance.

It is not clear to me that one can or needs to go further, nor is it clear where we will be driven if there are contradictions in the conceptions that have been set out. It is an unsure matter where speculation can come to rest. If it can come to rest only for a time and if it must come to rest in conceptions of being, then, for a time, it seems to me to rest in conceptions of beings such as those I have described.

Fourteen

Charles Hartshorne

Weiss After Sixty Years

Not too many friendships have lasted nearly sixty years. Chance, a word I like better than Paul does (and our differences are partly verbal), brought us together early in our long careers. Before that time, our intellectual histories had been vastly different. In the next few years, however, our intellectual exposures were more alike. We knew well some of the same teachers; but only Paul was still classified as a student. We read Peirce and Whitehead and talked to the latter— yet (such is philosophy), our mature speculations have diverged greatly. That is, no doubt, partly a consequence of our unlike early environments. For Paul's part in editing Peirce, I have only praise and gratitude. I can scarcely imagine having completed the job alone; and Paul was an admirable collaborator. Deciding to accept his offer to help and then later to accept him as coeditor were scarcely decisions, they seemed so obviously the things to do. In a cab five years ago, Paul and Jonathan Weiss and I reached an agreement that the greatness of Peirce, which we both appreciated, made what might have been a very difficult job relatively easy, at least in the interpersonal cooperation it involved. The importance of the job, not just for us and not particularly for our careers, but for the world, was perfectly apparent to both of us. That was enough common ground.

Weiss and I share a common faith in speculative philosophy or metaphysics as a reasonable enterprise. He had, I think, already derived something of this faith from Morris Cohen, who had himself been influenced by Peirce. Another trait that made it easy for us to work together was that we both mixed seriousness and hard work with a capacity for enjoying the humorous aspects of things. I have always found it difficult to quarrel with a witty and truly humorous person.

Weiss's founding of the Metaphysical Society and the *Review of Metaphysics* were brilliantly successful deeds of daring. Who knows what would have happened to efforts in and attention to my kind of philosophy without these accomplishments? What our philosophies have in common is most easily seen in his early works, *Reality, Nature and Man*, and *The God We Seek*. I particularly like *The God We Seek*. I also like his book on education dedicated to me and called *The Making of Men*. What divides us may be seen by comparing his *Modes of Being* and several later metaphysical writings to my *Creative Synthesis and Philosophic Method*, dedicated to him. The individualistic aspect of philosophy comes out in this comparison.

I have some understanding of why these later books of Paul's find appreciative readers. However, I am deep in a way of doing metaphysics that does not mix easily with his way. Translation from his thought to mine or vice versa is possible, but difficult. Technically, we differ considerably; but the essential human values that we try to express with these techniques, especially the ethical values, have much in common. I am also encouraged by the reflection that our philosophical disagreements are less drastic than those which separated the illustrious collaborators Whitehead and Russell. They indeed ended up far apart, yet their university trainings, as far as I can see, were even more similar than Paul's and mine. On one issue I agree partly with Weiss against Whitehead. Like Einstein, Whitehead gives a somewhat extreme view of the disconnectedness of contemporary events. Physicists seem to be changing their minds somewhat about this disconnectedness. One of them, Henry Stapp, who calls himself a revised Whiteheadian, has a view about this that *might* solve the problem. Currently, I am open-minded on this question—or, if you prefer, baffled by it. Disagreements between metaphysicians bother me somewhat because they give apparent support to the critics of metaphysics as a vain or misdirected enterprise; otherwise I do not think I would mind very much.

Paul's and my philosophies overlap in the following respects, among others. Neither of us simply accepts classical theism; but also neither of us is an atheist. (Just how far our ideas of God differ I am not prepared to say; the difference seems rather complex.) We agree in affirming freedom in the causally significant sense connoting an open future and contradicting Laplacean determinism. Here we have been influenced by Peirce. We both affirm, I explicitly and Paul at least implicitly, internal as well as external relations. Otherwise put, we reject extreme pluralism (Hume, Russell) and extreme monism (Blanshard). In this we resemble Peirce and Whitehead.

Our differences, partly real and partly verbal (as is usually the case in philosophy), appear especially in his Finalities and his idea of individual identity. What I call *ultimate contrasts* have some affinity with Finalities. For his five of these I have a greater, but indefinite, number of ultimate contrasts. Moreover, whereas he has God as a Finality I say that God is the *universal*, primordial, everlasting, and necessary *individual*, not a mere pole of an abstract contrast. Still, the contrast of God simply as such with creatures simply as such has some analogies with the other contrasts. And a divine essence exists that is abstract, indeed the most abstract of individual natures, which is why the divine existence can be necessary (existent unless logically impossible). For me the poles of a contrast—for instance, possibility and actuality—are not related symmetrically, whereas Weiss says they are interdependent. However, even here the issue is subtle. As abstract concepts, the poles are indeed interdependent in that both must have concrete exemplifications if either does: the particular cases, however, are related by one-way inclusion and dependence. An actuality includes, but is not included in, the possibility of that actuality; nor does the possibility depend on the actuality that depends on it. Yet there could not be actualities *without* possibilities, or vice versa.

The basic asymmetry of the contrasts is related to the asymmetry of the closed past and open future. Later events depend on earlier, not vice versa. Possibility is deeply temporal. Aristotle saw this well. That is why his wholly nontemporal deity was "pure actuality," devoid of internal potentiality or matter. Potentiality is essentially futurity; only the actual has a future. There is a significant relation of this to Whitehead's ontological or Aristotelian principle—that the general or abstract is real only in the concrete. Hence Aristotle's God, defined in purely abstract terms and immutable, is, as he should have seen, an empty abstraction (the bare "thinking of thinking"). He did see that it must lack knowledge of contingent individuals.

On individual identity Weiss exaggerates our differences. Of the exhaustive triplet of basic theoretical possibilities here, we both reject two and hence, by implication, accept the third. The triplet is formed by two extremes plus the view combining a less extreme form of what is positive in the extremes. The extremes are absolute or complete identity and absolute or complete nonidentity. The intermediate or moderate view is partial, incomplete, or relative identity. Absolute nonidentity, zero identity, is seen in Hume and Russell, who substitute mere similarity for even partial identity. Absolute identity is the view of Leibniz: regardless of the way it changes, an individual is at all times strictly the same individual. No matter how I, for instance, come to die, I have always been the individual who has that manner of death as part of the law of his being. Change becomes a monstrous paradox on this view. So also is the Hume-Russell view a monstrous paradox. Weiss and I agree, I think, on both points. But when he criticizes my view or Whitehead's, he implicitly imputes the extreme pluralist or extreme nonidentity view to us. Otherwise his arguments are *non sequiturs*.

Weiss's language emphasizes the relative identity and de-emphasizes the relative nonidentity; but this is, I hold, a rhetorical, not a logical distinction. We might, it seems, both admit that each aspect is of primary importance for some purposes, but not for others. No metaphysical language is equally convenient for all purposes. Whitehead's "societies" with "personal order" have "*identifying* characteristics," and the occurrence here of the verbal root of 'identity' is wholly relevant, since, according to Whitehead and me, previous members of the society are still real in and constitute elements of the later members. This is not mere similarity, it is partial identity, and only by way of emphasis does Weiss have anything more, if he rejects the Leibnizian or implicitly timeless view, as I think he does. *Completely, partially*, and *not at all identical* are exhaustive options. Let Weiss tell me how his partial identity or partial nonidentity differs from mine, and we might have a real disagreement.

The Buddhists raised this issue long ago and many Indian philosophers rejected their moderately pluralistic view. However, some of these antipluralists affirmed not only that you and I (for instance) are always strictly ourselves, they also affirmed that we are everyone else and Brahman as well. Can one make a clear case for a pluralism of persons that will not imply a genuine, though in some respects and for some purposes less significant, pluralism of successive states of one individual? To say that I at birth and I now are simply one numerical entity to which, however, diverse adjectives apply is, I think, to talk nonsense. The infant state was, and still more the present state is, more concrete than any bundle of adjectives can be, even if omniscience were to supply the adjectives. Concretely, these are two entities, the identity is partial or abstract. This is my challenge to

Weiss and a host of others. Sensible people, including Weiss, reject Leibniz and Hume. That is the big decision. The rest is (with one qualification to be considered presently) nuance and rhetoric, as far as I can see.

I was very pleased to have Bochenski's support for the affinity of Whitehead's view with Aristotle's. He was explicit and emphatic on the point. Emphasizing nuances or differences of emphasis has its place and keeps philosophers disagreeing merrily with one another; but it blurs the distinction between major differences that transcend linguistic preferences and keeps philosophers from arriving at anything like a common stock of sane positions between those absurd extremes in the avoidance of which wisdom is found.

Above all, shouting loudly, "I am always strictly the very entity I have always been and you are always simply not the entity" is to give apparent metaphysical support for self-interest theories of motivation. It also contradicts the biblical doctrine that we are, in Saint Paul's words, "members one of another" and should "love the neighbor as oneself," and the Buddhist principle of dependent origination, which holds that we are as united with one another as with our own past or future. This holds true also in the causal view of science. Extreme pluralism, whether of persons or their states, is not scientific, nor is extreme monism, in either application. If we ever got clear about such basic issues as this, we might indulge in the luxury of disputing about verbal nuances. But how clear are we about the basics?

When Aristotle says that a substance or individual cannot be "in" another individual, he falls into the extreme pluralist position of merely external relations. But then he cannot meet the monistic criticism that a relation external to both its terms becomes a third entity whose relation to its terms begins a vicious regress. Aristotle must deal with the plurality of successive states of the same individual either by treating them as mere adjectives (combined with the "essence," also an abstraction) or he must, to achieve clarity and consistency, like Whitehead and some Buddhists, admit internal relations, not only with one's own past but with the past of others. Aristotle, by whom we have all been influenced, at least indirectly, was certainly not an absolutist about the mutual interdependence of successive states of the individual, nor was he an absolutist about the mutual independence of individuals from one another. He was groping for a moderate position between monism and pluralism in both respects. How close did he come to finding it? How close does Weiss? Process philosophy has a definite solution for this problem. "Prehensions, the most concrete forms of relatedness," are one-way dependencies of actualities, connecting each to previous actualities in the same society and also, with certain differences, to actualities in other societies or commonsense individuals. I regard this as Whitehead's greatest, or at least his most original, achievement. Looking backward I am *still* the individual who was once a small child; for prehension of that child is still in the dim recesses of my present consciousness. But that child was not already the individual who would write this sentence; for nothing in the child's consciousness, no matter how faint or obscure, specified my present state. Aristotle—and Weiss—could agree with the previous sentence. And I hold they should affirm, and Aristotle came close to affirming, the second. But then they should consider that if we are aware of others, then to that extent (as Aristotle—but not Leibniz—admits) we depend on others and they are not wholly extrinsic to our being, related only as independent perfect clocks in a pre-established harmony.

My idea of metaphysics is that we must first find definite and exhaustive theoretical options, eliminate all but one, then see if the principles that achieve this can be generalized to solve related problems. Since the actualities composing our bodies also prehend, it is not only our consciousness that has to be considered but also the unconscious, more primitive types of sentience that single cells or molecules may have. We depend on our bodies because of the way we prehend their actualities. From Weiss's polemics against me one would scarcely know that he had ever heard of Whitehead's societies (personally ordered and also corpuscular) or of prehensions, and so on. Or that he sees the importance of the extremes, which are represented very definitely and precisely by two great geniuses, Leibniz and Hume, as well as by Blanshard, the complete monist (or Bradley if you prefer), concerning the unity *within and also between* individuals as setting a basic landscape for locating issues about individual identity and nonidentity.

I said above that there is one qualification to the charge that Weiss's disagreement with me about individual identity is merely rhetorical. Among the sensible, nonextreme views on this subject are those who, with Aristotle, Peirce, and Bergson, take change to be *continuous*, without finite gaps, and those who, with Whitehead, Von Wright,

James (in some writings), and Buddhists, assert such gaps. White-head's actual entities sharpened the issue, once and for all, and quantum physics plausibly gives the doctrine scientific relevance.

Common sense and ordinary introspection can be taken to support the Peirce-Bergson view I attribute to Weiss. However, one obvious objection was unwittingly supplied by Aristotle in his brilliant remark that a tree, which lacks awareness, is "like a sleeping man who never wakes up." He should have said, a sleeping and not dreaming man. If we can sleep without dreaming, without feeling or thinking anything, then surely not all our mental states change into their successors by infinitesimal degrees. Peirce thought that when we experience red, and then yellow, we experience an infinity of intermediate oranges in the transition. This seems to me a wholly baseless supposition. I regard Peirce's synechism as profoundly right as a doctrine of possibility, but quite wrong as a doctrine of actual change. If Weiss agrees with Peirce here, then my difference with him is substantial. Yet Peirce himself depreciates identity of persons as no more than a "vicinity," and in other ways.

In Weiss's argument that if I-now is not strictly identical with "I as when I made a promise," I am not responsible for keeping the promise or for having committed a bad act, he is implying that partial identity is insufficient for responsibility. But if one is absolutely identical with one's past selves and absolutely nonidentical with anyone else's past selves, why are we obligated to consider each other's welfare? I entirely reject the self-interest theory of motivation that this seems to assume. Besides, our basic obligation is to God ("love God with all thy being") and to ourselves or others as contributions to the divine life. Apart from our objective immortality in God, we are all but "passing whiffs of insignificance." Since this is so, mere self-interest is no more an ultimate justification than altruism. My obligation is to contribute to the future of life. If keeping past promises will do that and failing to do it will diminish my contribution, I will not be so silly as to cite my lack of *absolute* identity with my past selves as reason for doing otherwise. Such absoluteness is irrelevant. Relative identity, not only with myself but also with others—different relativities, to be sure—are the stuff of life. What is nonidentical in me now with me yesterday is sometimes relevant, sometimes not; but the distinction is not arbitrary or up to individual whims. My obligation to do my best in meeting obligations to myself and others, both as contributions to something cosmic and as everlasting, is indeed absolute.

A somewhat baffling difference between us is that between Weiss's "privacy" and my or Peirce's or Whitehead's "feeling" as minimal form of the psychical. With Peirce, Whitehead, Leibniz, and others, I take quality of feeling to be a minimal connotation of privacy. A stone or even a tree may lack privacy and feeling; but its molecules or cells would not therefore lack either. Paul separates privacy or inner quality from feeling. Russell and Roy or Wilfrid Sellars agree with Weiss here. I hold that the concept of absolutely insentient yet singular actuality is vacuous, has no positive meaning. Collectives, like stones, do not feel, but atoms do. Denial that they do does no real work. Feeling we know, any *positive alternative for inner quality* we do not know. Physics without psychology is a radically abstract view of things; what concrete reality adds if not experience as at least feeling (including sensation) no one has told us. Leibniz saw this first, many have seen it since.

Neither Weiss nor I have perfect understanding of metaphysical truth; for that is more than any linguistic scheme can achieve. In estimating Paul's contribution it is not enough to consider only his metaphysical system, the society and journal he founded (and he helped to found another), plus the editing and the books I have already mentioned. He has written two books of interest to artists and a book on sport that is read with interest by many people who might otherwise never look at a book with the word philosophy in the title. I learned from it and agree with its main point. Nor is the subject unimportant. There is also his latest book on politics that I have yet to read. His books on *Philosophy in Process* do not appeal to me; but there are those who like them. There are indeed many facets to Weiss's astonishingly creative career.

Notes

Introduction

1. Iris Murdoch, "Metaphysics and Ethics" in *The Nature of Metaphysics*, ed. D. F. Pears (London: Macmillan & Co. Ltd., 1960), p. 120.

Chapter One

1. Many other philosophers of our time have stopped short of the system, or even the science, as the highest level of integration. For example, the analysts, following close on the end of World War II, showed how much could be achieved by concentrating on the meanings of terms; earlier, the positivists had separated linguistically true from empirically true propositions, while the proponents and opponents of Gödel's theorem fastened on a single proof to determine the scope and consistency of a science.

2. Some brief exceptions are found. A short chapter on method commences the first major book, *Reality* (1938), pp. 3–16. A few pages of *Modes of Being*, pp. 81–83, are explicitly about method. Remarks on that elusive topic dot the rest of the writings but rarely dominate the discussion.

3. In readying many of his books for publication, Weiss submitted drafts to experts for critical comment and evidently made careful revisions in light of their cavils and suggestions. In some of his books, these comments have been printed in full. For example, *First Considerations*, a work not reviewed in this already overlong essay, devotes about one-quarter of its space to criticisms by six philosophers, persons who were not expected by the author to agree with him, together with his replies.

4. In a much later part of the book, *MOB*, pp. 533–40, Weiss discusses the need of each mode for the others.

5. It would be worthwhile, in a longer study, to connect this with publications of Weiss against war of all kinds.

6. This is expanded and altered in the last chapter of the book: "The four irreducible, distinct, but interrelated modes of being—Actuality, Ideality, Existence, and God—have much in common with Plato's motion, rest, other, and the same; with Aristotle's efficient, final, material, and formal causes; with the scholastic's substance, form, matter, and being; with Kant's quantity,

quality, relation, and modality; with Hegel's thesis, synthesis, antithesis [*sic*], and Absolute; with Croce's ethical, logical, economic, and aesthetic moments of the spirit; with Whitehead's actual occasions, eternal objects, creativity, and God. And if one were to add a fourth category of individuality to Peirce's original three, they correspond somewhat to a Peircean fourth, first, second, and third. There are, however, striking differences . . . " (p. 533). It seems to me that the mention of Kant's four "titles," as he calls them, is especially instructive, for Kant retained the same list throughout the three *Critiques* and in some of his other treatises as well, but systematically broadened the meanings each time the titles reappeared. But the combinations in Kant are, so to speak, indirect: The four meet as characteristics of judgments, categories, principles of the understanding, paralogisms, etc., determining their nature in concert or separately as the case might be.

7. One sort of complexity arises from the aforementioned combinability of the modes. In a later book, the four are subjected to what Glaucon would call "an overwhelming and baffling calculation" (*Republic* IX, 587e), which discovers not the moderately low numbers one might expect for the possible assortings of four modes, *i.e.*, six pairs if we leave out order, twelve if we include it, five trios if no order is required for groups of three, and so on. But with categories subsidiary to the modes, and including ordered permutations, there are no less than 4176 ways in which the modes enter into and interplay with and encounter the others (*GWS*, p. 293). If left at that point, this would afford plenty of leeway to compose a system both rich and impoverished—rich because so detailed and varied, impoverished because so lacking in connections with the world in which we live, the ways we live in it, and the ways we think about it. But Weiss emphatically does not leave matters at that point.

8. Thus the author says: "The various theses which are here isolated are all on a level, offered as equally basic and true. Those that are presented later should however help to articulate or develop those presented earlier, at the same time that they fixate some new facet of reality. Ideally it should be possible to make a start with any one of them and to utilize the others so as to articulate or develop it, at the same time that these others are used to focus on and to explain some further phenomenon" (*MOB*, p. 18). He is speaking of propositions, but it is obvious that they will change and behave as do their constituent *terms*. See also the Preface to *GWS*.

9. *Metaphysics* IV. 3. 1006a5–8.

10. There are resemblances, for instance, between Weiss's treatment of actualities in space in *Reality* and the mode Actuality in *Modes of Being*; and a short discussion of God and the ontological argument is included in his chapter on Multiplicity in the earlier book. It would, however, require extreme—and misplaced—cleverness to find close anticipations of the four modes

and their many features that Weiss was later to bring out, in any of the published books before 1958.

11. *Modes of Being* was first published in January 1958, but its Preface is dated more than a year earlier, December 1956. At that time, normal publication procedures usually required ten to twelve months between delivery of a manuscript and first copies off the presses, hence we may assume that the first one hundred pages (or slightly fewer) of *Philosophy in Process*, Vol. I, could have contained materials appearing in *Modes of Being*.

12. Lest it should seem that Weiss is under sway, in *Philosophy in Process*, of an obsession with a rule of four, let me point out that very frequently distinctions are made between two kinds of things, or three, or for that matter ten or some other number.

13. The last entry in *Philosophy in Process*, Vol. II, is dated March 6, 1964; the Preface to *The God We Seek* is dated May 1964; consequently the two works are almost exactly contemporary, and reveal the same concerns and resolutions, at least where *Philosophy in Process*, a work of vastly wider scope, deals with religion and theology. *The God We Seek* is in good part more popular in style than the other book or *Modes of Being*. For smoothness of transitions, for aptness of explanations and illustrations, and for absence of arcane technical terms, this is one of the author's best-written works.

14. *Summa Theologica*, Ia. QQ. 2–43.

15. It may be highly coincidental, and unimportant as well, but in *Reality* and *Modes of Being* the pronouns for God are written he, his, him, whereas in *The God We Seek* they become He, His, Him. (In *Philosophy in Process*, Vol. II, the capital letters are used.) Whether this is a mere typographical nicety or a change in attitude I cannot be sure. (All references to God are male.) Leibniz is so spelled in *Modes of Being* but receives a "t" in *The God We Seek*. Assiduous commentators will, I think, look in vain for any philosophical consequences in *that* variation.

16. Experience begins to emerge from epistemic aspects of man in *Modes of Being*. These are treated from 1.53–1.78 (pp. 52–71), but experience is not dealt with at any length in the book.

17. This list of other activities is given several times in the book, with minor variations.

18. It is advisable to interrupt a chronological order here to carry through a discussion of metaphysical topics. Indeed, the more closely one inspects the writings of Paul Weiss, the more evident it becomes that no single line of development exists; even the distinction between a period stressing combinatorial dialectic and a period or periods stressing experience and then its integration with the dialectic cannot be fully documented. There are these three tendencies, or themes, but Weiss develops them in what would ordinarily be called a contrapuntal fashion, but would more accurately be termed

similar to the development section in the *allegro* movement of a sonata or symphony.

19. This word is no longer capitalized, if that signifies anything.

20. The readability of *Beyond All Appearances* might be called into question, it being in several respects more difficult to follow than *Modes of Being* despite its resolution to begin with ordinary experience. The Introduction is abrupt and highly abstract, containing many such sentences as the following: "Each type of contextualized feature provides evidence of a distinct finality. To move from the feature to the finality, one must engage in a distinctive act of symbolization. This begins with texture, and penetrates, under the influence of the finality, into the finality" (p. xv). Granted that this is preparatory and will be explained later, it still places burdens on the reader beyond the necessary. There is a rapid listing of the forty "major theses" of the book, but without indication of how they are attached to the text itself. Each chapter is headed by a "controlling summary," which the reader should carry firmly in hand; yet it is still not a summary of the text itself. The many abstruse terms cry out for definition upon first mention, or for exemplification, or both.

21. The second expression is in each case an alternate sometimes used in the book.

22. The lines indicate what Weiss takes to be needed clarification of a confusion left over from *Modes of Being*. His mode Actualities concealed from him—and presumably his readers as well—a distinction between actualities, substantiality, and abstract or general being that is made in the later book.

23. Note the change that has taken place here. In *Modes of Being*, Existence was another name for becoming.

24. Op. cit., p. 268.

25. If this supposition is correct, we find some precedent for the usage in Aristotle, who in his *Categories* speaks of primary substance (*ousia*) as the individual man or horse, and of secondary substance as species or genus (ch. 5, 2a12–19). See *Aristotle's Categories and Propositions (De Interpretatione)*, trans. Hippocrates G. Apostle (Grinnell, Iowa: Peripatetic Press, 1980), pp. 64–65 for interesting commentary on this passage.

26. "Possibility" is capitalized, like the finalities. This may seem a deplorably trivial observation, but in reading a difficult text of this sort one seizes every hint available.

27. A book related to those on the other arts is *Sport: A Philosophic Inquiry* (1969), which may be thought something of an anomaly, but one should note that it is no mere invitation to share off-hour jogging, push-ups, and skeet-shooting with Paul Weiss. The book is a careful, 250-page study of the conditions of successful athletic participation, such as health, endurance, strength, accuracy, and coordination, along with a study of the role of competition,

professionalism, rules, and the like. Readers who consider it beneath the dignity of philosophers to take up such topics are reminded of Plato's *Republic* III, 403c–12b, and *Laws* VII, 813a–16c and VIII, 828a–35b, as the beginning of a long tradition of writers, mainly on the philosophy of education, who have included games, physical exercise, and occasionally military training in their programs.

28. The lists of those to whom Weiss was primarily indebted for stimulation and counsel, given in the prefaces to *The World of Art* and *Nine Basic Arts*, are long and are a register of eminent artists and critics of the past three or four decades.

29. Elsewhere (*WA*, p. 119) Weiss identifies the excellent work of art with the beautiful work of art.

30. Note the echoes of *Modes of Being*.

31. A painter of my acquaintance once said that each time he worked on a canvas he told himself, "This is It." Being a mediocre painter at best, he was of course wrong in practice, even if right in principle.

32. I have added the numbers to mark the four modes again.

33. Musicry is later (*NBA*, pp. 122–23) subjected to closer scrutiny. Ideally, it refers to a "neutral common time," which is the foundation of public clocks, private rhythms, emotion unions, and comprehensive decisions—a rather attenuated application of the four modes. Secondarily, it refers to each of the four, and to the disciplines that evolve around them: cosmology, narration, musical composition, and reconstructed time. The last meaning is that of musical composition alone. The composer is creative, but the performer is also, though in a different way, for both have their own sense of time.

34. The entire first chapter leads to this definition, a practice that Weiss does not often follow so explicitly in the other books discussed herein.

Chapter Two

1. *Sport: A Philosophic Inquiry*.

2. Cf. *e.g.*, Andrew Reck's reply in *FC*.

3. In his central work, *Modes of Being*, Weiss distinguishes, in addition to God, Actuality, Ideality and Existence (see below). In *Beyond All Appearances*, Actuality is split into Substance and Being (see below).

4. Weiss acknowledges his special debt to Kant (together with Aristotle and Whitehead) in the Preface.

5. As an aside worth repeating, Weiss once confessed to the author that (*per impossibile*) had God "in the beginning" taken him aside, shown him all the great works to come in the history of philosophy—"in all their glory"—

and asked him of which work he would like to be author, he would have replied, without hesitation, *The Phenomenology of Spirit.* Indeed, one could profitably read *Beyond All Appearances* as directly parallel with the *Phenomenology.*

6. See "Our Knowledge of What Is Real" in *The Review of Metaphysics* 18 (September 1964), p. 10.

7. See "The Origin of the Work of Art," *Philosophies of Art and Beauty*, eds. A. Hofstadter and R. Kuhns (New York: Modern Library, 1964), pp. 649–701.

8. This very apt expression is Owen Barfield's, *Saving the Appearances* (London: Faber & Faber, 1957), pp. 55 ff.

9. "What Is Metaphysics?" *Existence and Being*, ed. W. Brock (Chicago: Henry Regnery, 1959), pp. 325–61.

10. For what follows, cf. *MOB*, 3.02 ff.

11. See *WA* and *NBA* for a fuller development of these notions.

12. "Our Knowledge of What Is Real," p. 11.

13. Cf. "The Origin of the Work of Art." Though Weiss's speculative-constructive, systematic approach to philosophy is poles removed from Heidegger's ruminations, and although Weiss has little positive to say of Heidegger, these two thinkers share many central insights. The most essential difference between Heidegger and Weiss is Weiss's Platonic acceptance of ever-present, changeless truths-in-themselves.

14. Cf. Martin Heidegger, "The Way Back into the Ground of Metaphysics," *Existentialism from Dostoevsky to Sartre*, ed. W. Kaufmann (N.Y.: Meridian, 1956), pp. 206–21.

Chapter Three

1. Some examples of Weiss's humor: *Philosophy in Process*, Volume 5 (1971), 9–10: "Thales fell into a well, and came out saying everything is water. Anaximander was rather vague in his views, and concluded that the real was the indefinite. . . . Parmenides thought he was immortal and said that non-being altogether was not. Zeno was a devoted disciple, and argued that there was no motion." Ibid., p. 198: "Women are attracted both to heroes and to cripples. The ideal object of their affections is obviously a crippled hero, an eagle with a broken wing. How can she find one? By marrying a hero." Not only women and philosophers, but youth, too, are not spared Weiss's biting, even if chauvinist, wit: *Philosophy in Process*, Volume 6 (1975), 557: "A young philosopher—a contradiction in terms."

2. Weiss's own commentary on American philosophers and their German and English counterparts is in *Philosophy in Process*, Volume 5, p. 159: "German philosophers are deadly serious; they rarely say anything witty, and

rarely tell a joke unless it be to point up some idea. If they have genius, they do great things in philosophy; if they lack it, they are dull, and function either as disciples or as historians of ideas. English philosophers are not serious at all, but primarily witty, clever, and adroit. If they have genius, they say arresting things about rather minor matters; if they lack it, they occupy themselves with trivia, spoken about with some expertness. American philosophers are in between these two types, since they unite some wit or ease with considerable seriousness. If they have genius, they write a vitalized and understandable philosophy; if they lack if, they become academic, talking only to one another, and imitating the Germans or the English."

3. Fernand Van Steenberghen, *Ontology*, trans. Martin J. Flynn (New York: Wagner, 1952), pp. 46–69. John Edward Twomey, *The General Notion of the Transcendentals in the Metaphysics of Saint Thomas Aquinas* (Ph.D. diss., Washington, D.C.: The Catholic University of America, 1958).

4. Henri Pouillon, "Le premier traite des proprietes transcendentales: La 'Summa de Bono' du Chancelier Philippe," *Revue Neoscholastique de Philosophie*, Tome 42 (1939), pp. 40–77. Francisco Suarez, *Disputationes Metaphysicae* in *Opera Omnia*, Tomus 25 (Paris: Vives, 1866), Disp. III, Sectiones I et II, pp. 102–11.

5. Mark Jordan, "The Grammar of *Esse*: Re-reading Thomas on the Transcendentals," *Thomist* 44 (1980), pp. 1–26.

6. Thomas Aquinas, *Quaestiones Disputatae*, Volumen I: De Veritate, Cura et studio P. Fr. Raymundi Spiazzi, O. P., Editio VIII revisa (Taurini: Marietti, 1949), pp. 1–4.

7. Ibid., p. 2: "Alio modo ita quod modus expressus sit modus generaliter consequens omne ens; et hic modus dupliciter accipi potest; uno modo secundum consequitur omne ens in se; alio modo secundum quod consequitur unumquodque ens in ordine ad aliud."

8. Aquinas's account of transcendentals in *de Veritate*, q. 1, a. 1 may be outlined as follows:

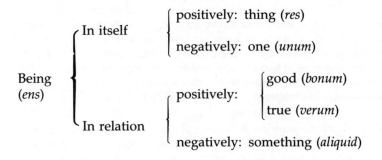

9. The parallels between Weiss's finalities and Aquinas's transcendentals may be outlined as follows:

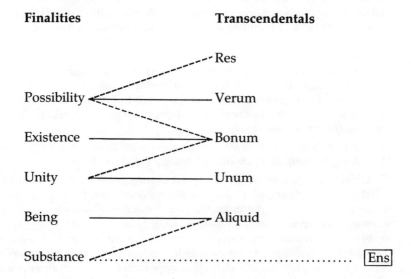

Finalities	Transcendentals
	Res
Possibility	Verum
Existence	Bonum
Unity	Unum
Being	Aliquid
Substance	Ens

(Solid lines signify an isomorphism between Weiss's finalities and Aquinas's transcendentals; broken lines signify overlaps between more than one finality or transcendental; the dotted line and the box, lastly, signify a superficial resemblance between the finality, Substance, and what is not a transcendental but rather being, of which the transcendentals are modes.)

10. Aristotelians in general would certainly bristle at Weiss's distinction between actualities in themselves, actualities themselves, and actualities by themselves. For example, actualities themselves are unique and, united with the finality substantiality, they are by themselves substantial densities. What characterizes the actuality in itself, corresponding to this uniqueness and substantial density is its insistency. Similarly, the actuality itself is intelligible or viewed by itself, *i.e.*, united with the finality, Possibility, it is an organized nature. The corresponding characterization of the actuality in itself is its opacity. What these remarks illustrate is that Weiss arrives at this description of actualities in themselves via a kind of via negativa. This way of characterizing actualities in themselves, so reminiscent of Kant's noumena, is troublesome in itself, but it also suggests difficulties in regard to the appearances of finalities. Strictly speaking, there are no appearances of actualities in themselves, but rather only appearances of actualities themselves, *i.e.*, affected by finalities, or actualities by themselves, *i.e.*, united with finalities. In other words, every appearance of an actuality is also an appearance of a finality.

To be sure, there is what Weiss calls a 'counterthrust' by the actuality in itself, constituting, along with a transcendent condition provided by a finality, actualities by themselves. But the fact that there are no appearances of actualities in themselves suggests a question about the topic of this paper. Are there appearances of finalities in themselves? The implications of the questions are hardly trivial. In the same way that actualities in themselves can only be given a negative description, so there is the danger that no positive account can be given of the finalities in themselves. Weiss states that "no actuality . . . ever succeeds in being just in itself," and his purely negative account of them suggests a similar fate for finalities in themselves, seriously sabotaging the viability of the entire ontological framework of actualities and finalities (*FC*, p. 47, sec. 8).

11. Thomas Reid, *Essays on the Active Powers of the Human Mind* (Cambridge, MA: Massachusetts Institute of Technology Press, 1969), p. 5.

12. Objective appearances are the result of the confluence of actualities and finalities, although one of the latter is always dominant. In some settings the shape dominates over the extended area localized by a body and in other settings the reverse is true. Neither factor, that of the actuality or that of the finality, exists without the other though they can, of course, be separated in thought. Nor can either factor exist independently of its source and Weiss's reasoning here plays on the claim that appearance is always an appearance of something. "An appearance is continuous with a reality, via a factor which the reality provides. The factor helps constitute the appearance and textures it" (*FC*, p. 33, sec. 35). This textual character permits us to advance to the realities behind appearances, although Weiss cautions that appearances are not mirrors of realities. Appearances always involve counterings, presumably by other finalities and actualities, if the appearance is predominantly a particular finality's appearance. We can move beyond the appearance to the finality or actuality constituting its dominant factor, but at some point "we find that we can go no further. The reality is then faced as brute, impervious" (*FC*, pp. 33–34, sec. 41).

13. *FC*, p. 35, sec. 50: "If the adumbration is given prominence there, one moves toward the objective appearance." *FC*, p. 35, sec. 55: "Adumbration is the converse of the act of contributing a factor to an appearance. . . . That is why we not only know the known but something beyond the known." See also, *BAA*, pp. 39, 62, 143.

14. One final feature of appearances should be noted. Weiss distinguishes appearances according to the grades of externalization of actualities and finalities. The lowest grade of appearance is *manifestation*, the next higher grade is a *display*, and the highest grade is an *expression*. These grades of externalization correspond to the degrees of internalization of finalities by actualities and thus to the types of actualities Weiss identifies, *viz*, things, living beings, and human beings, respectively.

15. *FC*, p. 65, sec. 22: "Evidence, via the evidenced, symbolizes its source."

16. Note that even in *First Considerations* passages (*e.g.*, p. 84, sec. 42) suggest that the process of evidencing applies to actualities as well. This problem is not inconsequential. The suspicion raised in n. 10 herein is simply enhanced if Weiss fails to speak of the *evidence* of actualities.

17. *FC*, p. 97, secs. 51–52; *BAA*, p. 62: "The reach of knowledge extends beyond the constitutive and possessive powers of the mind."

18. *FC*, p. 83, sec. 34: "Known or not, evidence is always related to the evidenced with a status and role which does not depend on its acknowledgment or deliberate use." *FC*, p. 85, sec. 48: "Evidence and evidenced are objectively turned toward one another apart from any use."

19. There is perhaps no single point that receives so much emphasis in Weiss's philosophy. *BAA*, p. 267: "The movement to the finality is one with the transformation of the initial content and oneself by the terminus to be arrived at." *FC*, p. 105, sec. 23: "A source must help a man yield what he had produced, if what he produced is to be made true of the source." *FC*, p. 109, sec. 17: "A user of evidence must allow himself to be controlled by what controls the evidence and evidenced." *FC*, p. 128, sec. 54: "A user of evidence forges a claim through its aid. That claim is honored if accommodated by the finality evidenced in that claim." For similar remarks in regard to each specific finality, see *FC*, p. 112, sec. 36; p. 127, sec. 45; p. 146, sec. 60; p. 157, sec. 50; p. 166, sec. 42.

20. *FC*, p. 64, sec. 14: "There are no evidences except so far as there are carriers of them."

21. *FC*, p. 65, sec. 21: "A source in the very act of providing evidence also provides a correlative term for that evidence. The source of the evidence thereby points the evidence, not to the source, but to an evidenced version of the source, relative to the evidence." *FC*, p. 87, sec. 67: "A source enables itself to be evidenced by giving the evidenced the status of a ground for the evidence." See also: *FC*, p. 85, sec. 48; p. 97, sec. 56.

22. For Weiss, evidencing is a timeless, ontological process in which five distinct factors can be identified: (1) the evidence controlling and specified by a particular appearance (or actuality), (2) the evidence detached from that specification (a carrier), (3) evidence and evidenced correlated, (4) the mutual relevance of evidence and evidenced, and (5) their common source (*FC*, p. 85, sec. 48; p. 66, sec. 32). The five steps Weiss identifies for the user of evidence simply correspond to these ontological factors in evidencing. *FC*, p. 85, sec. 48: "Men attempt to reproduce sequentially a single ontological state of affairs."

23. See n. 19 herein.

24. *BAA*, p. 250: "Were there no extensions embracing all appearances, the appearances would not be close or distant; they would not be contemporaries, or be in the relation of past to present, or present to future; and they would

not be part of operative causes or effects. The focused and the neglected are extensionally joined by the power of a finality beyond them, manifested as their common context. We are acquainted with that power just so far as we are acquainted with the context. When we release what we had focused on, we face both the focused and the region embracing the neglected, in a single attitude. That attitude matches the extensional relation that in fact connects them."

25. The correspondence of attitudes to contexts and contexts to finalities may be diagrammed as follows:

Finalities

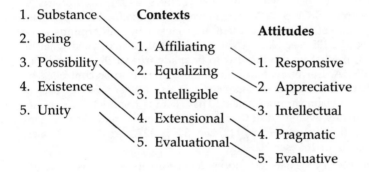

1. Substance   **Contexts**
2. Being   **Attitudes**
                 1. Affiliating
3. Possibility   2. Equalizing   1. Responsive
4. Existence   3. Intelligible   2. Appreciative
5. Unity   4. Extensional   3. Intellectual
                 5. Evaluational   4. Pragmatic
                                     5. Evaluative

26. Weiss groups various empirical endeavors to understand types of affiliating contexts as specializations of the single discipline of harmonics. Its counterpart under equalizing context is *a priori* economics.

27. Metaphysical emotions: appreciation and concern:

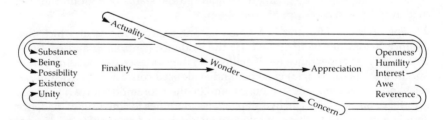

Actuality

Substance
Being   Finality ——→ Wonder ——→ Appreciation   Openness
Possibility   Humility
Existence   Interest
Unity   Awe
                                          Concern   Reverence

28. See n. 19 herein.

29. *BAA*, p. 236: "Finalities are altogether unlike familiar objects or the actualities these objects partly exhibit. They are not larger or nobler forms of these. Not palpable, each is more like an atmosphere than a thing. At once individual and universal, accessible and recessive, each is at once omnipresent

and all-pervasive. An approach to them justifies exclamation rather than simple affirmation, admiration rather than formalization."

Chapter Four

1. *R*, p. 6. On the links between philosophy and common sense, see ch. I, "On Method," in *Reality*. The themes of that chapter are often reworked in subsequent writing and combined with a dialectical method of establishing philosophical truths by refuting their denials on grounds of existential inconsistency. See, for example, the Introduction to *Nature and Man*, which connects the commonsense starting point with philosophical abstraction and the requirement of existential self-consistency.

2. The Aristotelian doctrines summarized here are to be found in *Categories*, chs. 1–5 and *Metaphysics*, Book Zeta. For a modern treatment of the centrality of substance in a commonsense categorization of the world, see Peter F. Strawson's *Individuals: An Essay in Descriptive Metaphysics* (Garden City, NY: Anchor Books, 1963).

3. Sir Arthur Eddington, *The Nature of the Physical World* (New York: Macmillan, 1929), p. ix.

4. David Hume, "Of Personal Identity," *A Treatise of Human Nature* bk. I, pt. IV, sec. VI.

5. A. N. Whitehead, *Process and Reality*, corrected edition, D. R. Griffin and D. W. Sherburne (eds.) (New York: The Free Press, 1979), pt. II, ch. VII.

6. Weiss's "new beginning" for a substantival process philosophy occurs in *Reality*, bk. II "Plurality and Process." The current essay summarizes my earlier attempts to draw the implications of the Weissian point of departure in "A Pluralistic Account of Space," *International Philosophical Quarterly* 11 (1971): 180–212 and "A Teleological Theory of Value," *Dialogue* 12 (1973): 629–45. In those attempts I owe major debts not only to *Reality* but also to *Nature and Man* and *Modes of Being*, as well as to Whitehead's *Process and Reality*.

7. On this point, see my "Time, Events, and Substance: Comments on Hurley and Whitehead" in *Physics and the Ultimate Significance of Time*, ed. David R. Griffin (Albany: State University of New York Press, 1986): 120–21, and "A Pluralistic Account of Space": 207–12.

8. Hume, *op. cit.*.

9. Aristotle, *Physics*, bk. I; Immanuel Kant, *Critique of Pure Reason* A182/B224 ff.

10. See my "Value as Richness: Toward a Value Theory for the Expanded Naturalism in Environmental Ethics," *Environmental Ethics* 4 (1982): 101–14.

Chapter Six

1. Iris Murdoch, "Metaphysics and Ethics," *The Nature of Metaphysics*, D. F. Pears (ed.) (London and New York: Macmillan and St. Martin's Press, 1957), p. 104.

2. Ibid., p. 115.

3. Ibid.

4. Ibid.

5. See my article, "Paul Weiss's Philosophical Journal," *The Review of Metaphysics*, 21 (June 1968): 699–713.

6. See my book, *The New American Philosophers* (Baton Rouge: Louisiana State University Press, 1968), pp. 322–24.

7. Review in *Time* (January 19, 1968), p. 93.

8. Elsewhere I have tried to do so. See my articles: "Paul Weiss's Concept of Being," *The Review of Metaphysics*, 25 (June 1972) Twenty-Fifth Anniversary Supplement, pp. 8–24; and "Objections to Some Supposed First Principles," in Paul Weiss, *First Considerations*, pp. 238–43.

9. Elsewhere, building on Weiss's theory, I have delineated liberty as a triadic relation holding between an actual, substantial agent, an existential situation, and a possible ideal, so that an adequate idea of liberty, subsuming both negative and positive concepts, signifies the freedom *of* the agent *from* the situation *for* or *to* possible ideal goals. See my article, "The Metaphysics of Liberty," in *Experience, Existence, and the Good, Essays in Honor of Paul Weiss*, Irwin C. Lieb (ed.) (Carbondale: Southern Illinois University Press, 1961), pp. 285–95.

Chapter Seven

1. This is one of the major theses of Weiss's *Man's Freedom*. I believe its presence in *Modes of Being* is a holdover and that the view gradually disappears from Weiss's later philosophy.

2. Because of the difficulty in maintaining cognitive force for evaluative modes of thought, I have argued that new paradigms of thinking need to be constructed that incorporate the Renaissance integration of quantitative and qualitative thought, but which integrate evaluative thought as well. The result of the Renaissance success in mathematical physics was the exclusion of value for the conception of "facts" and "possibilities." See my *Reconstruction of Thinking* (Albany: State University of New York Press, 1981).

3. This has been discussed in detail, with reference to both Aristotle and Weiss, in my *The Cosmology of Freedom* (New Haven: Yale University Press, 1974), pp. 141–63.

4. Because of this distinction between essential and conditional or nonessential traits in every actuality, Weiss is able to push metaphysics from the level of cosmological generalization at which Whitehead left it to true ontology. The one and the many is the royal road to the question of being. I discuss this in "Metaphysics," *Social Research*, 47 (Winter 1980), pp. 686–703.

5. I attempted to trace and analyze the ontological shift in Weiss's view in "Paul Weiss's *Philosophy in Process*," in *The Review of Metaphysics*, 24 (December 1970), pp. 276–301.

6. By phenomenology I mean a thoroughgoing description of what appears in daily life and under analysis; something like Hegelian or Peircean phenomenology, rather than Husserlian phenomenology, which tends to bracket out the most important features, *e.g.*, existence and value.

7. The theory of value sketched here develops ideas expressed in *The Cosmology of Freedom*, ch. 3, and *Reconstruction of Thinking*, *passim*.

8. See his brilliant discussion of causality, sec. IV of ch. I of *Modes of Being*.

9. This has been a theme of Weiss's since *Reality*, his first philosophy book, which presented itself as an Aristotelian counterfoil to Whitehead. See my comments and his response in *First Considerations*.

Chapter Eight

1. Christian Norberg-Schulz, *Intentions in Architecture* (Cambridge: Massachusetts Institute of Technology Press, 1965), p. 219.

2. Arthur Drexler, *Transformations in Modern Architecture* (New York: The Museum of Modern Art, 1979), p. 17.

3. Immanuel Kant, *Critique of Judgment*, trans. J. H. Bernard (New York: Hafner, 1951), par. 51, p. 166.

4. Hannes Meyer, "Building," *Programs and Manifestoes on 20th-Century Architecture*, ed. Ulrich Conrads, trans. Michael Bullock (Cambridge: Massachusetts Institute of Technology Press, 1979), p. 119.

5. Walter Pichler/Hans Hollein, "Absolute Architecture," *Programs and Manifestoes*, pp. 181–82.

6. See Karsten Harries, "The Dream of the Complete Building," *Perspecta*, 17 (1980), pp. 36–43.

7. See also Christian Norberg-Schulz, *Genius Loci: Towards a Phenomenology of Architecture* (New York: Rizzoli, 1979).

8. Vincent Scully, *The Earth, the Temple, and the Gods*, revised edition (London and New York: Praeger, 1969), p. 11.

9. Arthur Schopenhauer, *The World as Will and Representation*, vol. I, trans. E. F. J. Payne (New York: Dover, 1969), par. 17, p. 95.

10. See Karsten Harries, "Hegel on the Future of Art," *The Review of Metaphysics*, vol. 27, no. 4 (June 1974), pp. 677–96.

11. Friedrich Nietzsche, *The Will to Power*, trans. W. Kaufmann and R. J. Hollingdale (New York: Vintage, 1968), pars. 1 and 822.

Chapter Nine

1. Only later in *Sport*, two years later, does he pay attention to women in sport.

2. Weiss makes this clear in *Sport: A Philosophic Inquiry*, p. 246. "Like a religious man who turns from the world to open himself up to his God, the athlete places himself before whatever eternal and impersonal judge there is. He accepts as basic the position that he will be judged objectively, and irrevocably. The religious man is, to be sure, more actively occupied with his presumed judge than the athlete is. Through his faith he tries to come closer to his God, whose evaluations are of vital importance to him. The athlete, instead, is content to allow himself to be judged by men, and makes no effort to come in closer contact with whatever eternal judge there is. In compensation, he can often watch his judges in action, and is able to learn, as the religious man cannot, just how he compares with others."

3. Probably the best brief introduction to German theology of sport is Helmut Thielicke, *Sport und Humanität* (Tübingen: Hermann Leins, Rainer Wunderlich Verlag, 1967), brief bibliography in the concluding footnote, p. 43. The American David L. Miller, *God and Games: Toward a Theology of Play* (New York and Cleveland: World, 1969), pp. 197–206 has a considerable bibliography. An amusing piece is James V. Schall, *Play On: From Games to Celebrations* (Philadelphia: Fortress, 1971).

4. Paul G. Kuntz in *The Modern Schoolman*, vol. XLVI, no. 3, March 1963, pp. 251–70, and vol. XLVII, no. 4, 1970, pp. 433–53.

5. Paul G. Kuntz, "The Achievement of Paul Weiss," *Review of Metaphysics*, vol. XXV, June 1972, pp. 47–70, the Weiss issue based on the Symposium in Honor of Weiss's Seventieth Birthday, held at The Catholic University of America. There will also be in the *International Philosophical Quarterly* a review article of *Sport: A Philosophic Inquiry* titled, "Sports as Performing Arts: On Paul Weiss's Philosophy of Sport and Philosophy of Art."

6. This I argue in "The Aesthetics of Sport," a paper given at the Seventh International Congress of Aesthetics, Bucharest, Romania, August 28 to September 2, 1972, published (in · art) in *The Philosophy of Sport*, ed. Robert G. Osterhoudt (Springfield, IL: Cnarles C. Thomas, 1973), pp. 305–9.

7. John Huizinga, *Homo Ludens, A Study of the Play-Element in Culture* (Boston: Beacon Press, 1955) and Roger Caillois, *Man, Play, and Games*, trans. Meyer Barash (New York: Crowell-Collier, The Free Press of Glencoe, 1961). The

most thorough philosophic study is Ingeborg Heidemann, *Der Begriff des Spiels und das ästhetische Weltbild in der Philosophie der Gegenwart* (Berlin: Walter de Gruyter and Co., 1968).

8. The OED quotes from *Outing*, 1894: "Those men handle the little innocent rubber puck as Paderewski handles the black keys of a piano." J. A. Murray, *A New English Dictionary on Historical Principles*, vol. VII (Oxford: Clarendon Press, 1909), p. 1563.

9. The author has explored these similarities in two articles published recently. One, from the point of view of recent American aesthetics, is "The Aesthetics of Sport," a paper given at the Seventh International Congress of Aesthetics, Bucharest, Romania, August 28 to September 2, 1972, published (in part) in *The Philosophy of Sport*, ed. Robert G. Osterhoudt (Springfield, IL: Charles C. Thomas, 1973), pp. 305–9. The other, largely from the point of view of athletics and physical education is "Aesthetics Applies to Sport as Well as to the Arts," Center for Philosophic Exchange, SUNY, Brockport, November 1, 1973, *Philosophical Exchange*, Summer 1974, vol. 3, no. 3, pp. 25–39 and *Journal of the Philosophy of Sport*, vol. 1, September 1974, pp. 6–35. We need to note here that there are some authorities who find creativity and revelation in sports and who therefore would deny the proposition that sports are no more than crafts: Geoffrey Gaskin and D. W. Masterson, "The Work of Art in Sport," *Journal of the Philosophy of Sport*, loc. cit., pp. 36–66, and Carolyn E. Thomas, "Towards an Experimental Sport Aesthetic," ibid., pp. 67–91. Weiss himself argues that sport is more than a skill, and insofar as it is an "embodiment of the ideal in the shape of character," it "is somewhat analogous to the arts" (*PP* 5, p. 135). By "expend[ing] energy in controlled and disciplined ways [the athlete] strives for an excellence that goes beyond what mere exuberance... could produce" (*PP* 5, p. 380). But does sport fail to carry man towards the ideal excellence that art attains? If so, the difference is one of degree and not of kind.

10. Ralph Slovenko and James A. Knight, eds., *Motivations in Play, Games and Sports* (Springfield, IL: Charles C. Thomas, 1967), p. 28.

11. The most readily available summary is Book IV, Chapter I, "Greek Medicine as Paideia," on Hippocrates, Diocedes, *et. al.* in Werner Jaeger, *Paideia: The Ideals of Greek Culture*, trans. Gilbert Highet (Oxford: Basil Blackwell, 1947). Probably the best short, single work is Galen, "On the Small Ball." It can be found in F. A. Wright, *Greek Athletics* (London: Jonathan Cape, 1925), pp. 112–21. Galen begins: "How great an advantage for health gymnastic exercises are and what an important part they play in questions of diet has been sufficiently explained by the best of our ancient philosophers and physicians" Ibid., p. 112.

12. Robert W. Creamer, *Babe: The Legend Comes to Life* (New York: Simon and Schuster, 1974) compared with an excellent digest and appraisal of his records in baseball, W. Clyde Partin, "The Babe," a paper presented to the North

American Society for Sport History, May 12, 1974, London, Ontario, mimeographed, 54 pp.

Chapter Ten

1. My analysis of naming relies primarily on Weiss's chapter entitled "Names" in *First Considerations* and secondarily on his reflections upon what he calls the "assertum" in *Beyond All Appearances*.

2. *Critique of Pure Reason*, B 96/A 71.

3. The fact that Kant himself did not continue to so construe singular judgments in the *Critique* is important, but his analysis of how positing is operative in singular judgments was forgotten or overlooked by many philosopher-logicians in the face of the alluring prospects of extensional logical analysis. Weiss's conception of names, as well as his view that existence is a predicate, retrieves what is valuable in Kant's notion of "positing" while transforming the base from which judgments of existence can be verified: not simply the context of experience (as in Kant) but the contexts that are exhibitions of finalities.

4. All references to "On Sense and Nominatum" are drawn from *Contemporary Readings in Logical Theory*, Irving M. Copi and James A. Gould, eds. (New York: Macmillan, 1967).

5. "On Sense and Nominatum," p. 86. To achieve such "perfection"—to eliminate all conjecture in the understanding of linguistic inferences—Frege must eliminate the place of the hearer. In *Begriffsschrift*, he tells how such a hearer plays a part in our understanding of discourse: "In language the place occupied by the subject in the word-order has the significance of a specially important place; it is where we put what we want the hearer to attend to specially" (*Translations from the Philosophical Writings of Gottlob Frege*, Peter Geach and Max Black, eds., Oxford: Basil Blackwell, 1952, p. 3). But Frege turns away from such commerce of expressive selves in order to engage in the pursuit of a language that prescinds from the vagaries and spontaneities of "discourse." He states:

> In my formalized language there is nothing that corresponds [to the reciprocal action of speaker and hearer]; only that part of judgments which affects the possible inferences is taken into consideration. Whatever is needed for a valid inference is fully expressed; what is not needed is for the most part not indicated either; no scope is left for conjecture (Ibid., p. 3).

Weiss shows in his treatment of names not only that such precision makes ordinary identification problematic (see Strawson's "uniquely referring use"), but also how it vitiates inference itself and the possibility of metaphysical knowledge.

6. W. O. Quine, "Logic and the Reification of Universals," *From a Logical Point of View*, revised ed. (Cambridge, MA: Harvard, 1961), p. 103.

7. In the introduction to the fourth edition of *Methods of Logic* (Cambridge, MA: Harvard, 1982), Quine makes an important admission:

> Strictly speaking, what admit of truth and falsity are not statements as repeatable patterns of utterance, but individual events of statement utterance. For, utterances that sound alike can vary in meaning with the occasion of the utterance. This is due not only to careless ambiguities, but to systematic ambiguities which are essential to the nature of language. The pronoun "I" changes its reference with every change of speaker; "here" changes its reference with every significant movement through space; and "now" changes its reference every time it is uttered (p. 1).

Here he harkens back to his own Whiteheadian roots. Whitehead's cosmological scheme is constituted in the tension between an intensional interpretation of the universe (genetic analysis) and an extensional analysis of it (coordinate analysis). In a Whiteheadian scheme, $F(d)$ is construed intensionally, where d is a single prehension (utterance event in Quine's earlier comment) and F is the selection from the nonmathematical eternal objects. Such an event as $F(d)$ would become a content of later prehensive events. Where $F(d)$ is construed extensionally, it becomes a species of bound variable; the variable x which is substituted for d, stands for any number of points and F stands for an extensive region, constituted as a partial exemplification of a domain of mathematical eternal objects. In Whiteheadian language, Quine's reference to "bound variables" is a case in which one considers "extensive regions" as domains where prehensions are likely to occur; the reason I say "likely to occur" is that "instancing a class" is not equivalent to the "becoming of an actual entity." In Whitehead's view, without an intensional perspective (the genesis of events) there would be no way of ascertaining which eternal objects, whether mathematical or relational, are relevant to this epoch of the universe.

8. *Critique*, B 96/A 71.

9. See *Collected Papers of Charles Sanders Peirce*, Vol. IV, pp. 353–57 for Peirce's discussion of rhemata and what may legitimately be considered the subject of a proposition. Weiss, following Peirce, recognizes the case where a predicational class is secured by the abstraction of the subject. What remains is the individual construed as a function and an indeterminate class of variable predicates. In this regard, see Weiss's "The Metaphysics and Logic of Classes," *Monist* XLII (January 1932), pp. 112–54.

10. "On Sense and Nominatum," p. 81.

11. Ibid., p. 85.

12. Ibid., p. 91.

13. Ibid., p. 92.

Chapter Eleven

1. Martin Heidegger, "The Thinker as Poet," *Poetry, Language, Thought*, trans. Albert Hofstader (New York: Harper and Row, 1971), p. 4.

2. William James, *A Pluralistic Universe* (Cambridge, MA: Harvard University Press, 1977), pp. 94–95.

3. Ludwig Wittgenstein, *Philosophical Investigations*, trans. G. E. M. Anscombe (New York: Macmillan, 1953), p. 100.

4. This theme can be traced back to Weiss's discussion of "adumbration" in *Reality*. There, he tells us that adumbration is a mode of apprehension that isolates an "unarticulated concreteness" (*R*, p. 31). One will find variations on this theme in all of Weiss's subsequent writings. It is crucial for understanding how I can "apprehend" your ontological privacy without fully exhausting it.

Bibliography of Paul Weiss's Publications*

1926

1. "A Theory of the Comic." *Open Court*, XI (May), 280–87.
2. "The Man Who Was Seven." A Review of G. Santayana's *Dialogues in Limbo*. *The New Republic*, XLIX (May 12), 376–77.
3. "Human, All Too Human." A Review of Will Durant's *Story of Philosophy*. *The New Republic*, XLIX (July 28), 286.
4. "A Story of Philosophers' Correspondence." *The New Republic*, XLIX (August 25), 20–21.
5. "A Positivistic History." A Review of P. Masson-Oursel's *Comparative Philosophy*. *The New Republic*, XLIX (October 13), 226.
6. "The Minds of Yesterday." A Review of J. H. Randall's *The Making of the Modern Mind*. *The Nation*, CXXIII (November 17), 510.

1927

1. "A Critique of Science." A Review of P. W. Bridgman's *The Logic of Modern Physics*. *The Nation*, CXXV (August 3), 115–16.
2. A Review of J. W. N. Sullivan's *Aspects of Science, Second Series*. *The Nation*, CXXIV (April 27), 483.

1928

1. A *Preliminary Draft of a Bibliography of Contributions to Modern Logic and the Foundations of Mathematics*. Cambridge, MA, 1–12. (Mimeographed.)
2. "The Theory of Types." *Mind*, XXXVII, 338–48. Supplement II in Korzybski, *Science and Sanity*, 737–46.
3. "Relativity in Logic." *Monist*, XXXVIII (October), 536–48.
4. "Perception's Glassy Essence." A Review of A. N. Whitehead's *Symbolism: Its Meaning and Effect*. *The Nation*, CXXVI (February 1), 128–29.

---

*This bibliography has been prepared by Richard J. Getrich and updated by the editor. It does not include all published letters, interviews, and mimeographed drafts of published works.

5. "A Medieval Pragmatist." A Review of R. B. Burke's *The Opus Majus of Roger Bacon*. *The New Republic*, LX (June 13), 101–2.
6. A Review of Mortimer J. Adler's *Dialectic*. *Journal of Philosophy*, XXV (August 30), 500–2.

1929

1. *The Nature of Systems*. Chicago: Open Court Publishing Co. Appeared in *Monist*, XXXIX (April and July), 281–319, 440–72.
2. *Supplement to Bibliography of Contributions to Modern Logic and the Foundations of Mathematics*. Cambridge, MA, 6 pp. (Mimeographed.)
3. A Review of Sidney Hook's *The Metaphysics of Pragmatism*. *The City College Alumnus* (March), 99–100.
4. "The Ways of the Wise." A Review of A. Herzberg's *The Psychology of Philosophers*. *The New Republic*, LX (October 23), 275.
5. A Review of R. Carnap's *Abriss der Logistik*. *Bulletin of the American Mathematical Society*, XXXV, 880.

1930

1. "A Hebrew Scholastic." A Review of H. Wolfson's *Crescas' Critique of Aristotle*. *The New Republic*, LXIII (July 30), 323.
2. "Pragmatists and Pragmatists." Reviews of F. C. S. Schiller's *Logic for Use* and C. I. Lewis' *Mind and the World-Order*. *The New Republic*, LXII (March 26), 161–62.
3. "Entailment and the Future of Logic." *Seventh International Congress of Philosophy*. Oxford, 143–50.

1931

1. Hartshorne, Charles, co-ed. *Collected Papers of Charles Sanders Peirce*. Vol. I: *Principles of Philosophy*. Cambridge: Harvard University Press.
2. "Two-Valued Logic—Another Approach." *Erkenntnis*, II, 242–61 (with German abstract).
3. "Logic and System." Summary of thesis. *Summaries of Theses*. Cambridge: Harvard University Press, 217–19.
4. A Review of M. R. Cohen's *Reason and Nature*. *The City College Alumnus* (April), 61–63. Letter from Cohen, *Ibid.*, (May), 85.
5. A Review of William of Ockam's *De Sacramento Altaris*, tr. by T. B. Birch. *The New Republic*, LXVII (July 15), 242.

1932

1. Editor. *Collected Papers of Charles Sanders Peirce*. Vol. II: *Elements of Logic*. Cambridge: Harvard University Press.

2. "The Metaphysics and Logic of Classes." *Monist*, XLII (January), 112–54.
3. "G. H. Mead: Philosopher of the Here and Now." A Review of G. H. Mead's *The Philosophy of the Present. The New Republic*, LXVIII (October 26), 302.

1933

1. Editor. *Collected Papers of Charles Sanders Peirce*. Vol. III: *Exact Logic*. Cambridge: Harvard University Press.
2. Editor. *Collected Papers of Charles Sanders Peirce*. Vol. IV: *The Simplest Mathematics*. Cambridge: Harvard University Press.
3. "On Alternative Logics." *Philosophical Review*, XLII (September), 520–25.
4. "The Metaphysical and the Logical Individual." *Journal of Philosophy*, XXX, 288–93.
5. "A Scientist's Philosophy." A Review of Max Planck's *Where is Science Going? The New Republic*, LXXIV (March 15), 135–36.
6. "Ethics Before the Bar." A Review of F. S. Cohen's *Ethical Systems and Legal Ideals. The New Republic*, LXXVI (August 9), 348–49.
7. A Review of G. Cantor's *Gesammelte Abhandlungen mathematischen u. philosophischen Inhalts. Philosophical Review*, XLIII (March), 214–15.

1934

1. Hartshorne, Charles, co-ed. *Collected Papers of Charles Sanders Peirce*, Vol. V: *Pragmatism and Pragmaticism*. Cambridge: Harvard University Press.
2. "Metaphysics: The Domain of Ignorance." *Philosophical Review*, XLIII, 402–6.
3. "Baruch Spinoza." A Review of H. A. Wolfson's *The Philosophy of Spinoza. The New Republic*, LXXX (October 3), 220–21.
4. "C. S. Peirce." *Dictionary of American Biography*. Ed. A. Johnson. New York: Scribner's, 398–403.
5. Letter to *Journal of Philosophy*. XXXI (April 26), 251.
6. Letter to *Philosophy of Science*. I, No. 2 (April), 238.

1935

1. Hartshorne, Charles, co-ed. *Collected Papers of Charles Sanders Peirce*. Vol. VI: *Scientific Metaphysics*. Cambridge: Harvard University Press.
2. "Time and the Absolute." *Journal of Philosophy*, XXXII, 286–90.
3. "A Memorandum for a System of Philosophy." *American Philosophy Today and Tomorrow*. Eds. H. M. Kallen and S. Hook. New York: Furnam.

1936

1. A Review of F. H. Bradley's *Collected Essays. The New Republic*, LXXXVI (April 1), 230.
2. "The Nature and Status of Time and Passage." *Philosophical Essays for A. N. Whitehead*. New York: Longmans Green.
3. "The Business of Esthetics." A Review of M. M. Rader's *A Modern Book of Esthetics. The New Republic*, LXXXVI (April 22), 321–22. Letter, in answer to Rader, LXXXVII (June, 24), 208.
4. "Venture into Metaphysics." A Review of J. Wild's *George Berkeley. The New Republic*, LXXXVII (August 19), 52–53.

1937

1. "A New Philosophical School." A Review. *The New Republic*, XCII (September 1), 107–8.
2. "A Context Theory of Words." A Review of I. A. Richards' *The Philosophy of Rhetoric. The New Republic*, XC (April 7), 275–76.

1938

1. "The Self-Contradictory." *Philosophical Review*, XLVII, 531–33.
2. "Towards a Cosmological Ethics." *Journal of Philosophy*, XXXV, 645–51.
3. "Books That Changed our Minds." *The New Republic*, XCVII (December 21), 205.
4. *Reality*. Princeton: Princeton University Press.
5. "An Effective Logic." A Review of John Dewey's *Logic. The New Republic*, XCVII (November 23), 79–80.
6. "Toward Mysticism." A Review of J. Maritain's *The Degrees of Knowledge. The New Republic*, XCVII (October 5), 247–48.
7. "Thoughts Out of Season." A Review of B. Russell's *Principles of Mathematics. The New Republic*, XCV (June 22), 193–94.
8. A Review of Etienne Gilson's *Reason and Revelation in the Middle Ages. The New Republic*, XCVII (November 30), 110.
9. A Review of John R. Reid's *A Theory of Value. Ethics*, XLIX (October), 103–4.

1939

1. "The Locus of Responsibility." *Ethics*, XLIX, 349–55.
2. "The Year in Philosophy." *The New Republic*, CI (December 6), 204, 206–8.

3. A Review of *International Encyclopedia of Unified Science. Ethics*, XLIX (July), 498–500.
4. A Review of Rudolf Carnap's *Foundations of Logic and Mathematics. Ethics*, L (October), 119–20.
5. A Review of L. Bloomfield's *Linguistic Aspects of Science. Ethics*, L (October), 110–20.
6. "America and the Next War." *The New Republic*, C (June 28), 210.

1940

1. "The Essence of Peirce's System." *Journal of Philosophy*, XXXVII, 253–64.
2. "The Meaning of Existence." *Philosophy and Phenomenological Research*, I, 191–98.
3. A Review of James MacKaye's *The Logic of Language. Ethics*, L (April), 369.
4. A Review of A. Bowman's *A Sacramental Universe. Philosophic Abstracts*, Nos. 1, 4.
5. A Review of R. Demos' *The Philosophy of Plato. Philosophic Abstracts*, Nos. 1, 5.
6. A Review of W. Jaeger's *Paideia. Philosophic Abstracts*, Nos. 1, 6.
7. A Review of C. Perry's *Toward a Dimensional Realism. Philosophic Abstracts*, Nos. 1, 8.
8. A Review of M. Rader's *No Compromise. Philosophic Abstracts*, Nos. 1, 8.
9. A Review of M. K. Munitz' *The Moral Philosophy of Santayana. Philosophic Abstracts*, Nos. 1, 8.
10. A Review of M. Schoen's "A Scientific Basis for Moral Action." *Philosophic Abstracts*, Nos. 2, 7.
11. A Review of N. Berdyaev's *Spirit and Reality. Philosophic Abstracts*, Nos. 2, 4.
12. A Review of the Conway Memorial Lecture: *Ethics in Modern Art. Philosophic Abstracts*, Nos. 2, 7.
13. A Review of M. Lerner's *Ideas are Weapons. Philosophic Abstracts*, Nos. 2, 13.

1941

1. "God and the World." *Science, Philosophy and Religion*. Vol. I. New York: Columbia University Press.
2. "Adventurous Humility." *Ethics*, LI (April), 337–48.
3. "Midway between Traditionalism and Progressivism." *School and Society*, LIII, 761–63.
4. "The Golden Rule." *Journal of Philosophy*, XXXVIII, 421–30.
5. "An Introduction to a Study of Instruments." *Philosophy of Science*, VIII, No. 3 (July), 287–96.

6. A Review of W. T. Stace's *The Nature of the World*. *The Philosophical Review*, L (March), 236–38.

7. A Review of R. B. Brandt's *The Philosophy of Schleiermacher*. *Ethics*, LI (July), 490–91.

8. A Review of P. A. Schilpp's *The Philosophy of George Santayana*. *Philosophy and Phenomenological Research*, II (September), 124–26.

9. A Review of Justus Buchler's *The Philosophy of Peirce*. *Philosophy and Phenomenological Research*, II (December), 259–61. Letter in answer to Buchler, 261–62.

10. A Review of DeWitt Parker's *Experience and Substance: An Essay in Metaphysics*. *Ethics*, LI (July), 487–88.

1942

1. "Democracy and the Rights of Man." *Science, Philosophy and Religion*. Vol. II. New York: Columbia University Press.

2. "Freedom of Choice." *Ethics*, LII (January), 186–99.

3. "The Logic of Semantics." *Journal of Philosophy*, XXXIX, 169–77.

4. "Sources of the Idea of God." *Journal of Religion*, XXII, 156–72.

5. "Cosmic Behaviorism." *Philosophical Review*, LI (July), 345–56.

6. "Morality and Ethics." *Journal of Philosophy*, XXXIX, 381–85.

7. "The Purpose of Purpose." *Philosophy of Science*, IX, No. 2 (April), 162–65.

8. "Habits, Instincts and Reflexes." *Philosophy of Science*, IX, No. 3 (July), 268–74.

9. "The Ethics of Pacifism." *Philosophical Review*, LI (September), 476–96.

10. "Pain and Pleasure." *Philosophy and Phenomenological Research*, III, 137–44.

11. "Beauty, Individuality and Personality." *Personalist*, XXIII, 34–43.

12. "Charles Sanders Peirce." *Sewanee Review*, L, 184–92.

13. A Review of C. Hartshorne's *Man's Vision of God*. *Ethics*, LII (January) 238–39.

14. "Cosmology." *Dictionary of Philosophy*. Ed. Dagobert D. Runes. New York: Philosophical Library.

1943

1. "Issues in Ethical Theory: Some Presuppositions of an Aristotelian Ethics." *The American Journal of Economics and Sociology*, II, 245–54.

2. "The Social Character of Gestures." *Philosophical Review*, LIII (March), 182–86.

3. "Determinism in Will and Nature." *Journal of Liberal Religion*, IV, No. 4, 206–11.

4. "Scholarships Through Faculty Eyes." *Bryn Mawr Alumnae Bulletin*, XXIII, 10.

5. "Without Wisdom." A Review of P. A. Schilpp's *The Philosophy of G. E. Moore*. *The New Republic*, CIX (July 26), 114–16.
6. A Review of Henry Lanz' *In Quest of Morals*. *Ethics*, LIII (April), 231–32.

1944

1. "In Quest of Worldly Wisdom." *Approaches to World Peace*. New York: Harper and Row.
2. A Review of John Laird's *Theism and Cosmology* and *Mind and Deity*. *The Review of Religion*, VIII (November), 80–82.
3. "Art and Henry Miller." *The Happy Rock*. Ed. Bern Porter. Big Sur, CA: Porter Press.

1945

1. "History and the Historian." *Journal of Philosophy*, XLII, 169–79.
2. "Peirce's Sixty-Six Signs." With Arthur Burks. *Journal of Philosophy*, XLII, 383–88.
3. "The Human Nature of Man." *The Title*, I (May), 13–21.
4. "The Universal Ethical Standard." *Ethics*, LVI (October), 38–48.
5. A Review of P. A. Schilpp's *The Philosophy of Bertrand Russell*. Appeared in both *Philosophy and Phenomenological Research*, V (June), 594–99; and *The New Republic*, CXIII (December 3), 760–62.
6. A Review of Bertrand Russell's *A History of Western Philosophy*. *The New Republic*, CXIII (December 3), 760–62.

1946

1. "The Quest for Certainty." *Philosophical Review*, Vol. LV, No. 2 (March), 132–51.
2. "Philosophy and Faith." *Journal of Religion*, XXVI, No. 4 (October), 278–82.
3. "The True, the Good, and the Jew." *Commentary*, II, No. 4 (October), 310–16.
4. "A Parade of American Thinkers." A Review of Herbert Schneider's *A History of American Philosophy*. *New York Times*, December 22, 8–13.

1947

1. *Nature and Man*. New York: Henry Holt and Co.
2. "Et Tu Shimony." *Yale Literary Magazine* (May), 12–13.
3. "Social, Legal and Ethical Responsibility." *Ethics*, LVII, No. 4 (July), 259–73.

4. "Prophetic Blake." A Review of Mark Schorer's *William Blake*. *Quarterly Review of Literature*, III, No. 4 (August), 406–13.
5. "Being, Essence and Existence." *Review of Metaphysics*, I, No. 1 (September), 69–92.
6. "*Existenz* and Hegel." *Philosophy and Phenomenological Research*, VIII (December), 206–16.
7. "Our Knowledge of Right and Wrong." *Travaux du Congrès International de Philosophie Haiti*, 218–23.
8. A Review of the *Yale Literary Magazine*. *The Yale Daily News*. March 3, 2–3.

1948

1. "Alfred North Whitehead, 1861–1947." *Atlantic Monthly*, CLXXXI (May), 105–7. Reprinted from *The Harvard Crimson*.
2. "Immortality." *Review of Metaphysics*, I, No. 4 (June), 87–103.
3. "Job, God and Evil." *Commentary*, VI, No. 2 (August), 144–51.
4. A Review of Yves R. Simon's *Community of the Free*. *Ethics*, LXIII (April), 218–19.
5. "Otis H. Lee." *Review of Metaphysics*, II, No. 2 (December), 1–2. Appeared also in *Philosophical Review*, LVIII (September 1949), 465–66.

1949

1. "Sacrifice and Self-Sacrifice." *Review of Metaphysics*, II, (March) 76–98.
2. "Good and Evil." *Review of Metaphysics*, III (September), 81–94.
3. "Alfred North Whitehead." *Philosophical Review*, LXIII (September), 468–69.
4. "Some Epochs of Western Civilization." *Et Veritas*, IV, No. 2 (December), 8–18.

1950

1. *Man's Freedom*. New Haven: Yale University Press.
2. "Freedom and Rights." *Perspectives on a Troubled Decade, 1939–1949*, New York: Harper and Row.
3. Erich Frank's obituary. *Proceedings of the American Philosophical Association* (September), 80.
4. "Law and Other Matters." *Review of Metaphysics*, IV (September), 131–35.

1951

1. "Science, Superstition and Precision." *Freedom and Reason*. Conference on Jewish Relations, 309–21.
2. "Cosmic Necessities." *Review of Metaphysics*, IV, No. 3 (March), 359–75.

1952

1. "Some Neglected Ethical Questions." *Moral Principles of Action*. Ed. R. Anshen. New York: Harper and Row.
2. "The Prediction Paradox." *Mind*, LXI, No. 242 (April), 265–69.
3. "The Nature and Status of the Past." *Review of Metaphysics*, V (June), 507–22.
4. "The Logic of the Creative Process." *Studies in the Philosophy of Charles Sanders Peirce*. Eds. P. P. Wiener and F. H. Young. Cambridge, MA: Harvard University Press.
5. "Some Theses of Empirical Certainty." *Review of Metaphysics*, V (June), 627.
6. "The Perception of Stars." *Review of Metaphysics*, VI (December), 233–38.

1953

1. "Persons, Places and Things." *Moments of Personal Discovery*. Ed. R. M. MacIver. New York: Harper and Row.
2. "The Contemporary World." *Review of Metaphysics*, VI (June), 525–38.
3. "Grünbaum's Relativity and Ontology." *Review of Metaphysics*, VII (September), 124–25.
4. "The Past: Some Recent Discussions." *Review of Metaphysics*, VII (December), 299–306.
5. "On the Responsibility of the Architect." *Perspecta* 2. *Yale Architectural Journal*, 51–55.

1954

1. "Man's Inalienable Rights." *Ixyun*, V, No. 1 (January), 129–30.
2. "The Four Dimensions of Reality." *Review of Metaphysics*, VII (June), 558–62.
3. "Guilt, God and Perfection, I." *Review of Metaphysics*, VIII (September), 30–48.
4. "The Gita, East and West." *Philosophy East and West*, V (October), 253–58.
5. "Guilt, God and Perfection, II." *Review of Metaphysics*, VIII (December), 246–63.
6. *The Wandering Philosopher*. Mimeographed diary. 57 pages plus appendix.
7. "The Right of Might." *A. R. Wadia: Essays in Philosophy Presented in His Honor*. Madras: G. S. Press.

1955

1. "The Paradox of Necessary Truth." *Philosophical Studies*, VI, No. 2 (February), 31–32.

2. "Greek, Hebrew and Christian." *Judaism*, IV, No. 2, 116–23.
3. *Modes of Being*. Mimeographed, March, 1–56.
4. *Reality—A Selection*. Hebrew trans. Yehuda Landau. Jerusalem: Magnes Press.
5. "Real Possibility." Colloquium No. 6, *Review of Metaphysics*, IX, No. 4 (June), 669–70; *Response to Comments*, 682–84.

1956

1. "A Reconciliation of the Religions: A Non-Ironic Proposal." *Journal of Religion*, XXVI, No. 1, 36–44.
2. "On Being Together." *Review of Metaphysics*, IX, No. 3 (March), 391–403.
3. "The Real Art Object." *Philosophy and Phenomenological Research*, XVI, No. 3, 341–52.
4. "The Fortunate Philosophers." *Yale Alumni Journal* (June), 20.
5. "On the Difference between Actuality and Possibility." *Review of Metaphysics*, X, No. 1 (September), 165–71.
6. "The Nature and Locus of Natural Law." *Journal of Philosophy*, LIII, 713–21.
7. "The New Outlook." *American Philosophers at Work*. Ed. Sidney Hook. New York: Criterion Books.
8. "The Paradox of Necessary Truth Once More." *Philosophical Studies*, VII, No. 6, 88–89.

1957

1. "Ten Theses Relating to Existence." *Review of Metaphysics*, X (March), 401–11.
2. "Eighteen Theses in Logic." *Review of Metaphysics*, XI (September), 12–27.
3. "Report of the Visiting Committee in the Humanities and Social Sciences at MIT." Mimeographed. 43 pp.

1958

1. *Modes of Being*. Carbondale: University of Southern Illinois Press.
2. *Modes of Being*. Carbondale: University of Southern Illinois Press, 2 volume edition.
3. "Common Sense and Beyond." *Determinism and Freedom*. Ed. Sidney Hook. New York: New York University Press.
4. "The Semantics of Truth Today and Tomorrow." *Philosophical Studies* (January-February), 21–23.
5. "The Paradox of Obligation." *Journal of Philosophy*, LV, No. 7 (March 27), 291–92.

6. "On Being a Permanent Resident." Yale Senior Class Book, 337–39.
7. "Philosophy and the Curriculum of a University." *The Journal of General Education*, XI, No. 3, 141–51.
8. Summary and Comment, *Collected Papers of C. S. Peirce*, vii-viii. *Review of Metaphysics*, LXII (December), 327.

1959

1. *Our Public Life*. Mahlon Powell Lectures. Bloomington: Indiana University Press.
2. "Moving Toward Peace." Letter in *New York Times*, October 11, 10E.

1960

1. "Art, Substance and Reality." *Review of Metaphysics*, XIII, No. 3 (March), 365–82.
2. "Allies." A Poem. *Yale Literary Magazine*, CXXCII, No. 4–5, 145.
3. "Love in a Machine Age." *Dimensions of Mind*. Ed. Sidney Hook. New York: New York University Press, 193–97.
4. Letter to *Nation*, CXC. June 18.

1961

1. *The World of Art*. Carbondale: Southern Illinois University Press.
2. "History and Objective Immortality." *Relevance of Whitehead*. Ed. Ivor Leclerc. London: George Allen and Unwin.
3. *Nine Basic Arts*. Carbondale: Southern Illinois University Press.
4. "Elements of the Physical Universe." *Review of Metaphysics*, XV, No. 1 (September), 1–18.
5. "Thank God, God's Not Impossible." *Religious Experience and Truth*. Ed. Sidney Hook. New York: New York University.
6. "Man's Existence." *International Philosophical Quarterly*, I, 547–68.

1962

1. Letter. *Commentary*, February, 164–65.
2. "Wittgenstein." A play. *Spider's Web* (February), 37–59.
3. "Historic Time." *Review of Metaphysics*, XV, No. 4 (June), 573–85.
4. *History: Written and Lived*. Carbondale: Southern Illinois University Press.
5. "Weiss Asks Coffin: 'Is Christianity Necessary?'" *Yale News and Review*, I, No. 1 (September), 8–9.
6. "Twenty-two Reasons for Continuing as Before." *Philosophical Studies*, XIII (October), 65–68.

1963

1. "The Religious Turn." *Judaism*, XIII (Winter), 3–27.
2. *Religion and Art*. The Aquinas Lecture for 1963. Milwaukee, WI: Marquette University Press.
3. Letter. *Saturday Review*. March 23, 56.
4. "It's About Time." *Philosophy and History*. Ed. Sidney Hook. New York: New York University Press.
5. Letter. *Yale Alumni Magazine*, July, p. 3.
6. "Religious Experience." *Review of Metaphysics*, XVII, No. 1 (September), 3–17.
7. "Natural and Supernatural Law." *Political Science and the Modern Mind*. Detroit, MI: Sacred Heart Seminary.
8. "The Explanation of Man." *International Congress of Philosophy*, Mexico.
9. "The Use of Ideas." *Review of Metaphysics*, XVII, No. 2 (December), 200–4.
10. "Author to Editor." Letter. *Scholarly Books in America*, V (December), 2–3.

1964

1. "A Philosophical Definition of Leisure." *Leisure in America: Blessing or Curse?* Monograph. American Academy of Political and Social Science.
2. "The Right to Disobey." *Law and Philosophy*. Ed. Sidney Hook. New York: New York University Press.
3. "Our Knowledge of What is Real." *Review of Metaphysics*, XVIII, No. 1 (September), 3–22.
4. *The God We Seek*. Carbondale: Southern Illinois University Press.
5. Interrogation of Paul Weiss. Ellen S. Haring. *Philosophical Interrogations*. Edited by S. and B. Rome. New York: Holt, Winston and Rinehart, pp. 259–317; 345, 346.

1965

1. Letter. *Commentary*. April.
2. "C. S. Peirce, Philosopher." *Perspectives on Peirce*. Ed. Richard J. Bernstein. New Haven: Yale University Press.
3. Letter. *Yale Daily News*, October 14.

1966

1. *Philosophy in Process*. Vol. I. Carbondale: Southern Illinois University Press.
2. "The Good Child." Sonnet. *Yale Literary Magazine*.
3. *Nine Basic Arts*. Paperback. Carbondale: Southern Illinois University Press.

4. *Our Public Life*. Paperback. Carbondale: Southern Illinois University Press.
5. *Philosophy in Process*. Vol. II. Carbondale: Southern Illinois University Press.

1967

1. *Reality*. Paperback. Carbondale: Southern Illinois University Press.
2. Preface. R. S. Hartman. *The Structure of Value*. Carbondale: Southern Illinois University Press.
3. *The Making of Men*. Carbondale: Southern Illinois University Press.
4. *Man's Freedom*. Paperback. Carbondale: Southern Illinois University Press.
5. "The Economics of Economists." *Human Values and Economic Policy*. Edited by Sidney Hook. New York: New York University Press.
6. "Types of Finality." *Journal of Philosophy*, LXIV, No. 19 (October 5), 584–93.
7. Letter. *Yale Daily News*. November 7.
8. "Equal and Separate but Integrated." Presidential Address. Proceedings of the American Philosophical Association, XXXIX, 5–17.
9. *Right and Wrong: A Philosophic Dialogue Between Father and Son*. New York: Basic Books.

1968

1. *Modes of Being*. Paperback. Carbondale: Southern Illinois University Press.
2. Letter. *Yale Daily News*, April 12.
3. "Why College Students Revolt." *New York Times* Editorial, May 18.
4. "A Philosopher's View of Sport." *Yale Banner*, 186–94.
5. "The Nature of Violence." *Seventeen* (August).
6. "Sport and Its Participants." *Science*, CLXI (September), 1161–62.
7. "Some Paradoxes Relating to Order." *The Concept of Order*. Ed. Paul Kuntz. Seattle, WA: Washington University Press.
8. *Philosophy in Process*. Vol. III. Carbondale: Southern Illinois University Press.

1969

1. *Sport: A Philosophic Inquiry*. Carbondale: Southern Illinois University Press.
2. "What is Man?" *This Week*, November 2.
3. *The Making of Men*. Paperback. Carbondale: Southern Illinois University Press.
4. *Philosophy in Process*. Vol. IV. Carbondale: Southern Illinois University Press.

1970

1. *Philosophical Interrogations.* Paperback. New York: Holt, Winston, Rinehart.
2. *The World of Art.* Trans. into Hebrew. Tel Aviv: Yachad United Publishing Company.
3. "On What There is Beyond the Things There Are." *Contemporary American Philosophy.* 2d series. Ed. J. E. Smith. London: Allen and Unwin; New York: Humanities Press.
4. "Introduction to Metaphysics." *The Future of Metaphysics.* Ed. Robert Wood. Chicago: Quadrangle Books.
5. "Paul Weiss's Recollections of Editing the Peirce Papers." *Transactions of the Charles S. Peirce Society,* VI, No. 3–4, 161–87.

1971

1. "Age is Not a Number." *New York Times,* January 1.
2. "Architecture, The Making of a Metaphorse: Notes from a Symposium." *Main Currents,* 29 (September–October), 9–12.
3. Article on Paul Weiss with quotations. "Potomac Magazine" of the *Washington Post.* January 10.
4. *Sport: A Philosophic Inquiry.* Paperback. Carbondale: Southern Illinois University Press.
5. "Science and Religion." *Evolution in Perspective.* Eds. G. Schuster and R. Thorson. Notre Dame, IN: University of Notre Dame Press.
6. *Philosophy in Process,* Vol. V. Carbondale: Southern Illinois University Press.
7. "The Distinctive Nature of Man." *Idealistic Studies,* I, No. 2, 89–101.

1972

1. "The Possibility of a Pure Phenomenology." *Value and Valuation: Axiological Studies in Honor of Robert S. Hartman.* Ed. J. W. Davis. Knoxville, TN: University of Tennessee Press.
2. "Records and the Man." *Philosophic Exchange,* 1 (Summer), 89–97.
3. "A Response." *Review of Metaphysics,* 25, No. 4 (June), 144–65.
4. *The God We Seek.* Arcturus Books. Carbondale: Southern Illinois University Press.
5. "Wood in Aesthetics and Art." *Design and Aesthetics of Wood.* Eds. E. Anderson and G. Earle. Albany: State University of New York Press.

1974

1. *Beyond All Appearances.* Carbondale: Southern Illinois University Press.
2. "The Philosophic Quest." *Mid-Twentieth Century American Philosophy.* Ed. P. A. Bertocci. New York: Humanities Press.

3. *Philosophy in Process*, Vol. V. London: Feffer & Simons.
4. *Right and Wrong: A Philosophic Dialogue between Father and Son*. Arcturus Books. Carbondale: Southern Illinois University Press.

1975

1. "Bestowed, Acquired and Native Rights." *Proceedings of the American Catholic Philosophical Association*, 49: 138–49.
2. *Cinematics*. Carbondale: Southern Illinois University Press; London: Feffer & Simons.
3. *Philosophy in Process*. Vol. VI. Carbondale: Southern Illinois University Press; London: Feffer & Simons.
4. "The Policeman: His Nature and Duties." *The Police in Society*. Eds. E. C. Viano and J. Rowman. Lexington, MA: Lexington Books.

1976

1. "Reason, Mind, Body, and World." *Review of Metaphysics*, 30, No. 2 (December), 325–34.
2. "Substance and Process, Today and Tomorrow." *Philosophy Research Archives*, 2, No. 1204, 111–41.

1977

1. *First Considerations: An Examination of Philosophical Evidence*. Carbondale: Southern Illinois University Press; London: Feffer & Simons.

1978

1. *Philosophy in Process*. Vol. VII. Carbondale: Southern Illinois University Press; London: Feffer & Simons.

1980

1. *First Considerations, Addenda/Corrigenda*. Carbondale: Southern Illinois University Press.
2. "The Game as a Solution to the Problem of the One and the Many." *Journal of the Philosophy of Sport*, VII (Fall), 7–14.
3. "The God of Religion, Theology, and Mysticism." *Logos*, 1, 65–77.
4. "Recollections of Alfred North Whitehead." *Process Studies*, 10 (Spring–Summer), 44–56.
5. "Second Thoughts on *First Considerations*." *Process Studies*, 10 (Spring–Summer), 34–38.

6. "Some Pivotal Issues in Spinoza." *The Philosophy of Baruch Spinoza*. Ed. Richard Kennington. Washington, DC: Catholic University of America Press.
7. "Truth and Reality." *The Review of Metaphysics*, 34 (September), 57–69.
8. *You, I, and the Others*. Carbondale: Southern Illinois University Press; London: Feffer & Simons.

1981

1. "The Nature of a Team." *Journal of the Philosophy of Sport*, VIII (Fall), 47–54.

1982

1. "The Joy of Amateur Sport." *The National Forum, The Phi Kappa Phi*, 63 (Winter), 14–17.

1983

1. *Privacy*. Carbondale: Southern Illinois University Press.
2. *Nature and Man*. Lanham, MD: University Press of America.

1984

1. *Philosophy in Process*. Vol. VIII. Albany: State University of New York Press.

1985

1. *Philosophy in Process*. Vol. VII, Part 2. Albany:State University of New York Press.
2. *Sport: A Philosophic Inquiry. Supotsu to wa nani ka*. What is Sport? Trans. into Japanese by Akio Kataoka. Tokyo: Fumaido Shuppan, Showa 60.
3. "Things in Themselves." *Review of Metaphysics*, 39, No. 1 (September), 23–46.

1986

1. *Toward a Perfected State*. Albany: State University of New York Press.

Notes on the Contributors

RICHARD J. BERNSTEIN is the T. Wistar Brown Professor of Philosophy at Haverford College. He is the former editor of *The Review of Metaphysics* and *Praxis International*. His books include *Praxis and Action*, *The Restructuring of Social and Political Theory*, *Beyond Objectivism and Relativism*, and *Philosophical Profiles*.

ROBERT CASTIGLIONE, whose doctoral dissertation on Paul Weiss led to his Ph.D. from The Catholic University of America in 1971, is currently associate professor of philosophy at Rhode Island College. He published an analysis of *Privacy* in *Philosophy Today* (Spring 1984) and is preparing a biography and an analysis of Paul Weiss's work.

ANTONIO S. CUA is professor of philosophy at The Catholic University of America. He is coeditor of the *Journal of Chinese Philosophy* and past president of the Society for Asian and Comparative Philosophy and past president of the International Society for Chinese Philosophy. His works include *Reason and Virtue: A Study in the Ethics of Richard Price*; *Dimensions of Moral Creativity: Paradigms, Principles, and Ideals*; *The Unity of Knowledge and Action: A Study in Wang Yang-ming's Moral Psychology*; and *Ethical Argumentation: A Study in Hsüng Tzu's Moral Epistemology*.

DANIEL O. DAHLSTROM is associate professor of philosophy at The Catholic University of America. His principal publications are focused on German philosophy, especially Kant, Hegel, and Heidegger. He has published "Paul Weiss' Metaphysics of Human Experience" in *The Thomist* (October 1981). He is the secretary of the American Catholic Philosophical Association.

KARSTEN HARRIES is professor of philosophy at Yale University. He is author of *The Meaning of Modern Art* and *The Bavarian Rococo Church: Between Faith and Aestheticism*. He is currently working on a book exploring the ethical function of architecture.

CHARLES HARTSHORNE is emeritus professor of philosophy at the University of Texas at Austin. He coedited with Paul Weiss the *Collected Papers of Charles Sanders Peirce*. He has taught at Harvard, the University of Chicago, Emory University, and has held many visiting professorships as well. He is author of *Creative Synthesis and Philosophic Method* and, more recently, *Whitehead's View of Reality*.

THOMAS KRETTEK is a member of the Society of Jesus currently pursuing doctoral studies, concentrating on the philosophy of Paul Weiss, at The Catholic University of America. He completed a Master's and a Licentiate in Philosophy at Saint Louis University in 1977 and a Master's and a Licentiate in Theology at Regis College of the Toronto School of Theology in 1983.

PAUL GRIMLEY KUNTZ is professor of philosophy at Emory University. He was honorary president of the International Society of Metaphysics from 1974 to 1982 and has received many grants and awards for work in philosophy. He is author of several books and many articles in philosophy.

IRWIN C. LIEB, a former student of Paul Weiss's at Yale University, is University Professor at the University of Southern California and is a former vice president of the Universities of Southern California and Texas. He teaches and publishes on formal topics in metaphysics and is about to publish a major work on "time."

PETER MILLER is associate professor of philosophy at the University of Winnipeg. His areas of interest include cosmology, history of philosophy, value theory, ethics, and moral development. Publications include "Time, Events, and Substance" in *Physics and the Ultimate Significance of Time* (1985), "Temporal Concepts: A Schematic Analysis" in *Process Studies* (1979), "Axiology: A Metaphysical Theme in Ethics" in *Journal of Value Inquiry* (1983), and "What Aristotle Should Have Said: An Experiment in Metaphysics" in *American Philosophical Quarterly* (1972).

ROBERT C. NEVILLE is professor of philosophy and religious studies at the State University of New York at Stony Brook. Holding a Ph.D. from Yale University, he is author of several books, the most recent of which are *Reconstruction of Thinking* and *The Tao and the Daimon*. He is currently writing a philosophical theory of interpretation and value.

GEORGE KIMBALL PLOCHMANN is emeritus professor of philosophy at Southern Illinois University and currently adjunct professor of medical humanities at the Southern Illinois University School of Medicine at Springfield. He is editor of the Philosophical Explorations Series; coauthor of a philosophical and historical study of Southern Illinois University; editor and coauthor of an index to Wittgenstein's *Tractatus*, all for Southern Illinois University Press. He is also editor and coauthor of a collection of pedagogical studies in the humanities and author of a study in Plato, as well as of many papers.

ANDREW J. RECK is professor of philosophy at Tulane University and chairman of the department. His areas of interest are American philosophy, metaphysics, and history of philosophy. He is editor of *George Herbert Mead: Selected Writings*; *Knowledge and Value: Essays in Honor of H. N. Lee*; coeditor of *Studies on Santayana*; and author of *Speculative Philosophy*.

DAVID WEISSMAN is author of *Dispositional Properties* and *Eternal Possibilities* (both published by the Southern Illinois University Press), and of *Intuition and Ideality* (forthcoming from the State University of New York Press).

ROBERT E. WOOD, currently associate professor and chairman of the philosophy department at the University of Dallas, has published articles in the *Review of Metaphysics, Philosophy Today, The Modern Schoolman, Thought*, and *Listening*. He has translated two books and several articles from German, coedited the Horizons in Philosophy Series, edited the *Future of Metaphysics*, and authored *Martin Buber's Ontology*.

INDEX OF NAMES

INDEX OF SUBJECTS